FIRTH of FORTH

NORTH

N

horn

Inveresk

R. TYNE

TRAPRAIN
LAW

SOUTRA
HILL

law

MOORFOOT
HILLS

LAMMERMUIR
HILLS

BERWICK
UPON
TWEED

Tweedmouth

Lindisfarne
(Medcaut)

bles

Stow

GALA WATER

Galashiels

Carham

R. TWEED

O T A D I N I

R. TWEED

Melrose

Kelso

Pallin's
Burn

Bamburgh

EILDON HILL N.

TRIMONTIUM

rrow

WATER

Selkirk

Roxburgh
Castle

YEAVERING
BELL

R. ETTRICK

ALE WATER

DERE STREET

Jedburgh

CHEVIOT
HILLS

Alnwick

Alnmouth

Hawick

RUBERS
LAW

R. TEVIOT

S E L G O V A E

LEARCHILD
(ALAUNA)

HIGH
ROCHESTER
(BREMENIUM)

Otterburn

Dawston

LIDDEL WATER

NORTHUMBERLAND

Langholm

RISINGHAM

CARBY
HILL

BEWCASTLE

Netherby

HOUSESTEADS
(VERCOVICIUM)

H A D R I A N ' S   W A L L

Corwhinley

CORBRIDGE

R. TYNE

NEWCASTLE

Jarrow

CASTLESTEADS
(CAMBOGLANNA)

am

CARLISLE

Durham

* RIA*

Langdale

STANWICK

Scotch
Corner

CATTERICK
(CATARACTONIUM)

ARTHUR

AND THE

LOST KINGDOMS

Also by Alistair Moffat

The Edinburgh Fringe
Kelsae: A History of Kelso from the Earliest Times
Remembering Charles Rennie Mackintosh

ARTHUR
AND THE
LOST KINGDOMS

Alistair Moffat

Weidenfeld & Nicolson

LONDON

First published in Great Britain in 1999
by Weidenfeld & Nicolson

A CIP catalogue record for this book
is available from the British Library.

ISBN 0 297 64324 X

Printed and bound in Great Britain by
Butler and Tanner Ltd, Frome and London

Weidenfeld & Nicolson
The Orion Publishing Group Ltd
Orion House
5 Upper Saint Martin's Lane
London, WC2H 9EA

CONTENTS

ILLUSTRATIONS

The aerial survey of the Roxburgh site is reproduced by permission of HMSO. The other photographs are by Ken MacGregor.

MAPS

LINE DRAWINGS

ACKNOWLEDGEMENTS

This book has been forming for so long in my mind that it is difficult to remember some of the early kindnesses shown by people whose knowledge far outran my own. But I cannot forget how important my father, Jack Moffat, was in developing my own interest in the history of the Scottish Border country and in particular in place names. As much for his own amusement as anything didactic, he used to muse on names out loud, turning them over and over to get at what they meant. In every sense he made me think about these things before I passed them by. I owe him a debt of love that I can only repay to his grandchildren, and this book is dedicated to them.

Walter Elliot is a kenspeckle figure whose visceral and intellectual knowledge of the Borders is encyclopaedic. By an entirely different route he arrived at precisely the same conclusion as I did, and I am grateful for his kindness in sharing what he knows, and for reading this manuscript. He thoughtfully corrected some blunders but any inaccuracies that remain are entirely my own.

David Godwin should have been a farmer such is his ability to distinguish wheat from chaff. For his good humour, kindness and enthusiasm I am very grateful. Benjamin Buchan edited this book with tact and a sure touch, while Anthony Cheetham published it with brio and no little bravery.

No one helped me more in the process of writing this than Eileen Hunter. She showed me a path through the wilderness of word processing and made my life much easier. And as I navigated through options, files, tools and the rest, she kept me on the straight and narrow more than a few times. Many thanks and much love, Eileen.

My old friend George Rosie has borne several monologues on car journeys from Glasgow to Edinburgh with great fortitude, and his excellent film *Men of the North* for S4C and Scottish Television was partly a product of conversations on the M8.

To my Welsh-speaking friends I owe thanks for honest answers to puzzling questions and to Iain Taylor and Rhoda Macdonald more gratitude for wisdom and guidance in Gaelic. I hope none of them wince when they see passages from their beautiful mother-tongues rendered down into mine.

Harriet Buckley drew the illustrations for this book with patience and skill and also according to my suggestions. Therefore all that is good-looking about her drawings redounds to Harriet's credit and any mistakes originate with me. Ken MacGregor is an accomplished documentary film-maker as well as an excellent photographer, and several of his pictures are worth more than several thousands of my words.

Finally I want to acknowledge the tolerance of my family. I am glad that while I was writing this my wife Lindsay, and our children Adam, Helen and Beth, had other lives which they allowed me to visit when it suited me.

Alistair Moffat
Selkirk, 1999

To Adam, Helen and Beth
with all my love

Britain circa AD 150: tribal regions

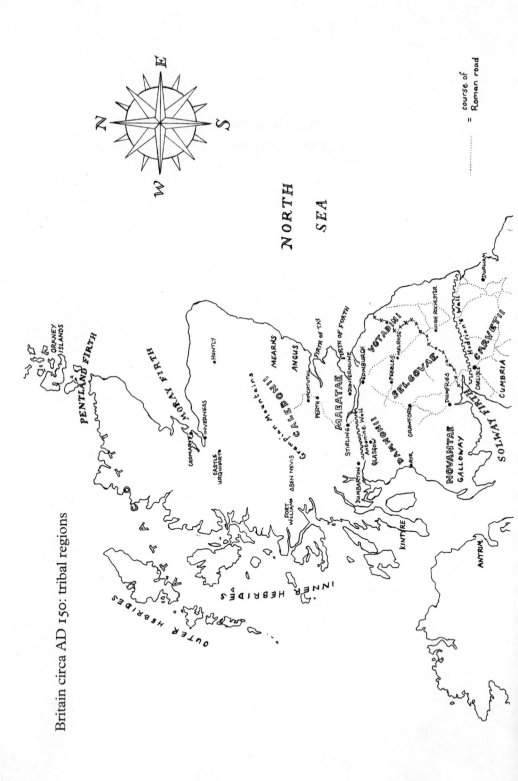

N E S W

NORTH

SEA

ORKNEY ISLANDS

PENTLAND FIRTH

MORAY FIRTH

• HUNTLY

CROMARTY

INVERNESS •

CASTLE URQUHART •

Great Glen

Grampian Mountains

Ben Nevis

FORT WILLIAM •

CALEDONII

MEARNS

ANGUS

• ARICHTUTHIL

PERTH •

FIRTH OF TAY

FIRTH OF FORTH

MAEATAE

DUNFERMLINE •

• EDINBURGH

STIRLING •

Antonine Wall

DUMBARTON •

GLASGOW •

DAMNONII

CRAWFORD •

• AYR

KINTYRE

NOVANTAE

GALLOWAY

SOLWAY FIRTH

VOTADINI

• PEEBLES

• MELROSE

SELGOVAE

• DUMFRIES

• HIGH ROCHESTER

Hadrian's Wall

CARVETII

CARLISLE •

CUMBRIA

• DURHAM

ANTRIM

OUTER HEBRIDES

INNER HEBRIDES

= course of Roman road

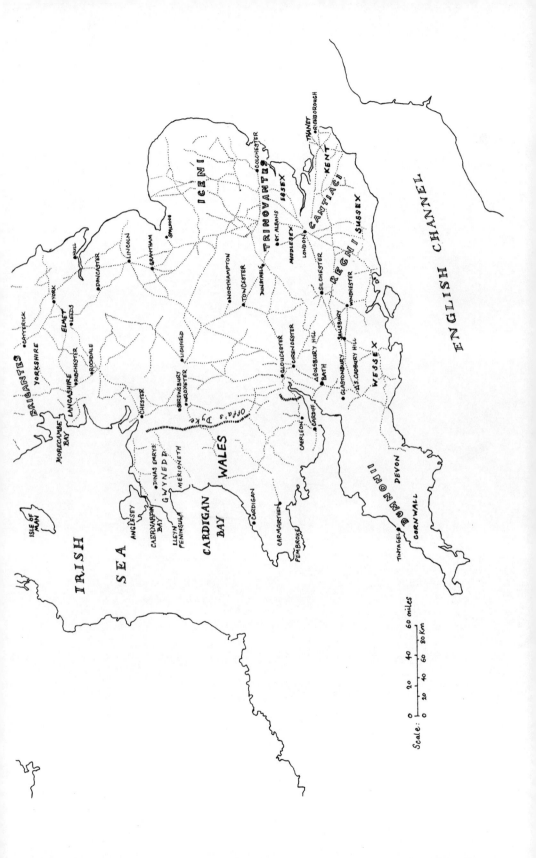

I

ANOTHER RIVER

This is a story of Britain; a tale of the events and circumstances that first defined Britishness, resisted homogeneity and made these islands a collection of nations whose languages have survived to describe several versions of our present, and remember a past different from the one we think we know. It is also the story of a time when written memory fails us and when archaeology is imprecise; what historians have called our Dark Ages.

This is the story of Arthur; perhaps the most famous story we tell ourselves, certainly the most mysterious and least historical. He was a heroic figure who cast a mighty shadow over our history, colouring our sense of ourselves more deeply than any other. And yet he is elusive, barely recorded on paper or vellum and certainly not noted in the chronicles of his enemies, those who eventually won the War for Britain. But Arthur touched the landscape, and it remembered him.

That is where I came across his story, in the hills and valleys of Britain. At first I did not realize what I was looking at. When I began thinking seriously about this book, what I had in mind was something quite different. Originally I intended a miniature. Richly decorated, vividly coloured, pungent and full of interest perhaps, but a miniature for all that.

I was born and brought up in Kelso, a small town in the Scottish Border country and, quite simply, I wanted to write a history of the place because it will always mean home for me and the sight of it still warms me even after thirty years of absence. I had no ambition past capturing something of the essence of Kelso by setting down in reasonable order a chronicle of the years of its existence.

But almost as soon as I began my research, a series of unexpected and puzzling questions threatened to detour my straightforward purpose. Kelso first comes on written record in 1128 when monastic clerks drew up the abbey's foundation charter. All of the villages, churches and farms detailed in the document must have been going concerns well before that date, and so I set about finding earlier references to the town and its hinterland. Scottish medieval records are notoriously scant but I was still surprised at the paucity of material. I could find only one mention of Kelso before 1128 in any sort of document at all. This was an English translation of a poem written in Edinburgh around 600. Not in Gaelic as you might ignorantly expect, or Latin, but in an ancient form of Welsh. Known as 'The Gododdin'[1] it tells the story of the warriors of King Mynyddawg and their disastrous expedition to fight the Angles at Catterick in North Yorkshire. One of the Gododdin princes is named as Catrawt of Calchvyndd. I realized immediately that this is the oldest name for Kelso and also its derivation. In Old Welsh, Calchvyndd means 'chalky height' and not only is part of the town built on such an outcrop but the street leading to it bears a translation, the Scots name Chalkheugh Terrace. And in the 1128 charter Kelso is spelled Calchou. Calchvyndd and Kelso are clearly the same place.

But I found myself more than surprised to read the early history of the south of Scotland in Welsh, and more, to read of Welsh-speaking princes, kings and kingdoms in a place I thought I knew well. Who were these people? Where were these lost kingdoms? It seemed to me that there was another river running.

[1] K.H. Jackson, *The Gododdin: The Old Scottish Poem* (1969).

Catrawt and his Calchvyndd led me to ask many questions, but in particular he suggested place-names as a rich source for the early history of Kelso and the Scottish Borders. What I found gradually revealed to me was something remarkable: a story of Britain and, more, the historical truth of the most famous secular story in the world, what people miscall the Legend of King Arthur. Neither a legend nor a king, I found him remembered by the land, in the fields, rivers and hills of southern Scotland, and by extension by the people who farmed, knew and named where they lived. Unremarked by history, little people who walked and worked their lives for generations under Border skies. And also by looking hard at a small place I began to become aware of a much larger picture until, after a time, I could lift up a map of the Border country and see clearly the watermark of Arthur.

Before I go on to the meat of what I have found, I should make some confessions and assertions. As a historian I am an amateur, in the old sense of loving it, and emphatically not in the new sense of being sloppy or less than serious. I am certainly not an academic historian, not time-served and with no folio of published papers to act as pencil sketches for the big picture. Anyway, what academic would want to do something so literally amateurish as to write the history of his home town?[2] Aside from a decent education, I only have two claims to bring to the reader's attention. The first is simple: since no one asked me to do this, I am not obliged to be anything other than my own man. I care nothing for academic reputation, the conventional wisdom or the weight of opinion. These researches are founded on common sense and sufficient erudition.

My second claim will take longer to unpack. It directly concerns my interest in the names of places, more properly toponymy, and how my knowledge of all this began.

When I was a little boy in the 1950s my dad took me with him in his van to summer jobs. He was an electrician who worked on Saturday mornings, often going out to the grand houses of the

[2] Alistair Moffat, *Kelsae* (1985).

3

Borders to fit a plug on a kettle or replace a lightbulb for ancient aristocrats with servants still suspicious of electricity. The toffs, as he labelled them, did not interest him much but my dad was fascinated by their land and their ability to hang on to it and shape it to their purposes. One Saturday he took me to a place called the Hundy Mundy Tower. Standing in the dank wood almost completely hidden, it was a chilly, creepy building resembling the gable end of a Gothic cathedral. My dad explained that it was a folly designed to finish a vista from the windows of a big house. The trees had been planted to add mystery and spurious antiquity. 'Power,' he said to me many years later, 'that is real power; being able to alter the landscape to suit one man's idea of a good view and invent a bit of history forbye.'

My dad knew the land around Kelso intimately and we talked a great deal about change, how it could obliterate history and how often the names of their places were all that remained of peoples who had long vanished into the darkness of the past. As he grew older and frail, I realized that much of his sort of understanding of the Borders would be obliterated too. Therefore I made extensive tape recordings with my dad and in rereading the typescript of this book I can hear the echo of his insistent voice clearly. No one else can, only me.

One more word before I set out my narrative. Much to the distaste, no doubt, of proper historians this piece of work is occasionally conveyed in the first person, not objective but nominative. In fact it is precisely names that make it so. I am a Moffat, first from western Berwickshire, earlier from Dumfriesshire. My mother's people are Irvines, Murrays and Renwicks from Hawick and the hill country to the west. All ancient Border families, people who stayed where they found themselves and found where they stayed to be beautiful. We have been here for millennia but, apart from playing rugby for Scotland, none of my family has gained great wealth, fame or notoriety. We have acquired few airs or graces. There is no need. We are all Borderers, and that is more than enough.

And that is precisely my claim. The landscape of the Scottish Border country is part of me, I know it in my soul. The red earth of Berwickshire is grained in my hands, the rain-fed fields of the Tweed valley nourished me and the hills and forests of Selkirk fill my eye. I know this place.

2

AN ACCIDENTAL HISTORY

Since this book began its life as a series of accidental discoveries, I should begin by describing the sequence of events that forced me to draw such an unlooked-for conclusion.

Despite my frequent puzzlements and pauses I completed my history of Kelso in 1985. I remember an excellent party, some daft speeches and a hilarious dinner with my mum and dad pleased as punch that I had dedicated the book to them. Because it was the name used by ordinary people I called it *Kelsae* and then below it for those who wanted a Sunday name: *A History of Kelso from the Earliest Times*. Except it wasn't. The earliest it got was 1113 when the future King David I of Scotland planted a settlement of austere French monks from Tiron first at Selkirk and then, moving them downriver in 1128, at Kelso. Being literate and careful men, they set down all the gifts given by David in a long foundation charter.[1] While the document is rich in detail, overflows with place-names, descriptions of natural features and much monkish precision, it was none the less frustrating to have to begin the history of such an ancient place as late as 1113. Particularly since the quarry I mined for material contained nuggets of information (much of which I

[1] *Kelso Liber* (*Liber S. Marie de Calchou*) (The Bannatyne Club, 1846).

failed completely to understand at first) about the lost centuries before the monks of Tiron came to the Borders and wrote down what they found.

My quarry was a collection of 562 documents or charters bound together in what is known as the *Kelso Liber*. Published by a nineteenth-century gentlemen's antiquarian association, the Bannatyne Club, the *Liber* is a singular thing. As a printing job it is remarkable as it sets out precisely the homespun, everyday Latin turned out by the monks of Kelso Abbey's scriptorium. They wrote on precious vellum and parchment and to save space they developed an inconsistent shorthand which, maddeningly, the printers and proof-readers had reproduced in all its inconsistency. However, once I had cracked its codes I found behind the idiosyncratic Latin a terse and sometimes elegant style and, with documents dating from 1113 to 1567, a surprising continuity of expression.

The twelfth-century documents of the *Kelso Liber* describe important places, a busy economy, and great wealth gifted to the Church. King David I moved the Tironensian monks from his Forest of Selkirk to Kelso so that he could concentrate economic, military, administrative and spiritual power in one place. He already held a massive royal castle across the Tweed from Kelso at Roxburgh, while beside it was his royal burgh of the same name. Established as an international centre for the trade in raw wool, Roxburgh was booming in the early twelfth century. It contained four churches, a grammar school, five mintmasters and by 1150 a new town forced the expansion of the town walls to incorporate it. David I needed literate men to help him administer his kingdom; he was very often at Roxburgh and so he moved his new abbey to Kelso for convenience and strength. And for a spiritual focus to confer prestige and dignity on all around it.

The foundation charters of Kelso Abbey list a long, immensely detailed and rich inventory of property, services and hard cash given by the king and by wealthy subjects anxious to impress him. Impossible to measure in today's values, perhaps the fabulous new wealth of the monks is best expressed by a telling comparison. By the end of the sixteenth century most, but not all, of what remained of the abbey's patrimony was appropriated by the Kers, a notorious Border clan based at a nearby stronghold, Cessford Castle. The Kers took a new title from the old castle and burgh, then became the Innes-Kers (Ker is pronounced 'Car') and are now the Dukes of Roxburghe (with an 'e'), one of the wealthiest and most widely landed families in Britain.

Twenty miles downriver was another bustling town much written about in the *Kelso Liber*. The port of Berwick-upon-Tweed was the main exit point and trading post for the raw wool shipped out to the primitive cloth factories of Flanders and the Rhine estuary. Colonies of Flemings and Germans were settled in the town in the early twelfth century and once again generous portions of the customs revenue, valuable property in the town, salmon fisheries in the Tweed estuary and many other rights and services were gifted by the king. These properties, incidentally, only escaped the clutches of the acquisitive Kers by dint of Richard III incorporating Berwick as part of England in 1483.

Being the supply end of an embryonic textile industry in Europe, Roxburgh and Berwick formed together the beating economic heart of medieval Scotland. When they addressed charters to their Scottish, French, Flemish and English friends, David I and his successors reflected a busy, expanding cosmopolitan society. And so long as the English and the Scots remained friends, Roxburgh, Kelso and Berwick boomed. But with the accidental death of Alexander III in 1286 and the drying up of legitimate heirs to the Scottish throne, the expansionist Edward I of England turned his attention northwards, and then followed it with his armies when he did not get his way. Centuries of intermittent border warfare ensued. Trade declined, international contact virtually ceased, and over time the Borders became a place where people crossed a frontier on their way north to do business in Edinburgh, or south to London. Berwick was split from Roxburgh, and ultimately the latter diminished to extinction.

It is easy to forget the bustle of the market place, the buzz of language – English, Scots, Gaelic, Flemish, French and German were all spoken as deals were struck in the Market Place of Roxburgh. It is all gone now, without leaving any mark on the landscape. Only the sheep are still there, quietly grazing where once their fleeces brought promissory notes of exchange from Flemish merchants.

What became increasingly clear to me as I read the *Kelso Liber*, all of it, was how important this place was. By any modern measure Roxburgh/Kelso was the capital place of Scotland in the twelfth century. It generated immense wealth, it minted the coinage of the young kingdom and the king set his seal on many hundreds of documents in Roxburgh Castle.

However, an important question hovered over all this. Why is this large city not noted in any source before 1113? How can it be that such an important place makes such a dramatic, instant historical appearance, like a medieval Atlantis emerging from the mists of anonymity? The truth is that Roxburgh was not built the summer before the monks arrived and sharpened their quills to write about it. Clearly the town had been established for a very long time before that. But the fact is that there are no documentary facts. Nothing to refer to except common sense and a knowledge of the place and its name.

While the consistency of expression, of grammatical form and of vocabulary over the 562 charters written between 1113 and 1567 in the *Kelso Liber* is remarkable, there is a quiet, barely discernible undercurrent of change which flows through that record of 450 years of experience in one place. When the Tironensians arrived in the Borders from France, they would have understood little of what local people had to say to them. As members of the French-speaking ruling élite imported into Scotland by David I, that may not have mattered much. Except in one vital area: land. Most of the abbey's new wealth was reckoned in acreage and in order to record their gifts clearly and safely, the clerks of the scriptorium needed to know two things: the name of the place they were to own and its

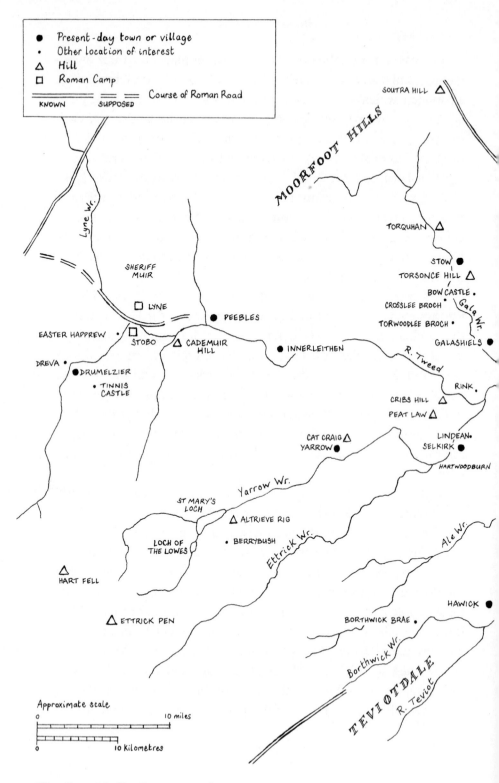

The Scottish Borders: central area

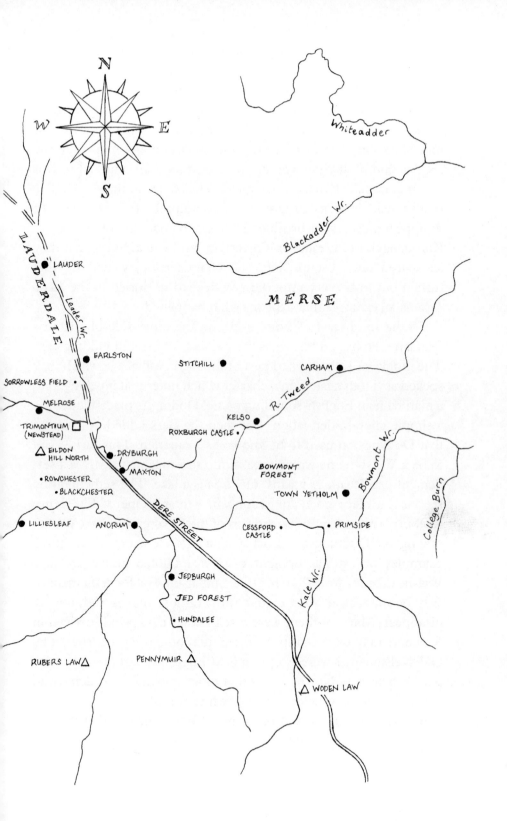

precise boundaries. A difficult business and the monks no doubt lost a good deal in the translation. There are nearly 2,000 place-names scattered through the documents and, even allowing for radical spelling variants, 112 do not appear on any map or in the recollection of anyone who knows the ground around Kelso. It is true that not all of the 2,000 names are located near the abbey. The monks held land as distant as Northampton, but even so 112 disappearances is surprising. The lost names are often exotic: Karnegogyl, Pranwrsete or Traverflat; but I began to see that they all shared one obscure linguistic characteristic, something that turned out to be very important to this story. Buried in the *Kelso Liber* is an example that explains what happened.

To the south-east of Edinburgh, on the other side of Arthur's Seat from Holyrood Palace, is the well-set suburb of Duddingston. The monks of Kelso owned part of the medieval village which they spelled as 'Dodyngston' in a charter which notes that it belonged to a man with an English-sounding name, Dodin. As place-names go, a simple enough derivation. But then the clerk added, for clarity, that Dodyngston used to be known as Trauerlen. This turned out to be a Welsh name which breaks into three elements: *tref* is a settlement or a stead, *yr* means 'of', *Llin* is a lake. The settlement by the lake, a place good for skating in winter. (One of Sir Henry Raeburn's most famous portraits is of the Reverend Robert Walker skating on Duddingston Loch.) The first elements in the three examples of extinct toponymic exotica quoted above are also Welsh: *Caer* for fort, *Pran* for tree, and again *Tref* for settlement.

It became clear to me that the 112 lost names did not all disappear. Many of them were discarded as new people arrived in Scotland anxious to stamp their identities on those properties. The Old Welsh names were swept aside as English speakers made these places their own. Nowhere was that more true than in Calchvyndd which the monks quickly boiled down to Kelso.

But what this process of renaming also told me was that the Old Welsh language culture was near the surface. Trauerlen was rejected by Dodin and the clerks of the abbey scriptorium but I am certain that it stayed for generations in the mouths of the ordinary people who formed the cultural bedrock of southern Scotland. People who understood Welsh names and, as I will show, who may have even retained remnants of the old language far into the medieval period.

There are some fossil remains of Welsh names that can easily be seen nowadays. The new people, like Dodin, took the best land but up-country in the more remote areas away from the population centres the old names persisted. Another *tref* makes the point. A sharp-eyed traveller on the A68 going south might notice a road sign near Lauder pointing to a by-road to Trabrown. In the collection of documents for Dryburgh Abbey[2] it has the give-away spelling of Treuerbrun or Tref yr bryn, or 'the settlement on the hill' or, since it is now a farm place, better as 'hillstead'. The name survived because the land was less sought after and the people in whose mouths Trabrown felt more comfortable retained the power to call it what they had always called it. These stubborn men and women form the basis of this story and the place-names they left to us will continually light our way through the voids of Dark Ages Scotland.

At the points in our history where documentary evidence is almost totally lacking, historians have for the most part regarded toponymy – the study of the place-names of a country or district – as a footnote rather than a guide. They have mistrusted the land as a text in itself and ignored our eternal, primal connection with the ground we live on. We are bound to leave our mark in more ways than an archaeologist can dig out and the names of our places beat out the rhythm of history more steadily and honestly than a stray text from a propagandist monk anxious to apply his partial slant to a piece of history somebody else told him. Too much importance has been attached to documentary history, too little to what the landscape can tell us.

[2] *Dryburgh Liber (Liber S. Marie de Dryburgh)* (The Bannatyne Club, 1847).

Here is a good example of how dry etymology can lead to daft conclusions even in a case where some play is allowed to toponymy. Melrose has been a holy place for at least a millennium and a half. Saints Cuthbert and Aidan and possibly Ninian had strong connections, as did the mother house at Lindisfarne. The original Celtic monastery lay in a loop of the River Tweed two miles to the east of the later Cistercian abbey so beloved of Sir Walter Scott. The name Melrose is everywhere written up as a reflection of the topography. From Gaelic the second element is *ros* for 'a promontory' – the loop of the Tweed – while the first is *maol* which means 'bare'. So Melrose is Mailros or, it is widely repeated, 'bare promontory'. That is a derivation produced by someone who has never visited the site and has missed an obvious connection with the known history of the place. Certainly Old Melrose lies on sufficient of an inland promontory to allow the second element, but 'bare'? The fields at Old Melrose, watered by the nourishing currents of the Tweed, are lush with corn each summer and in fallow years the farmer cuts some of the best hay in the Borders. It may be a promontory but it is not bare. What *'maol'* actually refers to is the men who lived at Old Melrose. In both Gaelic and Welsh it means not only 'bare' but also 'bald'. Celtic monks had a severe tonsure cut from ear to ear right over the crown of their heads. Melrose got its name because local people called it 'the promontory of the monks'.

The point of this example is a simple one. If scores of historians can fail to see the value of correct toponymy with a name and place as famous and important as Melrose, what else has been missed?

These are all questions that jumped out at me as I worked on my original book on Kelso. They told me that through the history of my native place another river ran and although I had little idea at the time where it would lead, it bothered me that so much that was obvious to me, a local amateur, was so ignored or, it seemed, wilfully misunderstood by the professionals.

Before I finished my history of Kelso, three more ill-fitting pieces of information disconcerted me enough to keep on interrogating the conventional wisdom.

In my researches I came across a spectacular liar. At first I thought I had made a sensational discovery. In the British Museum reading room catalogue I found an entry from a man who wrote under the name of Thomas Dempster. In 1627 he published a history of Scottish churchmen with the sonorous title of *De Viris Illustribus Ecclesiae Scotticanie*. The book records a dazzling succession of intellectual achievements and international contacts made by the abbots and priors of the monastery of Kelso. According to Dempster the twelfth-century Abbot Arnold wrote a treatise 'On the Right Government of a Kingdom'. His successors produced volumes on the freedom of the Scottish Church, appeals to the court of Rome, and in the late fifteenth century the Prior Henry was described by Dempster as an intimate friend of the Italian poet Angelo Poliziano and the philosopher Marsilio Ficino, both of whom were part of the Medici court circle during the zenith of the Florentine Renaissance. Clearly Prior Henry was a man of some erudition since Dempster tells us that he translated the work of Palladius Rutulius into Scots verse and carried on a lengthy and learned correspondence with the smart set in Florence.

All this would have been remarkable, if any of it had been true. I spent fruitless days searching through library catalogues, bibliographies and incunabula for any corroborative reference to these works. Not only did I fail to find the learned works themselves, I came across no trace of them either, no mention of their existence by any other writer. The extraordinary thing is that Dempster invented it all. He was an undergraduate at the University of Padua which, having a long tradition of foreign students, organized each group into different 'nations'. As a member of the Scots nation Dempster may have harboured a sense of cultural inadequacy in the company of relative sophisticates from France, Germany and Italy. Compared with the glittering intellectual achievements of the Italian Renaissance, an upbringing in backward, backwoods Scotland must have seemed dreich and unimpressive, leaving Dempster as only a listener in company, with nothing to talk about, no status. So he invented it. By writing his *De Viris Illustribus Ecclesiae Scotticanie* he hoped to borrow sufficient spurious lustre to allow him to pose as a substantial man, to be a talker, an understander, a member of the European intellectual mainstream. Poor man, so ashamed of his origins, he was forced into fiction to cover them up.

Since he wrote so much about Kelso Abbey – it is in fact the focus of his book, and has a correct sequence of abbots and priors in his list of illustrious Scottish churchmen – I think it is likely that Thomas Dempster came from Kelso or from the Borders. That belief is bolstered by the early part of *De Viris*. No doubt in pursuit of more reflected glory, he makes an interesting claim. Some of southern Scotland's earliest kings were descended from Romans who had 'worn the purple'. He goes on to say that they were, of course, cultured men even though they spoke a British language and their Latin was poor.

Either this is a fleeting glimpse of some research by Dempster into the work of very early historians (unlikely given the fiction he went on to produce) or it is a repetition of local traditions which were still in currency in the 1620s but are lost to us now. Despite my angry disappointment at how much time I had wasted on the inventions of Thomas Dempster, his references to British kings in southern Scotland whose forebears had worn the purple stayed with me, and intrigued me. They had the ring of remembered truth about them.

Traditions that carry the crust of old wives' tales around them are rarely worth more than passing interrogation. Black cats crossing our path as a good portent appeals only to the irrational in us all, but traditions which are held in common, which are repeated with some precision, which carry the weight of years upon them – these are worth parsing for historical meaning.

In the Scottish Borders each summer sees several unique

festivals. Associated with the towns of Selkirk, Hawick, Langholm and Lauder there occur what are known as the Common Ridings. Although surrounded by fun and endless opportunities for socializing, the core of these festivals is profoundly historic. For at least half a millennium and probably much longer the young men of the towns have ridden out in midsummer to check the boundaries of the common land. It is the origin of the phrase 'beating the bounds'. Particular trees were often used as triangulation points between other natural features such as streams and hilltops and to mark them out from others the riders beat the bark with swords and sticks so that they would recognize the same tree next summer. And as a matter of further incidental etymological interest the procession of riders is led by two Burgh Law men, or the Burley Men, who were no doubt often heavy-set individuals.

The Hawick Common Riding is one of the oldest and I often went to cheer on the riders with my mother. She was a native of Hawick or a 'Teri' as they nickname themselves. A strange word, it comes from a motto anciently associated with the Common Riding. On the plinth of a statue of a Hawick horseman, the complete phrase is inscribed: 'Teribus Ye Teriodin'. No one was ever able to tell me what it means. But when I realized how important the Welsh language underlay was to the history of the Borders, the meaning came easily. It is a Welsh phrase, *Tir y Bas y Tir y Odin*, not much changed by centuries of use. It means 'The Land of Death, the Land of Odin'. What that has to do with the Common Riding will be explained later, but the significance for me was pivotal. How had a Welsh phrase, not understood, become the unquestioned emblem of a place I thought I knew well?

Land, and its boundaries, is in essence what this story is about. As much as what the clerks of Kelso Abbey's scriptorium wrote down about the ground they found themselves in possession of, what people remember now in these traditions is important. And it was important 800 years ago. Here is an example of what I mean.

In 1202 King William the Lion of Scotland was asked by Pope

Celestinus III to arbitrate in a long-standing dispute between the monasteries of Melrose and Kelso over boundaries.[3] This had arisen as a result of the transfer of the abbey from Selkirk to Kelso in 1128. Seventy years later it still rumbled on. King William's reaction was to delegate.

> I brought together the ancient and honest men of the countryside into my presence and then I put the enquiry into their hands.
>
> At length they came to my court at Selkirk … I am bound legally to the evidence of the honest and ancient men of the countryside. I wish the monks of Kelso to give up for ever to the monks of Melrose two bovates of land, two acres and pasture for 400 sheep which the monks of Kelso used to hold. On that day discussion of the matter ended.

This dispute had ground on for seventy years because there was a great deal of very valuable land at stake, in today's reckoning perhaps two million pounds. And the striking thing is that William the Lion immediately fell back on tradition, on what ordinary people who lived in that place could remember. Something modern historians are loath to do. Indeed I doubt if a modern court of law would accept a tradition as absolutely determinant in a dispute of this scale, particularly if one side was able to produce a piece of paper to back its claims. I fear we dismiss tradition too readily in piecing together pictures of the past. I would be inclined to set greater store by the honest and ancient men of the country-side over against Thomas Dempster and his literary fancies any day. This is a point worth bearing in mind as my narrative progresses.

But first, one more piece of the unmade jigsaw which lay around the edges of my research into the history of Kelso. As I became more and more aware of how deeply the Welsh language under-pinned my work, I came across a piece of great British history: *The*

[3] *Melrose Chronicle* (trans. Joseph Stevenson) (1850).

Age of Arthur by John Morris.[4] A history of Britain from 350 to 650, it felt like a huge summary of a life's work; the sweep of the thing is majestic and the depth of learning is humbling. And yet it contains a remarkable error of geography. Not only does Morris believe profoundly in a historical Arthur, he also attributes to him a long period of British supremacy over the Angles and Saxons in the sixth century. Having successfully resisted the Germanic invaders, Morris believed that a strong British state and army existed over a wide swathe of the south Midlands including Dunstable and Northampton and stretching westwards to north of Gloucester. It had a king, wrote Morris, called Catrawt and it was known as Calchvyndd.

That set me thinking hard. Morris's footnotes and appendices are exhaustive and it was easy to see how he had got the location of Calchvyndd 300 miles wrong. Later Welsh poets and transcribers had appropriated the stories of 'The Gododdin' and applied them to the south-west, merging them with stories told in Welsh about Wales.

As I read more of the history of the Dark Ages, I could see that much of it had become even more skewed compass-fashion than John Morris's work. The Welsh-speaking peoples of southern Scotland had been almost completely forgotten, their history even removed and stuck on to that of other places. However, like many Scotsmen, I preferred to nurse this thought as a grievance rather than treat it as a spur to action.

Three months after the party for the publication of my history of Kelso and our family dinner, my dad died suddenly of a heart attack. I remember it was a foul February night when the young doctor phoned me. There were snow showers at first and then a blizzard blowing down on the north wind as I drove carefully south to be with my mother. There was a lot of late snow that winter and preferring to drive in the light I went to Kelso most Sunday mornings. I recall one journey in particular, like an experience sealed

4 John Morris, *The Age of Arthur* (1973).

within itself. I travelled slowly down the Leader valley into the Tweed basin and the heart of the Borders. A yellow slanting winter sun threw the shapes of the snow-covered ground into detailed relief. It was as though the landscape had been wrapped in clinging white tissue. I drove past the great prehistoric fort of Eildon Hill North. I could see the defensive ditches clearly circling the round summit, enclosing scores of ancient hut platforms. These were things I had never really looked at before, even though I had passed the hill a thousand times. I stopped the car at the turn-off down to Old Melrose and scrambled up the railway embankment on the opposite side of the road. At the foot of Eildon Hill North lay the Roman fort and town of Trimontium (there are three Eildon Hills) and although not one stone has been left standing upon another, I could clearly see the line of one of the walls in the snow-covered fields near the village of Newstead.

Even though nearly two millennia had passed since Agricola's legions had dug in at Trimontium there had to be a way to tell the story of what happened in the Borders before the Romans arrived, after they left and before the arrival of more outsiders with David I's French monks in 1113. We seemed to depend absolutely on other people to write our history for us. And more, there had to be a way of righting the imbalance in Dark Ages historiography, correcting the bias to the south.

Standing in the snow in the Borders in the February of 1987, it occurred to me that I should stop complaining and start working.

3

THE NAMES OF MEMORY

Let me begin with the Old Peoples. I do not know what else to call the communities who lived in the Borders before the Romans came. Until Pliny the Elder and Tacitus gave them names, locations, and some character, the Old Peoples left only shadowy marks on the landscape: great earthworks on the hilltops, burial sites, flint tools, cultivation terraces. And although the pains taken by archaeologists tell much that is useful about what they ate, how they sheltered themselves and where they built their huts, they tell us nothing of what they thought, how they felt, what they feared and what language they spoke. Because the Old Peoples left no written record they seemed to me to be dumb, grey figures in a distant landscape. I had read every history book I could find, gone to the National Library in Edinburgh to look at articles in periodicals even more detailed and learned. But still I could get no sense of who these people were.

At least that is how things seemed to me at first. But after a time I realized that I had been looking in the wrong place. What remains of the story of the Old Peoples is not to be found on the shelves of the National Library of Scotland. It lies all around us. If I wanted to hear the echo of how they spoke, some words of their language, then I realized that I should listen to the landscape. Names. Names of places, of natural features and most importantly the names of rivers. The Old Peoples gave the landscape names and many of them have survived. And since names are words, we can hear them talk by listening to the landscape.

Now, this will take a lot of explaining and a good deal of what I have found is highly conjectural. Names for peoples and places can be conferred in the most unlikely and confusing fashion. Here is a modern example of how this historical approach can go badly wrong.

Why do the Mexicans call the Americans Gringos? It is a strange term with an even stranger origin. When Davy Crockett, Jim Bowie and the other heroes of Texas's war against Mexico were besieged in the Alamo, they had a small force of about eighty Scots mercenaries with them. The Scots' marching song was the folk-tune 'Green Grow the Rashes O' and that is why Santa Ana's army and finally the whole of Mexico called the Americans Gringos.

Historians with an interest in etymology might believe that a recital of a nation's nicknames, or terms of abuse even, would provide a useful gloss to a study of that nation. However the Alamo story illustrates what a risky set of assumptions rumble around inside that way of thinking. The Mexicans believed that they were describing Americans when they were actually describing a band of Scotsmen, and they used an accidental term which says nothing much about any of the groups involved, except perhaps that early nineteenth-century Mexican soldiers had a poor grasp of English and knew nothing at all about traditional Scottish folk-songs.

So history from names is a risky business. Be that as it may, I am forced by the lack of anything else to go on to embark on this course. However, I hope that the process will not seem too laboured and the results not too scanty.

The oldest names in the landscape are river names. The rivers Thames, Tees, Tyne, Tweed and Tay have been so called for millennia. All begin with 'T' and all lie on the eastern coast of the country. That is because they were named by people who walked across the North Sea to Britain. The last Ice Age cleared the Tweed valley by about 7000 BC but it still left Britain connected to the continental land mass by low-lying, swampy plains which are now the North Sea. Archaeology on the banks of the 'T' rivers shows that those migrating were fisher people who used figure-of-eight flint and chart sinker-stones for their nets. They came to Britain in small, unrelated bands but they shared a language. They sought out navigable rivers and in boats they travelled up them into the interior of the densely forested unpopulated countryside. Archaeological finds of pottery and their places of burial trace the progress of the Old Peoples upriver and up-country. Densest along the banks of major rivers and particularly at the confluence of large tributaries, the finds gradually thin out inland and finally disappear at the foot of the watershed hills. Each time a band of these people came to a large river they called it the same thing: *tavas* is a Sanskrit root which means 'to surge'. All the names of the 'T' rivers come from the same word. In AD 80 the Roman historian Tacitus calls the Tay 'Tanaus' or 'Taus', a much clearer echo of the Sanskrit.

That means that after the last Ice Age Britain was first populated by a people who spoke an Indo-European language but were not yet Celts. The persistence of the names might be explained by the fact that the Celtic-language-speaking peoples who followed them understood what *tavas* meant, they understood the Old Peoples who pointed at the Tyne or the Thames and said what it was: the surger or surging river. A verb that became a name.

The Celts had another reason not to change the names of the rivers they found. They did not dare to. In Celtic story-telling rivers are magical phenomena possessed of cataclysmic power and often contain supernatural creatures easily given to anger and evil-doing. Gaelic legends still remember the Kelpies, water horses who drag the unwary to the depths. St Columba was the first to report the Loch Ness monster, while in Breadalbane there was, according to legend, an Uruisk tribe, half human, who haunted streams and waited at fords for careless travellers. So strong was this tradition that the Celts gave the chief of this tribe a name, Peallaidh, which they then preserved in Obar Pheallaidh, or Aberfeldy as it is now rendered down into English.

Rivers were thought to be sentient in those days long ago but even now, in what we are pleased to think of as more rational times, they still retain a power that can reach down the centuries and chill our bones. Here is an old Border rhyme which imagines the Tweed's tributary, the River Till, talking.

> Till said to Tweed
> Though ye rin wi' speed
> And I rin slaw
> For ae man ye kill
> I kill twa.

In the Border country, to draw a tighter focus, there is a network of names for various sorts of rivers which supply more words and more information. Tweed and Teviot are 'T' rivers, the arterial waterways of the area. They surge, are big rivers, navigable in small boats for much of their length. Then there is a second group of names: the Jed Water, the Kale Water, the Ettrick and the Gala Water. Just as modern English imposes a secondary classification of 'water' as opposed to river, so the Old Peoples gave them a lesser name. They are the babbling, talking rivers, large enough to be noisy but not navigable. Kale and Gala come from a similar Indo-European root, *kel*, meaning 'to shout' or 'to cry', while Jed and Ettrick are from *iekti* or *jekti* for 'to talk' or 'to babble'. Two of these ancient names have been joined to much younger words to form the town names of Jedburgh and Galashiels.

Then there is another lesser group of streams which have held on to Sanskrit names. There are two Allan Waters and two Ale Waters in Roxburghshire and Berwickshire. Their duplication in such a small area is interesting but the derivation is harder because it is hidden inside another name. On the Ale Water is the village of

Ancrum. In early monastic documents it is written in the more pulled-out version of Alnecrumba, or Alncromb or Alnecrum or Allyncrom. These show the old name of the Ale Water, which comes from the Sanskrit root *alauna* which means 'to flow' or 'to stream'. The clearest memory of this name appears outside the Borders in Roman military maps of the north of Britain. Three places bear the name Alauna and two of them lie on rivers where the modern name shows traces of the name given by the Old Peoples. The first and best known Alauna is Alnwick in Northumberland: the old town stands on the River Aln and although it has attached an Old Norse suffix, the example is there. Less clear is the Alauna in Cumbria. The unconnected name Maryport stands on a coastal site but the derivation falls into place with another river name, this time the Ellen which washes into the Irish Sea just below the town. The final example is near Ardoch in Perthshire but the reason that prompted the Roman reconnaissance units to name the place Alauna has been lost, probably covered over by later Gaelic place names.

In Berwickshire and north Northumberland there are more water-names such as the Blackadder and Whiteadder rivers that also come from Sanskrit roots.

All this shows that the Old Peoples spoke an Indo-European language like Sanskrit, which is close to the sort of Hindi now understood by ordinary people in India, and that they travelled and lived by water which they named with some sophistication. Although it is difficult to judge how numerous they were, they were certainly not anonymous. Five thousand years after they fought the currents up the Tweed, we in the Borders unconsciously use their words every day.

Also unconsciously, and particularly around Kelso, we complete in our everyday speech an extraordinary historical circle with the Old Peoples. Bina Moffat, my grandmother, used to buy kitchen utensils, and have knives sharpened by 'Muggers'. This is not as dangerous a practice as it might appear. By Muggers she meant Gypsies, and they often drove their carts into Kelso to offer their wares and services.

Muggers is a corruption of Magyars or Hungarians and it is a more sophisticated linguistic description than Gypsies. For they had little to do with Egypt or, come to that, with Bohemia. Their language does not fit neatly into the Indo-European group. Like Hungarian, Finnish, Basque, or Estonian, Romany is in its essence much less like the Mediterranean romance languages or the northern European Germanic. In fact it is a greatly corrupted dialect of Hindi with an eccentric admixture of words from several European languages. At some unrecorded time someone had understood this linguistic particularity and that is why my grandmother called the Gypsies 'Muggers', not because she believed they might steal her purse. That later American gloss no doubt derives in part from attitudes to these nomadic groups but in the 1950s in Scotland a Mugger was more likely to sharpen your knife than threaten you with one.

The reasons why Gypsies were not foreign to me as a child were part historical, part linguistic. Since the late Middle Ages certain tribes had from the king a grant of rights to overwinter at the village of Yetholm which stands eight miles from Kelso in the foothills of the Cheviots. They spoke Romany and referred to themselves as the 'Roma' or, if it was one person, a 'Rom'. Although they used it as a secret language or a cover tongue the Roma had become so familiar to generations of Kelso people that many of their words leaked into local dialect: basic terms such as *gadji* for man, *manishi* for woman, *pani* for water and *jougal* for dog. Two words that have transmitted themselves into modern drug culture via the film *Trainspotting* come from Romany: *bari* means good and *raj* means crazy. But perhaps the most telling piece of vocabulary for this story is a Romany word for river. They call it *tavvy*.

My grandmother had another name for the Muggers. After they struck their camp at Yetholm in the spring and they went on the road with their horses, carts and caravans, she called them the 'Summer Walkers'. Looking back now their lives and their language seem to me to whisper the story of the Old Peoples. Far from being strangers, perhaps they have wandered home.

4

THE HORSEMEN

Around 700 BC, several thousand years after the Old Peoples came, groups of horse-riding warriors were seen in the Tweed valley. They came from continental Europe and they spoke a language that I shall call P-Celtic. Tall, fair-headed and vigorous, they brought a military technology based on the horse and chariot which must have given them an immediate and terrifying dominance over the river-folk they found in southern Scotland.

It is impossible to know exactly when and in what numbers the P-Celts came but it is clear that their culture quickly overlaid the Old Peoples'. Their names are everywhere in the Tweed and Teviot valleys, describing all kinds of geographical features, as well as settlements, fortresses and, in time, the arrival of the Roman legions in AD 80. So widespread and so versatile, the names the P-Celts gave to the landscape suggest that they were indeed numerous and that they came to the Borders in successive waves.

Celtic languages fall into two distinct groups and the differences will need to be explained clearly at the outset. Mistakes can easily be made as one set of names are gradually adapted and changed by another, and then another. The two groups are most readily (but by no means wholly) differentiated by their treatment of the primitive Indo-European *qu* sound: what is approximately heard in the words equal or quiet. One group of Celtic languages retained this sound, making it later into a hard *c* or aspirating into a *ch*. These are the Q-Celtic languages which now survive as Irish and Scots Gaelic and no longer as Manx Gaelic.

The other group changed the *qu* sound into *p*. Around 700 BC this comprised Gaulish and what I will call Old Welsh, while now it comprises Welsh, Breton and (almost extinct) Cornish. The most handy distinguishing word is that for 'head': in Gaelic it is *ceann* with the *qu* sound retained, while in Welsh it is *pen* with it changed to a *p*. It is the origin of the phrase 'minding your Ps and Qs'.

The people who appeared in the Tweed valley spoke P-Celtic and gave names which sometimes they added to those of the Old Peoples; for example at the head of the river stands the high hill Ettrick Pen. But when, centuries later, Q-Celts came to the Borders, they changed P-Celtic names into their own cousin language. For example, Dun Medler, a place that will be very important to this story, became Drummelzier, sounding similar, meaning something quite different, hiding the vital information held in the original P-Celtic name.[1]

There are many other differences to note: in numbers *ceithir* is four in Gaelic and *pedwar* is four in Welsh; *pump* is five in Welsh, *coig* in Gaelic. But there are also many similarities which can bury meaning as well as attempts at dating. *Cadair* in Welsh and *cathair* in Gaelic both mean 'chair' or 'seat' as it is used in a topographical sense, like Arthur's Seat in Edinburgh. This makes P- and Q-Celtic toponymy tricky, and often entirely conjectural. But that is only as it should be. If our history was an open book, no one would read it.

In point of fact there is no book to open on early Celtic history; they were an illiterate people whose stories remained in the mouths of their bards until medieval monkish scribes and others took the trouble to write many of them down. But that is emphatically not to

---

[1] Mike Darton, *The Dictionary of Place-names in Scotland* (1994).

say that Celtic languages are loose or imprecise. The opposite is true. For the sake of recollection and ease of recital Gaelic and Welsh are formal in structure, even rigid, but they sound rounded and lyrical even to an uncomprehending ear. Compared to the relative harshness of English, these languages are a river flowing with the music of onomatopoeia, alliteration, rhythm and rhyme.

They are also the transports of memory. Even in their modern forms Gaelic and Welsh hold ancient secrets in their structure and vocabulary. Because they became literary languages relatively late in their development, and because they are now spoken by fringe cultures often rural in character, they have not changed as much as English. An old lady I met in Applecross described it neatly: 'English,' she said in Gaelic, 'is the commercial language; Gaelic is for talking about the day we are having.'

For the sake of respect for an old person I spoke to her formally using *sibh* for 'you' instead of the more familiar *thu*; something like the difference between *vous* and *tu* in French. For Celtic languages have retained not just the elaborate forms of politeness, they also appear to be as lexically tight as Ciceronian Latin. That is partly because they are actually close kin to the Italic group of dialects. Gaelic *athair* for 'father' is the same as Latin *pater* with the loss of the initial 'p'. This also happens when the Latin *plenus* for 'full' becomes Gaelic *lan*. And when the Indo-European 'e' mutates to 'i' in Gaelic, *verus* for 'true' becomes *fir*. There are hundreds of close similarities like this.

Which is not surprising when we see the long frontier that existed between both Latin and Greek and the Celtic languages. The root word *gal* shows how long. It means 'land of the Gaels or the Gauls' and it runs eastwards from Portugal (where now extinct Celtiberian was spoken) through Galicia over the Pyrenees to Gaul then over the Alps to Lombardy which the Romans called Cisalpine Gaul. Thence to Galicia in southern Poland, even to Galatia in Turkey. Of course *gal* appears in many places to the north-west of this frontier: Donegal, Galloway (from Gaidheal-

Gall which means 'the stranger-Gaels' or more simply the Q-Celtic Irish), Calais and the French term for Wales, Pays de Galles.

This long and ancient line of contact meant that the literate Romans wrote a good deal about the illiterate Celts, but before examining their sometimes prejudicial views I want to unpack one of the transports of memory carried even now by the Gaelic language.

Its colour spectrum is different. The Gaels see the same rainbows that English speakers see but they interpret them very differently. This is nothing to do with that whiskery piece of nonsense about climate affecting language. The Eskimos do not have forty-nine words for snow (that is racist-tinged balderdash), and the Gaels do not have twenty words for rain and a different language for colour because the sun never shines north of the Great Glen. They simply deal with it differently.

For example, English has no adjectives for 'streaked with irregular dark shades' which is *riabhach* in Gaelic; or a word for a colour somewhere between parchment and porridge, which is *odhar*; or for 'dark and blotchy', which is *lachdann*.

In using these and a dozen other adjectives, Gaels deal with colours at a level that would test the perceptional muscles of any English speaker. Like Latin, which has two words for 'black' (*niger* and *nerus* for matt and shiny) and two for 'white' (*albus* and *candidus* for matt and shiny respectively), the Celtic languages take this sort of description seriously. Not only is this because nature is nearer the centre of a Gaelic world than an English one, but also because it was about wealth.

If you could not produce a detailed description of a particular colour then you were likely to become a poorer man. That is because most of these adjectives come from a need to identify different colours and sorts of cattle. Particularly in the event of a dispute it was crucial to be clear that one's cattle were *lachdann*, *riabhach* or *odhar* or all three. Celtic society reckoned wealth in cows and it is no cultural accident that the most lavish term of endearment available to a Gaelic speaker is *m'eudail*. At the end of the twentieth century the polite translation is 'my treasure' but the actual, literal meaning is 'my cattle'.

The P-Celtic tribes of Britain operated a predominantly pastoral economy, running herds of sheep and goats as well as cattle. They hunted in the forests and supplemented their diet with cultivated cereal crops, sometimes grown at altitudes which seem impossible to us in these chillier times.[2] When Caesar reconnoitred Britain before his abortive invasion of 55 BC, he found that the recently arrived Belgic tribes of the south coast were growing corn, which his troops could easily steal and cart off to hungry Rome, but disappointingly, 'the people of the interior for the most part do not grow corn but live on milk and meat and dress in skins.' Across 2,000 years the sound of Caesar sniffing at these useless savages is audible.

However, the archaeological evidence does support this observation: there seem to have been no pre-Roman P-Celtic towns. Instead Britain is patterned with the remains of large enclosures which are often bounded by ditches and planted on hilltops.

Before going on to look harder at one of these places, I think it worth making another point. No literature, no towns, 'dressed in skins' and so on does not add up to backwardness or lack of sophistication. If the reader is still carrying around all the 'march of progress' baggage of imperial British historiography, or any of the weary savoir-faire of the wordly city-dweller, then little of what follows will make much sense.

Far from unsophisticated, the P-Celtic tribes of early Britain could in their minds encompass several worlds, and while the evidence is that their lives were short, it is a distortion to think of them as nasty and brutish. They were not savages; they developed an understanding of the rhythms of the earth and a set of acute sensibilities they used to describe it to each other. As we blow holes in the sky and cover the world with car parks, we should remember

[2] T.C. Smout (ed.), *Scottish Woodland History* (1997).

that these men and women believed in the sanctity of the land, understood its wildness and revered its great beauty.

Hills were often holy to the P-Celts and in the Borders there are several that stand by themselves, rising out of the river valleys to dominate the landscape. Chief among these are the Eildon Hills which the Romans called Trimontium. Archaeologists believe that by 1000 BC the rounded top of Eildon Hill North had been circled by a massive rampart of more than one and a quarter miles in length. The very act of being able to organize communal work on such a scale argues for social organization of complexity and reach as well as a clearly understood purpose in doing all that digging. Inside the ditches there are 300 hut platforms, suggesting a population of 2,000 to 3,000 at its zenith.[3] Generous estimates put the population of the Tweed basin at around 25,000 at that time, which allows a sense of how Eildon Hill North dominated more than just the landscape. It was one of the largest hill forts in Britain and certainly the biggest in Scotland. And yet it is awkward to reach, needing a stiff climb up to 1,400 feet to a summit that is breezy even on still summer days. No water source exists on the hill except rainwater and around the Eildons there is almost certainly insufficient arable land to feed such a large population all the year round.

Even though the name means 'old fort' in P-Celtic, it seems unfeasible as a defended settlement on that scale. The perimeter is simply too long and even if attackers could be beaten off, lack of water and food made a siege impossible to withstand. So what was it for? There are clues lying around the hill but before going on to draw them together, let me first suggest an analogy.

Q-Celts loved their cattle as much as their British cousins and one of the greatest early Irish poems is the 'Tain Bo Cualnge' or 'The Cattle Raid of Cooley'.[4] It is led by the far-famed warrior Cu

---

[3] Stewart Ross, *Ancient Scotland* (1991).
[4] Michael Foss, *Celtic Myths and Legends* (1995).

Chulainn and tells sometimes mystical, sometimes sexual tales of horsemen and charioteers and the magical rituals involved in the practice of the Celtic wars of the Heroic Age. As Irish kingship emerges out of legend into history, the Hill of Tara in County Meath comes into the light with them. It was the seat of kings, a place where laws were spoken – at one time and to many people so that there should be no doubt or variety of interpretation. It was a place where justice was dispensed and politics discussed. Rising high above the Tweed, visible clearly from all directions, the Eildons were also a site of huge prestige, the defining landmark of the Borders, and a place with many similarities to its distant Irish neighbour.

At Tara on particular days there was also much fun: horse races, marriages, feasts, feats of arms and entertainment with music and tale-telling. But more than that it was a place full of magic. To understand how the magic worked it is vital to see past the mythology of the 'Tain Bo Cualnge' and the derring-do of Cu Chulainn. The story contains a good deal about the course of pastoral life and in particular a sense of the stock-rearing year. Rather than taking account of the solar calendar centred on solstices or equinoxes, the prime points of the Celtic year revolved around the herds of sheep and cattle that were the core of life. Both groups of British Celtic languages also remember these pivotal dates in the original meanings of certain words, sometimes resisting half-hearted attempts to Christianize them, sometimes not.

In the strictly Presbyterian Gaelic dictionaries of the nineteenth century, Samhuinn is translated as 'The Feast of All Souls'. In fact it is nothing of the kind. Although the real derivation suggests a meaning of *samhradh* or 'summer', Samhuinn was not the end of a period but the start of the Celtic year.[5] Fat cattle too numerous to feed through the winter were killed and while some were reserved for immediate use for feasting, most were dried or salted. The

[5] Sheila Livingstone, *Scottish Festivals* (1997).

Eildon Hill North and its environs

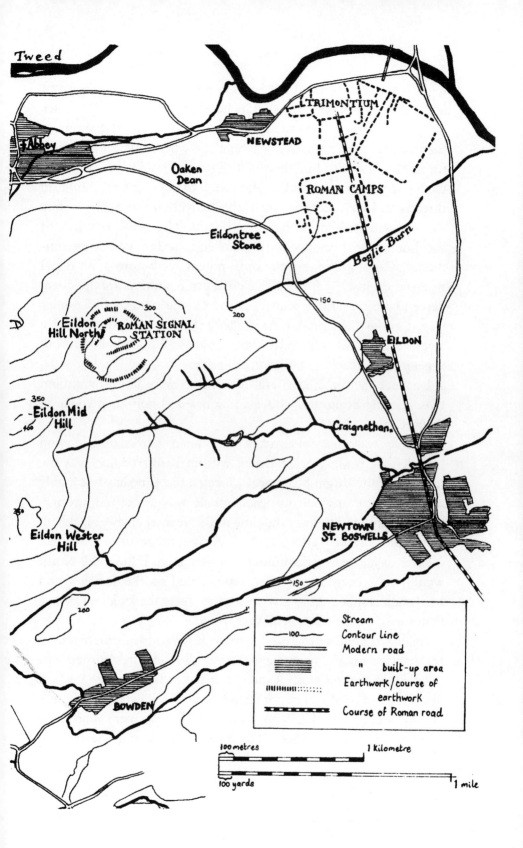

Tweed

TRIMONTIUM

NEWSTEAD

Abbey

Oaken Dean

ROMAN CAMPS

Eildontree Stone

Boglie Burn

150

200

Eildon Hill North

ROMAN SIGNAL STATION

300

EILDON

350

Eildon Mid Hill

400

Craignethan

250

Eildon Wester Hill

250

NEWTOWN ST. BOSWELLS

150

200

BOWDEN

～～～	Stream
——100——	Contour Line
═══════	Modern road
▬▬▬▬	" built-up area
ⅢⅢⅢⅢ····	Earthwork / course of earthwork
▪▫▪▫▪▫	Course of Roman road

100 metres   1 kilometre

100 yards   1 mile

night before the Feast of All Souls is better known as Hallowe'en and still known in Gaelic as Oidhche Shamhna which takes place on 31 October. The remnants of the Celtic feast of Samhuinn thankfully persist, particularly in Scotland where children still dook for apples, trying to pull them out of tubs of water with only their teeth. Apples were sacred to the Celts. Sticky buns are hung on threads and children coat their cheeks with sugar trying to bite them, again without using their hands. The great bonfires of Samhuinn have been historically moved four days later to accommodate Guy Fawkes, but the most potent symbolism of all is still reserved exclusively for Hallowe'en. Turnip lanterns are the direct descendants of Druid ghost fences. As the darkness of winter closed in the Celts placed the skulls of the dead on poles to drive away evil. Now children light candles inside hollowed-out vegetables to keep that tradition unbroken.

I believe that on Eildon Hill North fires were lit on Samhuinn Eve, feasting began the winter and kings and holy men spoke to their people.

Imbolc was on 1 February and again Christian accretion intrudes. St Bridget or St Bride, who in Irish tradition was the midwife of the Virgin Mary, was allocated the same day but it only reinforced the original purpose. Imbolc was associated strongly with fertility, traditionally the time of the year when ewes lactated. But it also became Candlemas Eve, the first of the ancient Scottish quarter days when agricultural rents were paid. Eildon Hill North would have been temporarily repopulated as the farmers and herdsmen climbed up to give their portions to the king and priests who stayed on the summit all year round.

Again the bonfires roared, a symbol of the sun as farmers waited for the winter to roll back. As the flames died and fires burned low, people took the warm ashes and blackened their faces both for luck and for disguise. As a feast of fertility, Imbolc allowed promiscuity among adults symbolically unable to tell their partners apart. The Romans had a similar feast at the same time of year: the Saturnalia.

In Scotland this custom was called 'guising' and in 1796 the *First Statistical Account for Scotland*, compiled by parish ministers, was trying hard to suppress the ancient rite. Here is an entry for the town of Lanark. 'A sort of secret society of Guisers made itself notorious in several of the neighbouring villages, men dressed as women, women dressed as men, dancing together in a very unseemly way.'

Guising took place on at least two of the ancient Scottish festivals but the Church of Scotland failed in its efforts in a total ban, confining it to Hallowe'en only and then only for children. Sadly this has degenerated into gangs of young people with the sketchiest of costumes roaming the streets extorting money from householders. In America they call it 'Trick or Treat'. Despite a degree of debasement it is nevertheless warming to see the rituals of Imbolc and Samhuinn still robustly alive.

1 May was Beltane, a springtime festival of light and optimism. Fertility ran through the ceremonies as ewes had lambed and cows were in calf. When the waxing sun rose even higher in the sky fires once again were lit to symbolize its power and people danced around them deasil, or in a sunwise direction. Then the herdsmen drove their animals through the Beltane fire, because they believed in its power to cleanse and protect them from evil.

As distinct from May Day, Beltane survived well into the modern period in Scotland and the fossil remains of Celtic rituals are easily seen. As late as the nineteenth century on high hills all over southern Scotland ritual bonfires were built, often using woods sacred to Druids such as rowan, oak or birch. Two fires were set with a wide passageway between and it was through this that our great-grandfathers drove their terrified beasts. An astonishing relict of our past, but not the only one.

The name of the Ayrshire town Tarbolton means 'the Hill of Beltane' and on the night preceding Tarbolton Fair, now held in June, young men re-enact long-forgotten rituals. They go around the doors with wheelbarrows and ask householders for a piece of fuel which they then take to the summit of a hill. There they build an altar to the ancient Celtic god Bel, or Belenos. When they light the three-foot-high altar a crowd gathers to watch the young men leap through the fire.

One more surviving example of Beltane should paint as complete a picture as we will need of the uses of Eildon Hill North. 1 May is still the approximate date for the beginning of the ancient journeys of transhumance, the movement of herds up on to the high pasture for the summer. Herdsmen went up with them and lived out on the hills in their shielings. Before they left they were given a Beltane bannock, a sort of custard-covered cake with scalloped edges in imitation of the rays of the sun. Then they held a feast which was a mixture of celebration and sacrifice. Travelling in the Tweed valley in the 1760s, Thomas Pennant observed a Beltane Feast:

> The herds of every village hold their Beltane. They cut a square trench in the ground, leaving turf in the middle. On that they make a fire of wood, on which they dress a large caudle of eggs, oatmeal, butter and milk, and besides these they bring plenty of beer and whisky. Each of the company must contribute something to the feast. The rites begin by pouring a little of the caudle upon the ground by way of libation. Everyone then takes a cake of oatmeal, on which are raised nine square knobs, each dedicated to some particular being who is supposed to preserve their lands, or to some animal, the destroyer of them. Each person then turns to face the fire, and breaks off a knob, and flinging it over his shoulder, says, 'This I give to thee, O fox, spare my lambs.' [6]

At Peebles, fifteen miles from Eildon Hill North, the Beltane Festival lives on but in order to fit in with a busy calendar of other towns' celebration of themselves, it has been moved to the middle of June.

[6] Thomas Pennant, *A Tour in Scotland* (1776).

Just as Beltane remembers the god Bel, so the last in the cycles of Celtic festivals is for Lugh and in Ireland it is still widely held as Lughnasa on 1 August. In Scotland the name has been rubbed smooth over time into Lammas and it was a favoured date for the old, pre-Christian practice of handfasting.[7] Despite the best efforts of the Kirk this persisted in country districts well into the nineteenth century. A sort of intimate engagement, handfasting involved a couple deciding to live together for a year's trial period. If it went well then they agreed to marry on the Lammas after handfasting, often forging a permanent relationship over the blacksmith's anvil or finding a wandering priest to pronounce the vows. If the trial year went badly then the couple could separate without social stigma being applied to either party and if a child were born out of that temporary union, he or she became the responsibility of the father. A sensible arrangement now happily revived among young people with realistic expectations.

Horses were almost as important as husbands (and in some equestrian families they still are) and in rivers and in the sea they were washed at Lammas time in a ceremony greatly frowned upon by the Kirk for reasons I cannot fathom. In any case it sounds like a similar purification act to that visited on cattle when they were driven through the fire.

These then are the four nodal points of the old Celtic year: Samhuinn on 1 November, Imbolc on 1 February, Beltane on 1 May and Lughnasa on 1 August. If Eildon Hill North was a huge ritual and royal site crowded to overflowing with feasting, celebration, lawgiving and magic, it must have had an economic function since the quarter-days reflected important points in the stock-rearing year.

Just as the sky gods of the Celts drove them to climb hills to be closer, they came down to earth to deal with matters of wealth and trade. At the foot of Eildon Mid Hill and its sister the Wester Hill there is a very extensive series of earthworks. They are difficult to

7 Sheila Livingstone, *Scottish Festivals* (1997).

see now since the ground has been heavily planted with thick conifer woods. But the Ordnance Survey traces their layout clearly. Zigzagging in several directions, the earthworks are mainly ditches with banks. Although they use the contours and features of the land, running out at the bottom of very steep slopes or just as they reach a stream, they cannot have been defensive. There is simply no military logic to their layout with ditches running at all angles, connected but not consistent in presenting an obstacle of any formidable aspect to an oncoming enemy. However it would not take a farmer a second glance to tell what this series of ditches represent. They are stock fields. Supplemented by occasional runs of hurdle fences, this complex was built to accommodate the cattle, sheep and goats of the herdsmen who climbed Eildon Hill North at Samhuinn Eve to feast and pray for a kind winter.

The dates of these ancient festivals evolved into cattle fairs which in turn attracted commerce of all sorts to them. Imbolc at Eildon Hill was remembered by the Fair of St Boswell, a local saint who left his name at St Boswells. Lughnasa or Lammas bred the greatest cattle fair in medieval Scotland. Also appropriated by a Christian saint, in this case James, it took place nine miles from Eildon Hill at another magic place. Where the arterial rivers of the Borders meet at Kelso, the Tweed and the Teviot circle a place still known as the Fairgreen and St James' Fair has a continuous history as a cattle and horse market from 1113 and long before. It has now skipped across the Teviot to a purpose-made ground and is dignified with the modern title of the Border Union Show, second only now to the Royal Highland Show near Edinburgh. But it is still held at the end of July (close to the day of Lughnasa), and there is still much feasting, drinking, displays of horsemanship and the herdsmen lean on their crooks to talk about the weather and the price of fat calves. Conversations once held at the foot of Eildon Hill.

Fairs were handy for Celtic kings. The regular dates and locations allowed their officials to control them just as medieval Scottish kings did. But much wealth was on the ground on those

days and it presented a tempting target for outsiders. The landscape to the south-west of the cattle enclosures around the Eildons
reveals an extraordinary reaction to that threat.

The three hills lie in a long loop of the River Tweed. Having
been joined by the Ettrick and then by the Gala Water it flows
north-west past Abbotsford and then turns due west towards
Melrose, Trimontium, Maolros, Dryburgh Abbey and then down
to Kelso and the fertile flatlands of the Merse before washing into
the North Sea at Berwick. This loop protects the Eildons to the
west, north and east, leaving the only exposed flank to the south.

Here the P-Celtic kings organized another huge communal
project. For at least four and a half miles (almost certainly more)
there runs an earthwork of unparalleled scale in the Borders and pre-
Roman Scotland. Consisting of two ditches and two banks, sometimes with an aggregate breadth of fifty-six feet, or for part of its
length two ditches with a high bank between them, it stretches south-
east from the Tweed near Abbotsford down to the Ale Water. There
are forts at either end, remembered toponymically at the south-east
as Rowchester and Blackchester, and at Cauldshiels Loch at the
north-west. Its design is unquestionably defensive, expecting attack
from the south either by cavalry or chariots or both. Local people still
remember the purpose of this huge earthwork because they call it the
Military Road even though it now leads nowhere.

The ditches and banks presented a real barrier to horse-borne
assault and their orientation reveals the threatening shadow of an
enemy based in the hill country south-west of the Eildons.

Cattle needed to be watered as well as protected. Seasonal
streams border the ditched enclosures at the foot of the Eildon Hills
but a more certain source of water lay in a series of wells concentrated around them, no doubt influencing the original choice of the
site. Now sadly disguised by Christian names, St Dunstan's Well,
St Mary's and Monkswell are all handily placed for the herdsmen.

They were also magic places, a source of much more than water.
But it is important not to see this as simply more information about

41

Celtic religion. the fact is that the Celts did not believe in their religion in the modern way; they lived it. Their sky gods, their earth gods all gave meaning, forward purpose and structure to their lives.

Here is a good example of how the religious practices of the Celts persist. All over the western world there are fountains, rivers, pools and wells full of coins. 'Three Coins in a Fountain' was a popular song for my father's generation and it combined the magic number of three with the ancient Celtic practice of throwing items of great value into water. These were material sacrifices intended to placate earth and water gods. The most reliable source for archaeological finds of bronze objects are watery places. Metal weapons were of great value to the Celts and they threw them away regularly and in some quantity. A hoard of spears, swords and arrowheads was discovered in Duddingston Loch in 1778. They must have belonged to the P-Celts who knew the place as Trauerlen. The most vivid memory of weapons thrown into water is the story of Excalibur. On Arthur's death Tennyson[8] gives the magic sword to Sir Bedevere who rides to the lake, wheels it above his head, closes his eyes and with both hands hurls the great blade into the deep. Where a hand shimmers through the surface, catches it by the hilt and draws it downwards. As good an account as any of the rituals of Celtic warriors. Excalibur, incidentally, is only one of many magic P-Celtic swords; its name means 'hard dinter'.

For another perspective on the world of Celtic cattlemen and their use of Eildon Hill North, it is worth turning to the *Ravenna Cosmography*. This is a set of Roman maps of their world compiled in the fifth century in Italy. They draw together the cartographic traditions of Ptolemy and Avienus and many others and because the empire had occasionally compassed southern Scotland, places there are plotted. One of them is Medionemeton. It means the 'Middle Shrine' and although the location is imprecise, it looks to me as though it marks Eildon Hill North. The Romans knew it as

---

[8] Alfred Tennyson, *The Idylls of the King* (1859).

an important shrine, probably the most important between Hadrian's Wall and the later Antonine Wall to the north. There exists clear archaeological evidence that the Great Hill was occupied in the first and second centuries AD. This was previously the period when the Roman legions were at Trimontium, their depot and camp which acted as the military headquarters for all of intra-mural Scotland. It lay astride Dere Street, the north–south artery of northern Britannia and around the camp was a *vicus* or town which served the material needs of the garrison as well as the travellers on the road. Including the legionaries and their cavalry auxiliaries, perhaps 5,000 people lived at Trimontium.[9]

Above them lowered the bulk of Eildon Hill North. It is impossible to imagine the Roman commander allowing a military or even administrative occupation of the hill of any permanence. According to the archaeologists the Romans seem to have permitted temporary occupation and even then maintained a signal station on the summit which doubtless doubled as an observation post. The Romans were practical local politicians and it seems likely to me that they allowed the kings of tribes friendly to them to maintain the yearly cycle of the festivals of Samhuinn, Imbolc, Beltane and Lughnasa. The cattle fairs would have made it logistically easy for Trimontium's quartermasters to levy tribute in kind and to provision their fort for the year.

The name of Medionemeton might be remembered in the name of a house: Cragnethan lies a hundred or so yards south of the hamlet of Eildon. But the substance of it and its historical continuity are much more striking and vivid. Close by runs the Boglie Burn, past the Eildon Tree, while over Eildon Hill there is the wooded ravine known as the Rhymer's Glen. This is the landscape of True Thomas, Thomas of Ersildoune, perhaps best known as Thomas the Rhymer.

He was undoubtedly a real person who lived at Ersildoune or

9 Walter Elliot, *The Trimontium Story* (1995).

modern Earlston, a small town to be found near the line of Dere Street less than three miles north of Eildon Hill. Another Bannatyne Club publication, the *Melrose Liber*,[10] reprints a charter of the 1260s where Peter Haig of Bemersyde is compelled to pay half a stone of beeswax each year to the chapel of St Cuthbert at Old Melrose. Among others the charter is witnessed by Thomas Rymor de Ersildoune.

His defining work was a fascinating poem usually titled 'The Romance of Thomas the Rhymer'.[11] While out hunting on the slopes of Eildon Hill at Hallowe'en, Thomas meets a beautiful woman riding a splendidly harnessed horse. Thomas is literally enchanted as she points out to him three roads.

> Oh see ye not yon narrow road
> So thick beset with thorns and briers?
> That is the path of righteousness,
> Though after it but few enquires.
>
> And see ye not yon braid braid road
> That lies across yon lily leven?
> That is the path of wickedness
> Though some call it heaven.
>
> And see ye not that bonny road
> That winds about the fernie brae?
> That is the road to Elfland
> Where you and I this night maun gae.

Thomas spends what he believes is one night in Elfland but is in earth time actually seven years. He makes love to the Faerie Queen and then escapes with the gift of prophecy.

Now this poem, this man and this episode are much more substantial than an echo of Eildon Hill's P-Celtic past. They are its

[10] *Melrose Liber (Liber S. Marie de Melros)* (The Bannatyne Club, 1837).
[11] J.A.H. Murray (ed.), *Thomas of Ercildonne* (1875).

lineal descendant. The place-names stand witness: the queen met Thomas by the Eildon Tree; the crack in the earth and the crack in time through which they slipped into Elfland is the Boglie Burn. A bogle is a Scots word for an elf or faerie, not always a benign one. Huntly Bank, where the poem opens, is on the other side of the hill near the cattle enclosures and Rhymer's Glen is a more recent toponymic affirmation of the story.

The poem was first reproduced in the early fifteenth century in England but when the Chaucerian crust is broken off, the real character of it is made plain. Thomas visited the Celtic Otherworld, entering it through a portal traditionally revered by their priests. He went on Samhuinn Eve when any barriers between men and the supernatural were lowered. And he came back with the gift of second sight, with the magic of a P-Celtic holy man.

The reality is just as engaging. Thomas's family name was Learmonth and as the records of his holdings at Earlston attest, he was a landowner of some substance. Someone who sounds like his son (unless the visit to the Otherworld conferred longevity as well as second sight) gifted lands to the hospital which lay on Dere Street at Soutra in 1294.[12] I believe that as a literate man Thomas was probably a collector of stories. He lived in a place that had seen great social change and at a time when political upheaval was about to erupt into bloody warfare.

At Earlston, Thomas found himself close to a linguistic frontier. Place names to the west and north of the town (like Trabrown) had survived long enough to be included in the great collections of monastic charters compiled in the Borders in the twelfth century. But the P-Celtic speech community must have dwindled dramatically by the 1260s when Thomas was active. Their stories were about to die with them when he wrote them down, and cast himself in them.

In 1286 King Alexander III of Scotland made an ill-advised

---

[12] *Soutra Cartulary* (Trinity House of Soutra), Advocates Library.

journey across the Forth to Fife to spend an uxorious night with his young and beautiful wife. He never saw her; his horse plunged off a cliff near Kinghorn and Scotland was plunged into centuries of intermittent warfare with England as their kings attempted to conquer and control the north of Britain. The stories have it that True Thomas predicted the death of Alexander III the night before it happened. In the Wars of Independence that followed, many other calamities were foretold by him.

Less black, much more hopeful are the prophecies contained in what scholars know as the 'Third Fytte' of Thomas.[13] In summary he predicts the return of Arthur who sleeps with his knights under Eildon Hill. There is, he writes, 'a good time coming' when 'the kind conqueror' will ride from the west and defeat the Saxons before reuniting Britain. No doubt as Edward I's armies burned and looted 'the Saxons' became synonymous with 'the English', but Thomas is clear about the use of the word 'Britain' and the sense of Arthur emerging with his horse warriors: 'a chieftain unchosen that shall choose for himself, and ride through the realm and Roy shall be called'.

'The Romance of Thomas' and the prophecies spread quickly around Scotland; place names related to the Rhymer are found as far north as Inverness and as far west as Ayrshire. To the Gaelic speakers of the Highlands he became a heroic figure; his origins grew mythic and he became known as Tomas Reumhair or Thomas the Wanderer.[14] His preservation of the P-Celtic legends of Arthur resonated with their ancient Q-Celtic cousins. There is a mysterious couplet in a classical Gaelic poem of circa 1600, which makes a clear connection.

'The leadership of the Gael in his customary step will fall to a champion of the warband of Britain.' Attributed to Thomas, this sounds like a repetition of a Merlin prophecy of the emergence of

---

[13] J.A.H. Murray (ed.), *Thomas of Ercildonne* (1875).

[14] Ronnie Black, various articles in the *West Highland Free Press* (1997/8).

someone very like Arthur. What is clearly traceable is the transmission through the cult of Thomas of this sort of story in the Gaidhealtachd of the highlands of Scotland. Echoes survived in tales of Thomas or his shade at markets searching for good horses, clearly with warfare in mind. At some point the prophet supplanted the prophesied and Thomas became Arthur. Another Gaelic poem translates as:

> When Thomas comes with his horses
> The day of plunders will be on the Clyde
> Nine thousand good men will be drowned
> And a young king will attain the crown.

As I hope to show this is a clear reference to the struggles of the P-Celts of southern Scotland.

There is much more Gaelic material in this vein, particularly from the seventeenth century but the phenomenon of Thomas the Rhymer shows how the Celtic magic of the Eildons kept its power long after fires ceased to be lit on the summit. Even when the Angles came to the Borders they remembered it when they used their own name, Aeled-Dun or Fire Hill. And, more, it shows how long in the memory of ordinary people the idea of Arthur as a P-Celtic messiah persisted.

The reactions of classical writers give a more rounded sense of pre-Roman Celtic society. It is important to remember that such authors knew the Celts well. Not only were the Cisalpine Gauls neighbours to the north of the Roman heartland in central Italy, these tribes also had the temerity to sack Rome itself in 390 BC. That sort of history encourages care in reading between the lines of sources in Latin.

Much prejudice and much suspicion salts the observations of writers such as Cato and Caesar. That aside, the Latin records of Celtic society are both extensive and attractive. For the sake of clarity I intend to differentiate between several social or racial differences and social organization. And also to emphasize that the British P-Celts and their European brothers shared these things, even as in the case of Druidism, Britain being the ultimate source of what the Romans found distinctive about the Celts. Therefore Cato writing in Rome in the middle of the second century BC has much to say that may be useful in colouring the human landscape of the Scottish Borders before his descendants and their legions arrived in AD 79.

The P-Celts were illiterate and while that means that very little of how they describe their experience at the time has come down to us, it does not mean that they were verbally unsophisticated. The opposite in fact. Cato was not the only Roman historian to be struck by the eloquence of the Celts. It was a function of illiteracy. It involved the training of memory in a way that book-readers cannot now imagine. Important speech had to be formed in a manner that could be easily recollected. The devices of metre, rhyme, alliteration, symbolic lists were all harnessed to the construction of an enormous house of Celtic memory. While much of this is now in ruinous decay, historians are too reliant on written record and too ready to dismiss the history held in common memory. Much that is truly old in Border culture is remembered, not scripted and not taken from a text of any sort.

Eloquence is still believed to be a Celtic characteristic, particularly among people anxious to believe in their Anglo-Saxon roots. But it is denigrated now as 'blarney' or in phrases like 'he talks a great game' or 'all mouth' and so on. This sort of prejudice, I hope to show, is one of the many unattractive consequences of the Celtic wars in Britain. The obverse is, of course, the adoption of English as a written medium by the Celts and the consequent outflowering of so-called English literature in the twentieth century: Joyce, Yeats, MacDiarmid, Heaney, Stevenson, O'Neill, Dylan Thomas, Barrie. There is a much longer list available but it suffices to ask where the blarney is in all that.

Reckless bravery ran through Roman descriptions of the Celts, particularly during Caesar's invasion of Gaul.[15] Protected by the absolute certainty of an afterlife, warriors fought to the death and, as we shall see, to the last man. There are even reports from the historian Polybius of a class of Celtic spearmen who went naked into battle. Wearing only a torc around their necks, these men believed that their nudity protected them, and that their souls were immortal.

Drunkenness was also associated with battle and in later poetry scenes are painted of warriors feasting and drinking prodigious amounts of mead, beer and wine over long and sustained periods. There was a clear sense that being out of one's mind could be a spiritual experience, perhaps best caught in the curious phrase 'being beside himself with drink'. But there is no doubt that in modern times Celtic blarney-men such as Brendan Behan and Dylan Thomas have been only too ready to fill the stereotype.

Inebriation was and is the extreme expression of a general sense of there being a prideful, insolent Celtic temperament (I knew one Welsh rugby player who was described as temperamental; that is, 50 per cent temper and 50 per cent mental) which can find eloquent expression in unlikely places.

What also struck classical writers, partly because it differed so profoundly from their own attitudes, was how Celtic society treated women. They were powerful figures in their own right and Celtic memory is lit by their presence. A British example shows the cultural differences sharply. When Prasutagus, King of the Iceni tribe in East Anglia, died in AD 60 he had no son and the Roman provincial administration refused to recognize any rights that his two daughters and his Queen Boudicca might have. When the governor's staff arrived at the Iceni capital to begin the process of incorporating the kingdom into the empire as part of the directly controlled province of Britannia, they seem to have met some argument from Boudicca and her courtiers. Their response was

[15] N.K. Chadwick, *The Celts* (1970).

incomprehension; women could have no place in government. Ignorance turned to atavism and, far from succeeding to his kingdom, Prasutagus's daughters were brutally raped while Boudicca was stripped and publicly flogged by a centurion of the governor's praetorium.

The P-Celtic Iceni saw this appalling outrage as a spark to ignite a savage rebellion. Colchester was taken and burned and after the Roman garrison had barricaded themselves into the stone temple they were overcome after a siege of two days and slaughtered. Both St Albans and London fell to Boudicca and southern Britannia was aflame. The governor Suetonius Paullinus hurried east from campaigning in Wales and it needed all his legionaries' experience to defeat the Iceni chariots at a battle near Towcester. Even allowing for the excesses of propaganda, the historian Dio Cassius paints a vivid picture of Boudicca:

> She was huge of frame, terrifying of aspect and with a harsh voice. A great mass of bright red hair fell to her knees: she wore a great twisted golden torc, and a tunic of many colours, over which was a thick mantle, fastened by a brooch. Now she grasped a spear, to strike fear into all who watched her.[16]

The Boudicca rebellion offers a pungent sense of difference between the Mediterranean world and that of the Celts. Ever practical, Caesar left a clear description of the way the Celts ordered their society and the sorts of people they recognized.[17]

The basic unit of Celtic military organization seems to have been the *pagus*, a group of comrades-in-arms which perhaps evolved from ancient ties of blood and marriage. Gradually the military unit came to denote a piece of land; incidentally *pagani* is the derivation of 'peasant' or more clearly heard in the French *paysan*. It also came to mean 'heathen' or 'non-Christian' by transfer

[16] Dio Cassius, *Roman History* (ed. Boissevain) (1895).
[17] Caesar, *De Bello Gallico* (ed. Locks) (1842).

because in its early centuries Christianity was mostly confined to townspeople who thought of 'peasants' and 'pagan' as virtually identical terms.

In Gaul and Britain a 'people' or a tribe like the Iceni was made up of several *pagi* who recognized a king or a sub-king. In turn a tribe was centred on a place, usually fortified in some way, which the urban Romans miscalled an *oppidum*. This was the tribal capital and in France and England some cities still bear their ancient connections: Paris was the capital of the Parisi, Canterbury of the Cantiaci and so on.

Caesar divided the Celts into three groups under the king: *equites, druides* and *plebes*. The strict definition of *equites* is 'horsemen' and although in Rome it had come to bear a looser meaning of 'aristocracy', I believe that Caesar chose the word more carefully. He wanted to describe a caste of horse warriors, either cavalry men, or charioteers, the élite Celtic fighting force. Certainly they were aristocrats, landowners, patrons as well but they first acquired their defining eminence on the back of a horse.

The Druids were more than simply the ancestors of the mistletoe-bearing white-robed priests who gather now at Stonehenge at the solstices. This was a powerful stratum of people, pan-tribal according to Caesar and holding allegiance only to their beliefs and their brotherhood. They were the priests who officiated at the great festivals of Samhuinn, Imbolc, Beltane and Lughnasa on sacred sites like Eildon Hill North. Druids kept no chapels or temples, rather they held that wooded glens and in particular oak groves were places where the gods were close. Hard by the Eildon Tree lies Oaken Dean, an old name.

The Romans believed that the Druids underwent a twenty-year training, memorizing a vast store of unwritten and arcane knowledge. And lest anyone believe that these men were anything other than hugely powerful, it seems certain that Druids conducted human sacrifice. The Romans believed Britain to be the centre of the cult and in AD 60 the provincial governor attacked the

Druidical centre of Anglesey and destroyed the sacred groves on the island. Generally tolerant of most religions within the empire, this merciless treatment was unusual and must have represented a belief that the Druids formed a potential focus for trouble.

In addition to their priestly function, they also acted as bards, historians, lawyers and doctors and were vital to the cohesion of the Celtic peoples. But for all that the Druids remain a shadowy group, few of whose names have come down to us. In Scotland in the sixth century there seems to exist only one report of a man who held such an influential role. When St Columba went to the court of the Pictish King Brude at Castle Urquhart near Inverness,[18] his success at conversion was complete when the Druid Briochan was dismissed. He may have been the last Druid in Scotland to exert political power.

The Plebs were as usual the largest group and the least noticeable. The bedrock of Celtic society, as farmers and craftsmen, their daily toil allowed the horse warriors to make war and the Druids to make politics. There seem also to have been slaves but even less is known of them past the reasonable supposition that they were prisoners of war.

So far much of this story has been told by analogy and by the use of sources written by outsiders and sometime enemies of the Celts, the Romans. Two other pieces of history written by winners add something to the picture. In 731 the Northumbrian monk Bede completed his *Ecclesiastical History of the English People*.[19] Writing at Jarrow, only sixty miles south of the Tweed, he had disappointingly little to say of Scotland. Even though that was not his purpose – he dedicated the book to King Ceolwulf of Northumbria, and wanted to legitimize with a proper history the Anglo-Saxon conquest of England – it is still surprising.

Bede begins with a general description of the island of Britain; it contained five languages and four nations: the English, British,

---

[18] A.O and M.O. Anderson, *Adomnan's Life of St Columba* (1961).
[19] Bede, *Ecclesiastical History of the English People* (Penguin, 1955).

Irish and Picts. Naturally he leads with the English even though it is highly unlikely that they were more populous than the British P-Celts. By 'Irish' he includes Scots and clearly he sees both the British and the Picts as separate peoples. Each group, he notes, has its own language and the fifth is of course Latin. By 870 the *Anglo-Saxon Chronicle*,[20] an even more one-sided version of history than Bede, lists five languages and then goes on to name six: 'English and British and Welsh and Scottish and Pictish and Book Language'. It seems that by the ninth century Welsh was growing away from the P-Celtic mother-tongue of England and southern Scotland. Wales had held its borders and under kings such as Hywel Dda and Rhodri Mawr it was developing politically. By 'Scottish' the chronicler meant Q-Celtic or Gaelic and by Pictish it is likely (but impossible to be sure since there are no written records) that a northern dialect of P-Celtic was spoken in the Highlands.

Under pressure from the Anglo-Saxon élite it is clear from every side that P-Celtic in England was dying by the ninth century. Even as early as 450 in Gaul a Christian bishop reports that the leading aristocratic families were trying to throw off the 'scurf' of Celtic speech, condemning it as a language of home and hearth while Latin was the lingua franca, a language for serious people. This set of attitudes must have been mirrored much later in England, particularly in the towns where English established itself quickly as the language of everyday government and of power. And also with Bede and the *Anglo-Saxon Chronicle* it became the language of record. No competing version could possibly be forthcoming from the illiterate Celts, not until the early Middle Ages when, through many pairs of interested hands, versions of their poetry began to be written down.

The job of suppression was not difficult; it is easy to prevent a dumb person from communicating. The Celts became the

---

[20] *Anglo-Saxon Chronicle* (ed. and trans. Michael Swanton) (1996).

peasants, the pagans, the people in the hill country, the men of the wild margins of Britain. As a postscript to all these lost messages, it is cheering to note that it was thought important, even at a distance of 450 years, to vilify, even to demonize Britain's last truly powerful P-Celtic king. Many admire his eloquence, no one doubts his physical courage, some think him dominated by his wife, but few in the audience are on the side of Shakespeare's Macbeth.

Having coloured a Celtic background as vividly as sources allow, I want to pause and say something more about why the telling of this story is, in my opinion at least, important. With the passing of the last Ice Age and the coming of the Old Peoples and the Celts, Scotland (as well as England, Ireland and Wales) was peopled anew. And preserved in uncultivated upland peat-bogs, bodies of these early settlers have been found sufficiently intact to allow scientists to characterize their DNA. Two large-scale studies have been completed in Northumberland and Shetland to compare the chromosome patterns of more than 2,000 years ago with the people living in the same areas today.[21] In Shetland there was general disappointment that the present inhabitants were in fact not descendants of the daring Viking adventurers who had come and colonized the islands for half a millennium. Rather they had many Celtic chromosomes and researchers could have laid the DNA make-up of prehistoric Shetlanders over that of the present inhabitants and detected little, if any, difference. In Northumberland, the findings were also identical, despite the invading Angles establishing a powerful Dark Ages kingdom based at the stronghold of Bamburgh.

This scientific evidence is backed by historical common sense. Britain is an island only recently easily reached. For two millennia the twenty miles of the English Channel has discomfited Julius Ceasar, defied Napoleon and Adolf Hitler and even when the weather allowed crossing, comparatively few invading people

---

[21] For the most recent research, see article in the *Glasgow Herald*, 13 April 1995.

came. Jutes, Saxons, Angles, Danes, Vikings and Normans were mostly men who came in small boats. Unlike continental Europe, where anyone who can walk can migrate or invade, Britain has not seen its population base overrun by the great tribal migrations of the first millennium AD. We are who we were, two thousand years ago.

However scant and half-formed these stories may be, they are what the medieval re-inventor of the Arthur myth, Geoffrey of Monmouth, called the Matter of Britain. It is no accident that the P-Celts are often called the British. It is no accident that Arthur, our greatest hero, was British, not English. Why do we not celebrate the Saxons, the Vikings or the Normans? After all they were winners, they established their control over the larger part of England. Yet we do not identify with them or their heroic journeys and victories. It is the British, it is Arthur, fighting a gloriously losing battle, we venerate.

I believe that the answer to this conundrum is a simple one. We are not Saxons, for the most part, or Vikings either and Normans hardly at all. We are the children of a defeated Celtic culture. And we live a sort of myth history, something from that ancient time between remembering and forgetting. Between sleep and waking, we try to hold on to a sort of Arcadia, resisting cold Anglo-Saxon pragmatism. Almost nothing at all is actually known about our greatest hero. There are few facts about Arthur and yet he is the centre of one of the most powerful secular stories the world has ever known. He casts a mighty shadow, but it has little substance except in our minds. That, as much as any DNA test, makes Britain a Celtic nation. We remember with our blood and without words we pass on our characteristics, our fears, our loves to our children. Early German and Austrian psychologists believed that we held these things in our subconscious and they called it folk memory.

5

THE ENDS OF EMPIRE

Archaeologists' finds show that the P-Celts first rode into the Tweed valley some time around 700 BC. Their language can be read on the Ordnance Survey, and their early history sketched with examples from the collective of Celtic nations, but that is all. No written records survive and consequently there are few events or stories to hear.

Not until AD 80, when Gnaeus Julius Agricola, the governor of Britannia, marched his legions over the Cheviot tops, do we hear the scrape of a pen on the history of the P-Celts.[1] As apologist, war correspondent and propagandist, Agricola brought his son-in-law Tacitus to Britain. The resulting biography offers the first historical glimpse of Scotland from an outsider. Given Tacitus's prior ignorance and his purpose in writing a hagiography of Agricola, his survey of Scotland shows characteristic Roman precision and an almost forensic objectivity. The mixture of anthropological interest in the natives, pity for their miserable plight, imperial arrogance and mild surprise at their ability to resist or do anything sensible at all, reminds the reader of early British imperial history. But the most striking tone in Tacitus is one of business. Like the East India

[1] Tacitus, *Agricola* (ed. J.G.C. Anderson) (1922).

Company or the Hudson's Bay Company, the Romans adopt a cool, efficient and businesslike approach, clear in their objectives and not much interested in what the natives did, or how they reacted. After 300 years of imperial expansion stretching from the Persian desert to the Black Forest, they had developed a colonizing method whose template they laid over Scotland. Or tried to.

Here it will be useful to grasp something of Roman imperial policy in Britain. Because southern Britannia was valuable, fertile and relatively easy to control, its governors had been content to leave a client kingdom semi-autonomous in the north of England. Stretching from Lancashire over to the southern Pennines into Yorkshire was the kingdom of the Brigantes. The name is P-Celtic and comes from the root word *Brig*, which can mean precisely a summit but more generally hilly or mountainous. The Brigantes were the Hill People and it is cheering to observe a surviving remnant of their existence in the name Pennine which comes from the P-Celtic *pen* for head. With Cumbria and Cornwall the Pennines form what might be called the ancient 'Gaidhealtachd' of England.

Strong women figure in the early history of Britannia: Boudicca of the Iceni had already made her bloody mark in AD 60/61, and Queen Cartimandua of the Brigantes indirectly sparked another rebellion. As a faithful client of Rome, Cartimandua had surrendered the British resistance leader Caratacus when he fled north for sanctuary. The son of Shakespeare's Cymbeline or Cunobelin, he had tried and failed to raise an insurrection in the south. Cartimandua's husband Venutius was outraged by his wife's treachery and he began the process of changing Brigantia from a client/buffer kingdom into the enemy of Rome.

In his campaigns Tacitus writes that Venutius summoned 'help from outside'. That can only have come from one direction: southern Scotland. It is the first, shadowy historical appearance of these tribes and, as we shall see, it was not a happy one. In 71 the governor of Britannia, Q. Petillius Cerialis, marched the Ninth Legion north from Lincoln to a place they called Eboracum, or York, or Ebor as the Anglican Archbishop still styles himself. It comes from the Celtic for yew tree, *iubhar*, which, because of the traditional use of its elastic branches, came by extension to mean the 'bowmen'. York was to become the military headquarters of northern Britannia, a place that has never lost its strategic significance, and about which more will be said later.

At Stanwick, near Scotch Corner (in itself a historic reference) where the ancient highway branches west up over Stanemore to Carlisle, the Irish Sea and Galloway, archaeologists have found a reoccupied hill fort which was enlarged hugely to an area of over 800 acres. This is level pasture land including a substantial water supply and it was defended by a perimeter of massive dykes. Here Venutius's army of northern tribesmen mustered from the Yorkshire Dales, the Redesdale Hills, the Cheviots, the Ettrick Forest and from Cumbria and in the enclosure they fenced and pastured their horses.

When the legionaries arrived at Stanwick, Venutius discovered that he had created a defensive structure whose great length made it impossible to defend. He was quickly brushed aside and the Roman fighting machine rumbled on, with those who escaped the slaughter at Stanwick fleeing before them.

There is a pungent archaeological footnote here which is worth pausing for. Down in the ditches of Stanwick, among the debris of fallen ramparts, a series of human skulls were found. When the Brigantes and their Scottish allies realized that the Romans were forming to attack the huge, looping perimeter, their Druids built ghost fences. Placing skulls at important points on the turf walls, they tried to use their magic to protect the tribesmen and their horses and repel the advancing legionaries. Once again their gods failed them.

The instability of the Brigantes under Cartimandua and Venutius persuaded reluctant Roman strategists that the security of the empire would be best served if the whole island of Britain were conquered and fully absorbed. In order to protect the valuable plains in the south, the Romans began a process of subduing the hill country that bordered them. Four legions were stationed in Britannia, a fighting force of 50,000 men, nearly 10 per cent of the entire imperial army. Clearly Rome considered Britannia valuable.

The legions paused at York after overcoming Venutius in AD 71, dug in and consolidated their hold on Brigantia. Then they turned west to Wales which they subdued after a dogged resistance. With their flank thus protected, the Romans swung north again towards Scotland knowing something about the horse-riding tribesmen who had come to fight with their allies at Stanwick. Perhaps they were intent on punitive measures.

Tacitus is silent on this since his attention was caught by the arrival of Agricola, his father-in-law, back in Britain as governor in AD 77 and avid for glory.

Remembering all the time that Tacitus tells only a Roman story, shining Mediterranean light on a culture that left no written record, no sense of its version of events, it is necessary to look once again at the land and its names, and how it offers another interpretation.

High up in the Cheviots, where the grey-green hills lie folded like the blankets on a sleeping giant, near the source of the talking Kale Water, where no one lives now, the P-Celts left us a name which marked the moment of the Roman invasion. When the legions climbed through the hills, their scouts came across a well-defended fortress on top of Woden Law. They marched around it and, about a mile away, built a series of camps at a place the P-Celts called Pennymuir. It means 'at the head of the walls'. The field name Pennymuir Rig straddles the southern wall of what was probably the second camp.

More pointed is the origin of another name thirty miles to the north-west. Peebles is an oddity, quite unlike other names around it. The market town lies at the foot of another P-Celtic stronghold on Cademuir Hill. When the Romans penetrated up the Tweed valley, they camped near Peebles. Looking down from their fortress, the P-Celts watched the legionaries pitch their leather tents. *Pybyll* is P-Celtic for tent and the name Peebles remembers something that the Romans did when they first arrived in the Tweed valley in 80.

Agricola's first campaign was faultlessly executed. The Ninth Legion left Corbridge and followed a route up Redesdale and over the Cheviots which later became Dere Street and which is now the A68. When Agricola and his scouts gained the top of Redesdale they could see the dominating feature of the landscape of the Tweed valley which lay below them. Rising out of the woods were the three summits of the Eildon Hills. Like an arrow the Romans made straight for them, Agricola instructing his engineers to survey the line of march for a road, much of which is still visible today.

Broadly, the road and fort system tracks the progress of the Roman conquest of Scotland but the direction it took and the comparative ease with which it was accomplished allow sensible conjecture on the politics. Agricola's military intelligence had clearly added to his existing knowledge of the tribes of southern Scotland. Tacitus only resorts to the adjectives *novae* or *ignotae* when he describes the tribes beyond the Forth and Clyde line or across the Irish Sea. The men of the Borders were neither new nor unknown.

The Selgovae of the hills of Teviotdale and Tweeddale were the clear object of Roman strategy. They had been with Venutius at Stanwick and, like the hill peoples of northern England, they were certainly hostile to Rome. The line of Roman advance shows that. At the Eildons, Agricola established a huge base at the foot of the great hill fort. It commanded a long view up the Tweed valley, was near the mouths of other Selgovan valleys: Ettrick, Yarrow, Gala Water were the major arteries. And the fort also acted as a road depot, situated on Dere Street, halfway between the Cheviots and the Firth of Forth.

Agricola then struck north up the Leader valley over Soutra Hill and down to Inveresk, his route close to the eastern borders of the Selgovae. On the west the Twentieth Legion marched north from Carlisle up what is now the A74 planting forts and garrisoning them as they went. Then at Crawford they turned to the north-east over the hills to the Esk valley and went on from there to link with the Ninth Legion on the shores of the Forth in AD 81. It was a clinically executed pincer movement tightly circling the hill country of the Borders and with forts at each valley mouth, Agricola locked the Selgovae into their upland fastness.

The Romans had already used this method of containment successfully in the Pennines and Cumbria against the Brigantes and also the hill peoples of Wales. On his drive northwards Agricola ignored the east of Northumberland and paid no attention to the lower Tweed valley, the Lammermuir Hills or East Lothian. A more easterly route would have made campaigning much easier; the terrain is relatively flat and if the line of the A1 had been followed then the fleet could have supported and supplied the column, as it was to do later. Also these ignored areas represented the most valuable, fertile ground, far more attractive and productive than the rough bounds of Annandale and Teviotdale. The very likely truth is that Agricola was indifferent to the eastern tribe, the Votadini, because he had done a deal. Either cash was paid or a treaty made, or both. In any case the east is remarkable for an almost total absence of Roman forts or roads. In addition it is very likely that it suited the Votadini to see their aggressive neighbours, the Selgovae, receiving so much attention from the invaders. And if Agricola had explained to them what his overall campaign plan was, then they would have been happy to see northern hostiles also dealt with by their new allies. Which in a historical way is disappointing. If the Votadini had been unfriendly to Rome then Tacitus would have told us more. As ever we will have to depend on names and local knowledge.

In the southern half of Scotland, the Romans found four tribal groupings in all: the Novantae in Galloway, the Damnonii in the Clyde valley, the Selgovae in the central Southern Uplands and the Votadini in Lothian and the Tweed basin. These names were not conferred on the tribes but derived from what the Romans discovered about them and much must be made of their meaning.

Novantae first. It compares with the tribe centred in Middlesex called the Trinovantes.The root is transparent for once. The P-Celtic word *newydd* is related to the Latin *novus* which is in turn connected to the English 'new'. But how can a tribe be titled 'thrice-new'? Better to slacken off the meaning a little to allow 'vigorous' or 'lively', both possible for the Welsh word *newydd*. So, the Novantae are the vigorous people, a description the legions might have accepted after the campaign of 83 in Galloway.

Damnonii is much more difficult. Again it compares with an English example where there were Dumnonii in the south-east, a name that survives as Devon. Domnan is a Q-Celtic personal name, close to Columba's biographer Adomnan and a group of warriors in Irish myth history known as the Fir Domnann.

There is a tradition that they were so called because they were diggers, the men who deepened the earth. However, before the conjecture becomes impossibly strung out, let us remember that modern Gaelic retains the word *domhain* which means 'deep' and old Q-Celtic has *dubros* for the same thing. Go back to Devon and Cornwall where the tradition of mining for iron ore and tin is millennia old and that should complete a tidy circle around the Irish Sea. The Damnonii of the Clyde valley were known as the diggers or, better, the miners. (Sad to reflect in passing that the closure of the North Lanarkshire coalfield ended a tradition stretching back two or three millennia.)

While names and places shifted, fell out of use and were got wrong, it is consistency of memory that is most striking. One windy winter Saturday I went up the Yarrow valley to look at some standing stones. About half a mile west of Yarrow Kirk, on the right-hand side of the road to Moffat, there are two massive unhewn stones. A strong local tradition remembers that they are monuments to two warrior chieftains, and further, that their followers were not so honoured, their bodies being disposed of in the marshy pool in the haughland to the north, known still as the Dead Lake.

Three hundred yards to the west of this place, called the Warriors' Rest, there is a large flat stone with an inscription on it which is now very weathered and difficult to read. However a nineteenth-century antiquary wrote it down before it faded. It solves part of the puzzle:

> *Hic Memoriae et*
> *Bello Insignisimi Princi*
> *pes Nudi*
> *Dumnogeni Hic Iacent*
> *In Tumulo Duo Filii*
> *Liberalis*

The stone commemorates two men who fell in battle in that place. For my immediate purpose, it shows the remarkable persistence of a name related to the tribe of the Damnonii and that there were princes who claimed to be sprung from that royal line 500 years after Tacitus notes the name. For a later purpose this memorial to a forgotten battle will be a telling part of a larger picture.

Immediately to the north of the Dead Lake is a field known as Annan Street. Like the eponymous river in Dumfriesshire, the first part might simply stand for a P-Celtic word for water much in the way that Britain's several rivers Esk and Usk are corruptions of the Q-Celtic *uisge* for water. Mind you, another corruption of the same word is a deal more interesting: that is, 'whisky'. Street is also straightforward. As in Dere Street or Watling Street, it is an English term for a Roman road. So, Water (Roman) Road. Or a Roman road by water. No matter how ingenious the lexical juggling, the topographical facts cannot be bent to fit this name. There is no Roman road in this hilly and windy valley and while Annan may be an old P-Celtic name replaced later by Q-Celtic Yarrow (from *garbh* meaning 'wild'), why has it survived in the name of a field 200 yards from the river?

And, more intriguingly, there is a very long earthwork lying about a

The Yarrow Stone

mile due west of Annan Street known locally as the Catrail. Nineteenth-century local historians believed that it marked a physical boundary between P-Celtic speakers and Anglian or English-speaking incomers.[2] While this has been discredited recently, it seems no more unlikely to me than the walls built by the Emperors Hadrian and Antoninus Pius. In any event the disposition of P-Celtic and Anglian place-names to the west and east respectively of the earthwork is uncannily consistent. And to complete the pattern of competing toponymy, there is a Victorian printing of the Ordnance Survey of the Yarrow valley which was surveyed in 1855 and which describes the Catrail as a Pictish earthwork which is, in turn, what Catrail means in P-Celtic – a fortress, or, sometimes, simply home.

I have taken a long detour away from the derivation of the Damnonii to show how field-walking and intimate local knowledge can put colour on a dreich historical landscape. I shall come back to Annan Street and the Catrail later, but suffice it to say for the moment that Yarrow Kirk was an important place in sixth-century Scotland: a battle fought, princes buried, boundaries set and most remarkably a traditional reading of the ground surviving 1,500 years, and hardly noticed at all in historical accounts.

Which in a tidy sort of way swings the focus south and east of the Damnonii to the Selgovae, for Yarrow Kirk lies in the centre of their territory. From the angle of Agricola's advance in AD 80 and his strategic aim of splitting the Novantae from the Selgovae, their western boundary probably lay along the modern A74 and the A702 as it branches north-east towards Edinburgh. The Votadini bordered with them to the north and east, although precisely where is not clear, and to the south the lands of the Selgovae petered out in the worthless wastes of the south-western Cheviots, where their neighbours were the Brigantes.

That reading of Tacitus places the Selgovae in the Ettrick, Yarrow, Jed and Teviot valleys and in the hill country of upper

---

[2] T. Craig Brown, *History of Selkirkshire* (1885).

Tweeddale. And their name came from the way in which that wild habitat forced the tribe to live. It comes from P-Celtic *hela*, to hunt, more clearly seen in the Q-Celtic cousin-word *sealgair* for hunter, at least in its spelling.

Although one name is a fine thread to hang a picture on, the hunters and more particularly where they hunted offer a splash of colour in the landscape if several different pieces are brought sensibly together.

Let us begin in Rome in 80. It is June, the grand opening of the new theatre known as the Coliseum, and the description of the inaugural games left by the poet Martial. Deep in the dark holding pens under the floor of the arena sits a large brown bear. Frightened and exhausted after its long journey, the animal roars and growls as its handlers hook their long wooden staffs on to its collar. They goad and push the bear along the tunnel to the arena and the baying Roman crowd. Blinking into the blinding Mediterranean sunlight, the bear is let loose and the announcement rings around the Coliseum, 'a bear from far Caledonia' sent to Rome by the governor of Britannia Gnaeus Julius Agricola, doubtless to publicize his conquest of southern Scotland and by extension the land of the Selgovae, where bears lived in the forests.

A fine thread right enough, but two bits of solid information can be drawn: by June 80 Agricola had only just begun to campaign in southern Scotland but the place is known as Caledonia; and although the bear could have been got in any number of ways, its capture signals some sort of relationship (defeat, tribute) with the tribes and also says something about their habitat.

The Selgovae were hunters who lived up-country, in the wild lands, the less valuable areas. As ever names tell a story where documents are lacking, and pollen archaeology describes an ancient landscape.

When the legions marched over the Cheviot tops and looked down into the Border valleys, they saw a great forest broken only by hilltops and rivers. The climate was warmer 2,000 years ago and trees were able to grow on ground up to 2,000 feet. The principal species were alder, oak, ash, Scots pine, elm and birch – tall, mostly hardwood trees naturally regenerating, giving cover not only for bears but also wolves, elk, deer and myriad smaller species. The Selgovae had plenty to hunt.

This tree-covered wilderness is remembered in the names Ettrick Forest, Jedforest and Bowmont Forest, although the meaning of 'forest' needs to be looked at twice. It comes from monastic Latin *forestis* which means a large uncultivated tract of land usually but not always tree-covered. Often in later times it meant ground governed by forest law which protected its use as a royal game reserve. More closely *forestis* means 'the outside wood' as it does for Sherwood Forest or the New Forest. It compares with *parcus* which means 'walled-in forest'. There is a good example of this in Selkirk where a large area of rough pasture on the edge of the town, between it and the Ettrick Forest, is called the Deer Park. For completeness the Deer Park is now part of Hartwoodburn Farm, or in another way, the farm by the burn in the Stag's Wood. It is a neat illustration of primitive forest management with a domestic deer park for breeding and easy hunting, next to the great wood where stags ran wild. A good strong echo from the time when people lived by the hunt.

Selgovae has not left much of a toponymic trace on the land. Selkirk is thought to be an Anglian word: *schelch* for wood and *chirche* for a church or kirk. The last element is beyond doubt but there is obviously a connection between the P-Celtic *hela*, the Q-Celtic *seilg* for hunt and the Anglian *schelch* for wood. Perhaps it is not stretching common sense too far to hear the Selgovae live on in the name Selkirk, the Queen of the Forest as she is known locally? The only other possible descendant is the mysterious place called Segloes included in a list of meeting places for tribesmen licensed by the Roman occupation. But the name is a confusion. It is a corrupted version of Locus Selgovensis. It is one of two places located in southern Scotland which appeared in the Roman list. The first is Locus Maponi in the territory of the Novantes and can clearly be connected to Clochmabenstane, which is a standing stone on the flatlands near Gretna in Dumfriesshire and which remained an important meeting place well into the seventeenth century. A granite boulder, seven feet six inches high, it was associated with Apollo Maponos, the Romanized name of the P-Celtic sun god.

Locus Selgovensis is much harder to find and archaeology and logistics are a surer guide than place-names in this case. East of Peebles where the Lyne Water runs into the Tweed there is an ancient meeting place known as the Sheriff Muir. Via river valleys it is accessible from the northern hills, from Clydesdale through the Biggar Gap to the west, from the south down the upper Tweed valley and from the east from the Tweed again. For these logistical reasons the Sheriff Muir remained the muster point for the Peeblesshire Militia until the late eighteenth century.

Across the Lyne Water, wedged in a v-shape where the Meldon Burn feeds it, there is archaeological evidence of a massive wooden stockade enclosing an area of twenty acres. The posts were ten to twelve feet high and the area was entered by a wide passageway. It may have been an enclosure for stock gathered there for the cycle of the Celtic festivals. At all events the Lyne ceremonial complex is in the centre of Selgovae territory, accessible to all its outposts and a place sensitive enough for the Romans to build a large fort nearby to keep watch on their old enemies.

Two miles further up the Tweed there is another Roman fort near the farm of Easter Happrew. On flat and low-lying ground, with no evidence of defensive structures of any sort, which lies between the farm and the Sheriff Muir, there have been some extraordinary recent finds of Roman material. High-quality brooches, coins, copper alloy weights for use with scales, gaming counters, a mass of potsherds, and dozens of pieces of Romano-Celtic horse gear have all been found in a large area measuring 700 metres by 250/300 metres. Most striking are two small casts of horses' heads harnessed with Roman bridles. This rich store of new discoveries is compelling evidence of a commercial civil site adjacent to the Roman fort, what is known as a *vicus* or small town.

These new finds are reinforced by the plotting by Ptolemy of a place that sounds very much like the Locus Selgovensis. He calls it Corda and puts it approximately at Lyne. The meaning is from a P-Celtic word which simply means 'a meeting place' or sometimes 'a council'.

The distribution of place-names and their dating shows how people changed the landscape, and sometimes who they were and when they did it. Broadly, the surviving P-Celtic names given by the Selgovae describe a great wood, the natural features within it, and sometimes where they lived. In the upper reaches of the Ettrick and Yarrow valleys, to the west of the Catrail, lie Berrybush, an anglicized P-Celtic name hiding the meaning *bar y bwlch*, 'the summit of a pass', and Altrieve for *eltrefe* for 'old settlement'. There are two places where the original P-Celtic meaning was lost: Loch of the Lowes is essentially Loch of the Loch and Cribbs Hill is Hill Hill. *Pen* for 'head' names many hilltops – Ettrick Pen, Pennygant Hill, Penmanshiel – while the P-Celtic word *pren* for tree is everywhere: Prin near Innerleithen, Pirnie near Maxton. Primrose in Roxburghshire has nothing to do with a little yellow flower; it means *pren y ros* or 'the tree on the moor', while Primside means 'white tree'. This speaks of a densely forested area where special trees were boundary markers, meeting places or in a pre-Christian era, objects of worship. In Scotland now, ancient trees are still venerated and often given names. Each year the riders taking part in the Jedburgh Common Riding visit the Capon Tree, held to be the last survivor of the old Jedforest, and at Kelso the townspeople walk to the Trysting Tree on St James' Fairgreen.

But toponymy tells us that the P-Celts gave their names to the Great Wood. Only when the Anglians and then later the Normans came to the Border country do the names for clearings, fields, glades and open pasture appear in any number. These are a fascinating group with the likes of Hundalee for 'the clearing of the dogs' or Sorrowlessfield near Melrose, which was believed to be the only farm in the Borders not to lose men in the disaster at Flodden but was really named for William Sorules in 1208.

These are not, however, part of this story and must be left for another day. The reason to pause on the nomenclature of the Great Wood is to lay down a background to the next part of this story. The forest is where the Wild Man of the Woods was to be found, among the warlike Selgovae, before the Anglians or the Saxons came, in that time when everything important was remembered, nothing written down. But it is a story that has not been forgotten and is known now all over the world, and began in the Great Wood, the Forest of Caledon, the Ettrick Forest.

The last of the tribes encountered by the Romans in the south of Scotland were called the Votadini. They claimed territory from West Lothian around the coastline and down to below Berwick-upon-Tweed, while inland Dere Street (now, more or less, the A68) divided them in the west from the Selgovae and to the south they may have extended as far as the north Tyne. Like the other tribes, their centres occupied hilltops: Edinburgh, Traprain Law and probably the Eildon Hills on the banks of the Tweed.

Votadini had changed to Gododdin by AD 600 and the later rendering allows a meaning. *Goddeu* is a P-Celtic word meaning 'the forest' or more loosely 'the land of trees'. It has not survived into contemporary usage, except, eccentrically, in Gaelic, twice. The first meaning is only resonant: *giuthais* is a Scots pine, literally 'juicy tree', because of its abundant and useful resin. The second is related to *goddeu*. Scottish Celts saw the Scots pine as the king of the forest, the wildman of the woods, the tree of heroes, chieftains and warriors; a single species symbol of the Great Wood that once covered most of the land. Now there are only remnants of the pinewood left, along with the oak, ash, willow, juniper and alder, one of the six species truly native to Scotland. The second meaning is crucial to this story. The Firth of Forth is called Linn Giudain, but only by the more learned of the Gaelic speech community. It is a name that has almost, but not quite, fallen out of use. As we will see later in this tale, it is a vital survival.

According to Tacitus, the Novantae, the Damnonii, the Selgovae and the Votadini occupied all the land between the Antonine Wall and Hadrian's Wall. From AD 80 until AD 410, when the Emperor Honorius was forced to abandon the province of Britannia to its fate, these people were exposed constantly to Roman culture but only intermittently subjected to military occupation. Precisely because the four tribes were awkward, difficult to subdue, aggressive, the Romans opted for an arms-length policy.

What should be drawn from this is a straightforward point· the P-Celts retained their political and military organization while learning a great deal from the efficient fighting machine that was Rome. Their first teacher was Agricola and his campaign in the Borders seems to have gone forward without much difficulty. Except for an echo of battle in place names just audible down 2,000 years. The Ravenna maps show a place in southern Scotland in the territory of the Selgovae. Called Carbantoritum, its derivation is illuminating. *Carbad* is a Celtic word for 'chariot' and the second element of the name can mean a ford but more likely a slope. 'Chariot-slope' sound a likely battle reference and toponymy finds a resonance in a very likely place.

The Liddel Water runs south-west through Liddesdale into the River Esk which joins the Solway near Carlisle. The valley was the refuge of notorious sixteenth-century cattle thieves or reivers and the site of many clan strongholds, the most famous being Hermitage Castle. Liddesdale was also a back door into the Teviot valley and the rich farmlands of the Borders. The reivers knew this and nearly a thousand years before them so did the P- and Q-Celts. In 603 Aedan MacGabrain, the Gaelic King of Dalriada, brought a coalition army of the north and west to battle against the Angles under Ethelfrid, King of Northumbria. It was a crushing defeat for Aedan and Bede notes that: 'From that day until the present, no king of the Irish in Britain has dared to do battle with the English.'[3]

This pivotal battle was fought at Degsastan or Degsa's Stone. The name has been truncated into Dawston, a tiny hamlet in Liddesdale. Eight miles further down the valley, near Newcastleton, stands Carby Hill or 'Chariot Slope'. I find it difficult to believe that the warlike Selgovae would have submitted meekly to Agricola without a fight. Carby Hill was a stone-built fortress placed in a strategic position which the hill tribes would have wanted to maintain. I believe they drove their chariots downhill at the Twentieth Legion on their march northwards, and were defeated at the mouth of one of their hill valleys. Interestingly the neighbouring hill to Carby is Arthur's Seat.

Having overwintered on the Tay in 83, the 30,000-strong Roman army made its way north carefully. Supported by the fleet, the soldiers dug in each night in temporary turf and palisade camps. Each legionary carried implements in his kit which he could use quickly and expertly to dig and stack turf to form a ditch and bank, on top of which other men set a fence of sharpened wooden stakes. These camps are almost always square in shape, with four entrances set in the middle of each side. Scotland is studded with them and aerial photography has discovered many which are invisible on the ground.

Agricola knew that the northern tribes had formed into an alliance to oppose his advance, and as he moved through Angus and the Mearns, the native war-bands skirmished with his outliers. Their strategy seems to have consisted in avoiding pitched battle. Knowing that the Roman legions were formidable, well-equipped and well-resourced fighting machines, they preferred to wear down and weary their enemy, all the time extending supply lines from the base at Inchtuthil on the River Tay.

These tribes were called the Caledonii by Tacitus, probably because that is what they called themselves or where they came

---

[3] Bede, *Ecclesiastical History of the English People* (Penguin, 1955).

from. It is an interesting name but perhaps best seen working backwards. 'Scotland' is the English word for Alba. It obviously means Land of the Scots, the Q-Celtic-speaking people who migrated from Ulster to Argyll to form the early kingdom of Dalriada and whose dynasty ultimately ruled most of modern Scotland. But what does 'Scot' mean? There is a Q-Celtic root which offers clues. *Sgud* is a Hebridean word which means 'a ketch' or more generally 'a small boat'. There is also a meaning revolving around the notion of a spy or a scout but that sounds to me like a borrowing from English. Much more likely is an Argyll word *sguich* which has an ancient meaning of 'booty, spoil, or plunder'. Argyll itself as a name is from Earra Ghaidheil or the coast of the Gael, that is to say, the first landfall of the Scots as they sailed, no doubt in small boats, from the Antrim coast. 'Plunderers' seems a good deal more likely than simply 'boatmen'.

Alba is more complicated. It is what the Gaelic-speaking Scots called Scotland when they landed and what Gaelic-speakers call it now. The way it is pronounced in Gaelic is the key to its meaning: the B is said more like a P and half an extra A is inserted between the L and B, almost making it Alapa. It is from the same root that named the Alps, the Latin word *albus* (meaning matt white). A word English remembers when describing people with white hair and pink eyes. But the use of *albus* has nothing to do with that or, in fact, with Scotland. Here is how it came about.

In 366 the historian Rufus Festus Avienus translated the works of the Greek geographer and philosopher Eratosthenes. He flourished much earlier, around 276 BC, and in compiling his gazetteer he used the work of Himilco the Carthaginian who lived circa 500 BC. He claimed to have sailed through the Pillars of Hercules and turned north. Two days' voyage from somewhere Himilco calls the Oestrymnides Islands there lies the Sacred Isle peopled by the race of the Hierni, and that near them stretches the Isle of the Albiones.

At a distance of 866 years, through at least one pair of hands, it is unlikely that the name Albiones did not become shopsoiled on the way. However there are references to Albion in the work of four classical geographers, including the more-or-less reliable Ptolemy. All these men approached the island theoretically from the south and in all probability they translated the name given to the island by the P-Celts of Gaul. Because the first feature their sailors saw on the shortest crossing of the English Channel was the White Cliffs of Dover, they called the whole island 'white-land' which Avienus and others before him translated into Latin as Alba. The Q-Celtic Scots adopted the Latin name for all of Britain and gave it to the bit of it that they colonized. So the meaning of the Gaelic name for Scotland has nothing to do with what they found and everything to do with England.

Aside from in the mouths of the 65,000 Scots who make up the pitifully small Gaelic speech community, the name of Alba has not survived widely. Adomnan, the biographer of St Columba, writes in the seventh century AD that the Scots of Britain (as opposed to the Scots of Ireland) are separated from the Picts by *'montes dorsi Britannici'*.[4] The mountains of the back of Britain, or the spine of Britain, are translated into Gaelic or Q-Celtic as Druim Alban, with Alba taking a genitive case. And on some maps the western ridge of peaks stretching from Ben Ime, near Arrochar by Loch Lomond up north to Ben Nevis, Fort William and the Great Glen are marked as Drumalban. There is another use in an old name (and aristocratic title) in Perthshire. Breadalbane comes from the Q-Celtic Braghaid Albain, meaning 'the uplands of Alba'. But it is much further south that a seeming repetition occurs. Near Lanark and close to where the River Douglas runs into the Clyde there is a small village called Drumalbin. On the edge of the Southern Uplands, in the rolling countryside of the Clyde valley, it is a curious thing to find. It certainly cannot be Adomnan's *'montes dorsi Britannici'* which lie far to the north. But *druim* in Q-Celtic can mean ridge as well as back and the spelling of Drumalbin with the

---

[4] A.O. and M.O. Anderson, *Adomnan's Life of St Columba* (1961).

penultimate 'i' might mean 'of the Scots'. 'The ridge of the Scots' rather than 'the back of Scotland'. I will return to this.

Ptolemy writes of 'Albion, a Prettanic isle'. Other geographers use the term 'Britannic Isles' to include Ireland, and by Julius Caesar's time the island is regularly called Britannia. But Ptolemy preserves the origins of the word best in his spelling. It comes from Pretani, probably a soldier's nickname for the inhabitants of the island. It means 'the people of the designs'. Caesar notes that both skin-painting and tattooing were widespread among the P-Celts of the south-east of England and so, before they knew any better, they got the name Pretani from the Romans. Therefore Britain is a Latin name for a Celtic custom for a country that thinks itself Anglo-Saxon. Celticness endures in more than DNA and, despite the designs, more than skin-deep.

But Britain has a particular meaning in this story. When I come to say something about the lost Welsh kingdoms of southern Scotland, I will sometimes use the traditional term Britons because they were the northern remnant of a pan-British P-Celtic culture. That is why the only use of the word Britain in place-names is in Scotland. Most famously in the ancient capital of the Welsh kingdom of Strathclyde at Dumbarton, or Dun Breatann, the fortress of the Britons. Less well known is Clach nam Breatann at the head of Loch Lomond, the Stone of the Britons, either a northern boundary of the P-Celts or a battle-site, or probably both. There is Balbarton in Fife, the Stead of the Britons; in Aberdeenshire Drumbarton, the Briton's ridge; and in Dumfriesshire another Britons' ridge at Drumbretton.[5]

The oldest name for Scotland is Caledonia. It is what Tacitus called the country north of the Forth and Clyde line, which his father-in-law invaded in AD 83/84. The Caledonii were the principal tribe under which all of the north had united to resist the Roman invasion. They were probably also the first group

5 W.J. Watson, *The Celtic Placenames of Scotland* (1926).

Agricola's legions encountered and as so often happens, the invaders gave that name to all the peoples of the area. The place-name of Dunkeld remembers the Caledonii, as do the mountains of Schiehallion and Rohallion, and this puts them broadly in modern Perthshire, in the front line against the Romans.

The root of the word is *caled*, P-Celtic for 'hard'. It is a reference to the rocky geography of highland Perthshire, the screes, the stony passes and the bare, treeless mountain tops. If Alba means 'white-land' then Caledonia stands for 'rock-land'.

However, that name began to lose its specificity very quickly as Roman geographers extended its meaning south to cover the lusher, green countryside south of the Forth and Clyde. Even allowing for the vagaries of classical cartography and the unreliability of third- or fourth-hand reporting, the ancients' drawing of Caledonia equated very approximately with the extent of modern Scotland.

After months of cautious advance, Agricola finally forced the Caledonii to stand and fight in open battle. Tacitus tells us the name of their leader. He is Calgacus, meaning the swordsman, and he is the first Scotsman whose name has come down to us. In classical style Tacitus gives him a speech to his troops before battle is joined. This is a familiar device used by Roman historians to underscore the scale of the military triumph about to be achieved. Although the words, the syntax and the ideas are the literary invention of the historian, the careful reader can sift some grains of authenticity from what Calgacus is said to have said:

Shielded by nature, we are the men of the edge of the world, the last of the free. Britons are being sold into Roman slavery every day … When that happens there will be nothing left we can call our own: neither farmland, nor mines, nor ports. Even our bravery will count against us, for the imperialists dislike that sort of spirit in a subject people. Therefore as we cannot hope for mercy, we must take up arms for what we cherish most. We will be fighting for our freedom.[6]

Mons Graupius[7] is the unknown site of the battle where Calgacus and his tribesmen took on the might of Agricola's legions. They were, of course, defeated on that day, but not decisively. No one knows for a certainty where the battle was fought but sensible conjecture and a knowledge of the logic of Roman campaigning places it somewhere near the town of Huntly in the north-eastern corner of Scotland.

Mons Graupius was the high-water mark of Roman power in Britain. A year later Agricola was recalled to Rome and the imperial frontier in Scotland retreated south.

The Romans did not invent Scotland but they did establish a tradition of differentness. Caledonia can be characterized, albeit in general and blunt terms, by the way in which the invaders reacted. They found the northern tribes too hostile, their terrain so difficult to control that they built two walls and mounted a series of unsuccessful punitive expeditions. Hadrian's Wall was a remarkable response to the problems caused by the Caledonian warriors. Probably the largest Roman monument in Europe, it represented expensive exasperation and a determination to keep out the northerners from the valuable province of Britannia or at least control them. The essential truth to be drawn is that the Romans could not conquer Scotland and by AD 211 they had given up trying.

Although Agricola's recall had everything to do with court politics in imperial Rome and little to do with his work in Britannia, it did have the effect of diverting the agreed military strategy. If the conquest of the whole island could not be managed quickly then the Romans needed to consolidate what they had won. Agricola's

---

[6] Tacitus, *Agricola* (ed. J.G.C. Anderson) (1922).

[7] Graupius is a name like Grampian, which is what the civil servants of St Andrew's House decided to call that bit of local government when all the old counties were disestablished in an act of unparalleled vandalism in 1974.

campaigns had defined the political realities of the north. In the Pennines and the Southern Uplands were hostile tribes of hill men whose territory had been contained by encircling roads and fort building at the mouths of their glens. In the river valleys of the Tweed and probably the Clyde, compliant client peoples had been cultivated in the shape of the Votadini and the Damnonii. Beyond them, north of the Forth and Clyde line, lay the confederacy of the Caledonii, defeated at Mons Graupius but not conquered, and definitely dangerous. Unlike the tribes of continental Europe who could move if attacked and displaced, the Caledonii had nowhere to go, no alternative but to stand and fight – ferociously. That is what Tacitus understood when he put those words into Calgacus's mouth. The Caledonii truly were the men of the edge of the world.

If the whole island could not be conquered in the wake of Agricola's campaign, then the question facing imperial planners was simple: where to draw the line. When the Emperor Titus took the decision to limit conquest to southern Scotland, it seems that he took the advice of Agricola and fortified a frontier on the Forth–Clyde line. Not only was this the shortest border possible at thirty-seven miles, but it also marked a cultural and linguistic divide between the P-Celtic tribes to the south and the Picts, who probably spoke a cousin language, to the north. There is strong archaeological evidence that Agricola built forts a little further north of what later became the Antonine Wall in order to protect a redoubt at the east end of the frontier. The line from Drumquhassle at the southern tip of Loch Lomond up to Mentieth and across to Doune protected a small but strategically vital kingdom based on the valley and estuary of the River Forth.[8]

Tacitus certainly believed that the Forth–Clyde line was a real border, describing the country north of it as if it were a different island '*summotis velut in aliam insulam hostibus*'. And he went on to describe the Caledonii as 'these new and unknown peoples' having

---

[8] Sheppard S. Frere, *Britannia* (1967).

red hair and large limbs. They reminded him of the Germans on the Rhine frontier.

While there are more than hints of exaggeration and flattery in what Tacitus writes of his father-in-law, there is a ring of truth in his claim that Agricola personally reconnoitred and selected sites for forts in Scotland and routes for roads. If he did, he had a brilliant eye. His ability to judge the lie of the land was unerring and many of Agricola's sites and roads remained in use for centuries, even up to the present day.

On the Ordnance Survey, however, the Trimontium fort seems undistinguished. The site is close to the foot of Eildon Hill North but it does not seem particularly elevated or defensible. Disappointing to walk around, a collection of hedges and fields, it is a deceptive place. What Agricola recognized were three things. Knowing that danger lay to the west in the hill country of the Selgovae, the site commands a long view up the Tweed valley to Melrose and Galashiels. The Romans had not only the technology to build roads, they also knew how to construct bridges. Trimontium fort had to be near a place where Agricola's engineers could get his army across the Tweed. Hard by the site there are three relatively modern bridges, two road and one rail, which confirm the Romans' decision. And finally with a garrison of more than 1,000 soldiers Agricola needed to be able to supply them easily. Carts and herds and services could readily reach Trimontium compared with, for example, the inaccessibility of Eildon Hill North which towered above the fort. And on the flat pasture around the walls the horses of his cavalrymen could graze without having to be moved out of sight.

The fort was built in 80 and, with a break between 105 and 140, it was occupied until 211. A recent find of an intaglio bearing the image of the Emperor Caracalla has advanced the end date of Roman occupation to the early years of his reign. During the whole of this period Trimontium's role was a complex one. It certainly operated as a military base with its troops acting as colonial police-

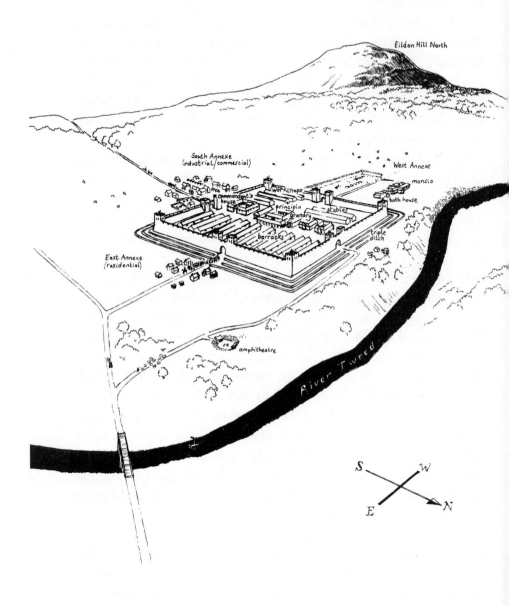

Trimontium during the Roman occupation

men, and, in the British imperial phrase, showing the flag. Close to the great hill fort, it was a powerful symbol of the Roman presence among the tribes of southern Scotland, particularly for the Selgovae to the west who remained hostile. Trimontium was also a road depot astride the north–south artery of Dere Street but also at the centre of a radius of other routes. There are 500 miles of Roman roads in Scotland and, according to milestone finds, distances were reckoned to and from Trimontium. The Romans also used Eildon Hill North as a signal station. With mirror and fire they could send messages south to Ruberslaw eighteen miles away and thence down to army command at York. It is also very likely that the Romans used the River Tweed to bring materials to Trimontium. For example, wine was bulky and heavy and desirable. Brought by ship to Berwick-upon-Tweed and then up the Tweed by barge to the fort, it was much the easiest way to supply the thirsty legionaries and their officers.

Trimontium also had a clear economic function. It was expensive to maintain a large garrison and as far as possible the tribes around the fort were compelled to pay for this. The 'Exactor' or tax collector would ensure a supply of corn, hides, meat and other commodities. There is some evidence, too, of an early trade in furs and wool.

But the most important role for the commander at Trimontium was political. Having come to an arrangement with the chiefs of the Votadini before the invasion, the Romans needed to cultivate a support role for these tribesmen, both in keeping the Selgovae in check and also in creating southern Scotland as a buffer zone between the valuable province of Britannia in the south and the unconquered, probably unconquerable, Caledonians to the north. This role for the Votadini was to prove determinant. The Romans strove to twin their imperial policy aims with the more localized interests of the tribesmen. They taught them a great deal: from statecraft to cavalry tactics and much else that endured. Two hundred and fifty years after the Romans left Trimontium, Arthur and his cavalrymen fought and thought like them.

The centre of the fort was enclosed by a twenty-foot-high turf and stone rampart which itself was protected by a series of ditches dug in front of it. Inside were twelve barracks buildings which suggest a garrison of a thousand soldiers, the *principia* or head-quarters building in the centre, flanked by two granaries, and the commander's house in the southern section.

To the west of the main rampart stood a huge half-timbered building known as the *mansio*. It was a trading station in the style of the factories of the East India Company or the merchants of the Hudson's Bay, and it also acted as a residence for important travellers. Local tribal chiefs no doubt visited the *mansio* to agree their tax arrangements with the Imperial Revenue Department. Beside this building stood the bathhouse; almost as large as its neighbour, its location is confirmed in dry summers by a dark patch in the grass where charcoal was dumped.

Trimontium went through at least seven phases of rebuilding, often as a result of political events elsewhere. When the Antonine Wall was occupied between 142 and 163, it acted as a supply base and when it was abandoned it became an outpost forward of Hadrian's Wall. This involved both increasing and shrinking the size of the garrison as well as changes in the fortification.

The archaeological record of building and rebuilding is very com-plicated and for clarity and direction I want to concentrate on only one aspect of Trimontium: its primary function as a cavalry fort.

During the occupation of the Antonine Wall, a crack mounted regiment was based at the fort. They were the Ala Augusta Vocontiorum Civium Romanum, a specialized cavalry unit recruited from northern Spain and the south of France. The Voconti were a Celtic tribe and their prowess was not unusual. The Romans had a long tradition of creating cavalry regiments from the Celtic peoples they conquered. The design of Roman harness is of Celtic origin and the army quickly adopted the kinder snaffle bit used by these warriors.[9] The author of a Roman military handbook,

[9] Karen Dixon, *Roman Cavalry* (1994).

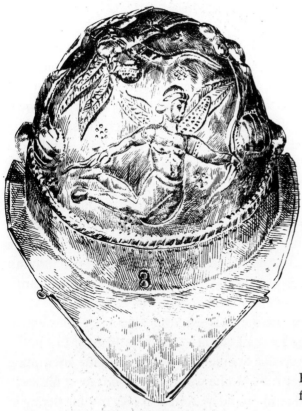

Roman cavalry helmet
found at Trimontium

A visor-mask from
Trimontium worn
by a cavalry trooper

Vegetius, tells us that the imperial army preferred to recruit rural peoples, believing them to be tougher and stronger than townsmen. In his *Epitoma Rei Militaris* compiled in the fourth century, he wrote that for cavalry regiments huntsmen were particularly preferred, having some native skill with their horses and boldness in riding them. It was a Roman habit to levy forces from local tribes and there is no doubt that Votadinian huntsmen would have been brought into the Roman cavalry and instructed in their methods.

At Trimontium a great deal of harness has been found, some of it magnificent. Thrown into wells as votive offerings by Celtic soldiers, several beautifully worked cavalry helmets and face masks have been retrieved. And in the town that developed around Trimontium, there is clear archaeological evidence of the manufacture of horse leather and metalwork on a large scale.

At the same time as the Ala Augusta Vocontiorum were at Trimontium, a huge force of cavalry arrived in Britain. In 175 the Emperor Marcus Aurelius was fighting on the Danube attempting to subdue the Iazyges tribe but he was forced to cut short his campaign, make hurried terms and depart to deal with trouble flaring in Syria. As part of the treaty the Iazyges had to provide 8,000 Sarmatian cavalrymen for the imperial army. These were oriental horsemen who had moved westwards from the steppes in a folk migration. A fascinating group, they were famous for mounting *tamgas* or pictorial charges where they had attached flags to their long lances which bore strange, pre-Christian devices. Many of these have found their way into the unique heraldic system of Poland, which in turn has fuelled the tradition that with its long history of cavalry warfare, the Polish aristocracy are descended from the Sarmatians.

At all events these cavalrymen were quickly deployed and 5,500 were sent to Britannia where their skills were urgently needed. They must have been a remarkable sight to the garrison of Hadrian's Wall. Probably stationed in Britain for twenty years, their stallions and mares would have changed the cavalry horse stock of the north dramatically, since they arrived in such numbers. And their skills as horsemen would have added to the fighting repertoire of both the Roman regiments in Britain and their P-Celtic allies in southern Scotland.

But they brought something else which became part of the British tradition in two ways. The Celtic slashing sword or *spatha* had until then been the main weapon of a horsed warrior. The Sarmatians fought with long lances, perhaps six feet, held in both hands, such was their horsemanship. The Romans called this a *contus* and adopted it immediately. Another innovation was equally striking. As part of their *tamgas* the Sarmatians had developed what the Romans called the *draconarius*. This was a hollow, open-mouthed dragon's head attached to a lance with a long tube of red or white material attached to it so that when a horseman galloped, the whole thing would fill with air. For extra effect, reeds were inserted into the dragon's mouth so that when air passed through them, they seemed to hiss.

When the Emperor Constantius I entered Rome in triumph in AD 294 after regaining control over Britannia, which had been prey to a number of usurpers, his procession was described by the historian Ammianus. 'And behind the manifold others that preceded him, he was surrounded by dragons, woven out of purple thread and bound to mouths open to the breeze and hence hissing as if raised by anger, and leaving their tails winding in the wind.'

The *draconarius* was adopted by all the cavalry regiments in the Roman army in the fourth century. A charge of Romano-Celtic cavalry must have raised terror in those who stood against it. First a horn, or *carnyx*, would sound and the troopers would form a line, trot, and then at another horn move up to canter. The dragons would billow behind them and when the horses began to gallop, they would hiss above the thunder of hoofbeats. These were sights and sounds enough to make the strongest infantryman turn and flee for his life: the worst possible thing to do in the face of charging cavalry, as Arthur's enemies were to discover.

Roman cavalry trooper wielding a *spatha*

The Sarmatians' introduction of the *draconarius* and its colours to Britain have a curious resonance in the Red Dragon of Wales. The P-Celtic word *draig* is a straight borrowing from the Roman word, but I cannot make any secure connection here. In later Welsh poetry Arthur's father was Uther Pendragon or Uther Head-Dragon, and in early myths of Merlin he is shown revealing to Vortigern two dragons fighting. One is red and represents Wales and the other white for the Saxons. The white defeats the red. There are no dragons in Britain before the Sarmatians, and plenty around Arthur whose cavalry force would have carried them into battle.

What is certain is that a large detachment of Sarmatians was back in Britannia around 250. They were based at Ribchester on the Ribble in northern Lancashire where they were later granted a block of land where as veterans they could settle – with their horses. There is evidence that the Roman army expected to recruit from these settlements and given the skills of the Sarmatians and the quality of their horses, it is likely that they did so.

Not only did these men add to the sum of native horse and cavalry knowledge, their terrifying standard also gave us a peculiarly British name for a cavalry trooper, a dragoon.

In the *Epitoma* Vegetius repeats to the point of distraction that the essence of Roman military success is not necessarily superior bravery but superior training. Nowhere is this more important than in cavalry regiments where both horse and rider must be kept in a constant state of fitness. Archaeologists have shown at Trimontium that there was a parade ground designated for equestrian training. This is certain because an altar has been found dedicated to goddesses specifically revered by Celtic cavalry regiments in the Roman army. These were the Matres Campestres and the only altars found for them lie in southern Scotland between or on the Roman walls.

A division of the Vocontians erected the Trimontium altar in a place that has now disappeared. The equestrian parade ground lay on a flat piece of ground about 200 yards east of the fort. In the late nineteenth century, railway engineers drove a deep cutting through it and simply removed thereby the possibility of any more archaeological investigation.

A clearer connection can be read in an inscription at the fort of Benwell on Hadrian's Wall: 'To the Mother Goddesses of the Parade Ground and to the Spirit of the First Cavalry Regiment of Asturian Spaniards styled ... Gordian's Own Terentius Agrippa, prefect, restored this temple from ground level.'

The Matres were goddesses of Celtic origin; the inscription speaks of their association with the 'spirit' of a cavalry regiment and it thanks a 'praefectus', a cavalry commander, for the restoration of the altars. This sounds like an exclusive cult which may be the ancestor of the Horsemen's secret societies which flourished in the Borders and elsewhere until the early part of this century. When horsepower was what actually drove the agriculture of Britain, secret initiation ceremonies were held for young men who were about to learn to work with horses. Much of this was concerned with recipes for certain feeds which would produce particular equine behaviour. But there was also the remnant of a deity to whom respect and allegiance was sworn. When that happened, the young men became party to something they called the Horsemen's Word. This was ENO or ONE said backwards, and it represented the oneness of man and horse and the oneness with the cult of horsemanship. Perhaps a faint echo of the Matres Campestres, and the spirit of the Asturian cavalry.

Aside from the outdoor parade ground, Vegetius advised strongly that cavalry regiments should also have an indoor riding school. Archaeologists have found that around 180 the headquarters building inside Trimontium's walls was demolished and replaced by a large hall, certainly big enough for a group of riders to use to maintain fitness in bad weather. Incidentally, one of the exercises in Roman equestrian training was horse vaulting. Riders were expected to be able to mount quickly by running up behind their pony, placing their hands on its hind quarters and vaulting

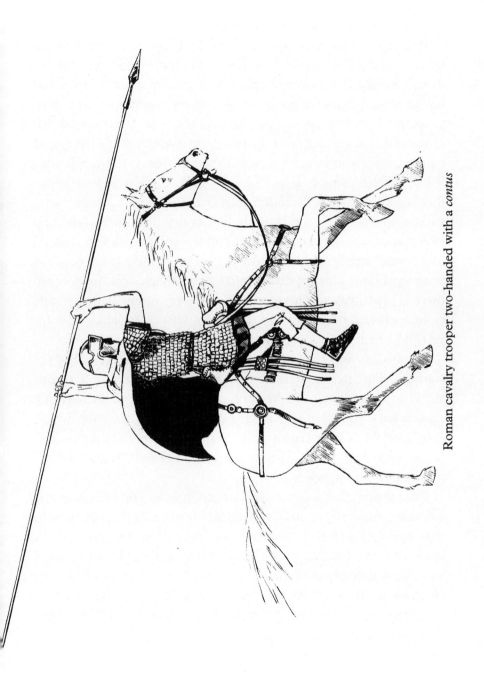

Roman cavalry trooper two-handed with a *contus*

into the saddle, which at that time had no stirrups to get in the way. This is the origin of the use of the gymnastic vaulting horse.

All cavalry regiments, particularly on forward postings, needed to organize a horse-supply programme. They could not wait for fresh mounts to become available in the course of nature. Therefore the Romans created military stud farms to breed what replacement horses were needed. A cavalry regiment of 480 men probably had 550 horses active to allow for lameness, quick replacement and death. At Trimontium skeletons of both small native ponies and larger slender-limbed horses have been found. While there is some evidence of cross-breeding it is generally true that cavalry horses were much smaller than the great black beasts we see now carrying the Household Cavalry down the Mall. The largest were about fourteen hands and the smallest eleven. Riders' legs would dangle lower than the bellies of all of these animals but in an age before stirrups that would have mattered less. In any case there is evidence that these ponies were very tough: a 14.2 hands animal was reported carrying a trooper and his kit, weighing twenty-two and a half stones, over 800 miles with no loss of condition.[10]

The P-Celts were already a society that used the horse widely for warfare. The Romans trained them and in southern Scotland showed how policing and warfare could be carried on successfully on the back of a horse. This began a very long tradition which embraced the Border reivers and which persists in the present day. But more sharply, as we shall see, it also embraced Arthur and his troop of cavalry warriors.

Trimontium was a focus for interaction of all sorts between the Votadini and the Roman occupation, but what lay directly in both their interests was the continued containment of the Selgovae to the west. This tribe and their allies to the north and south were a constant source of serious trouble. At the accession of the Emperor Hadrian in AD 117, there was war in north Britain. The Selgovae and their neighbours, the Novantae, had formed an alliance with

[10] Karen Dixon, *Roman Cavalry* (1994).

the Brigantes and as the imperial biographer remarked: 'The Britons could no longer be held under Roman control.' An inscription at Jarrow confirms that the rebellion of the hill tribes was put down with routine efficiency. But what happened next was remarkable.

In order to separate the Brigantes from their northern allies in the southern Borders, the Emperor Hadrian ordered the construction of a stone wall to run from the Tyne through the Hexham Gap to the shores of the Solway. It is the largest Roman monument to have come down to us anywhere and an extraordinary response to the raids of these tribes.

In Germany, Hadrian had built a wooden frontier fence which had little military value, except that it defined the frontier, kept out unauthorized people and channelled travellers to particular entry points. The design of the Wall had similarities with these fences and shows that it was a political statement more than a military solution. It was not a fighting platform like a city wall with the ability to withstand a siege. The Wall was more like a fortified patrol route affording sentries a vantage point from which they could observe the country both to the north and south in reasonable safety. It controlled movement, had a substantial garrison but it was not built to defend southern Britannia from the north like a huge rampart. It was in reality a fire-break between the Brigantes in the Pennines and the Selgovae and Novantes in the Southern Uplands. These populations must have been large and vigorous to prompt a stone structure on this scale, and the movement of people through the Wall constant and sufficiently substantial to necessitate such an intensive network of forts and disposition of troops, perhaps as many as 10,000 men.

It did not work. After the initial building phase was completed in 128, there was more trouble in the north. The new Emperor Antoninus Pius decided to reoccupy southern Scotland and to construct another wall, this time built with turf, on the line of Agricola's original frontier between the Forth and Clyde. By 142 reconquest was complete.

The *draconarius*

Two walls, two huge construction projects in fifteen years is, given Roman practicality, on the face of it surprising, even inefficient. Hadrian's Wall was not built in the wrong place if the object was to separate the Brigantes from the Selgovae and Novantes. And yet the Antonine Wall implies that it represented a considerable strategic error. The likelihood is that the Votadini had been left stranded too far north of Hadrian's Wall and were having trouble containing the Selgovae without Roman help. There is a passage from the Greek writer Pausanius that offers clues:

> Antoninus Pius never willingly made war; but when the Moors took up arms against Rome he drove them out of all their territory ... Also he deprived the Brigantes in Britain of most of their land because they too had begun aggression on the district of Genunia whose inhabitants are subject to Rome.

If 'Brigantes' is taken to mean the hill tribes of the Pennines and southern Scotland as a group and that 'Genunia' is part of the territory of the Votadini then Antoninus Pius had a pretext for invasion. 'Genunia' may have some very loose connection with the name Gododdin.

But that did not work for long either. Between 181 and 184 the hill tribes crossed Hadrian's Wall (the Antonine Wall having been abandoned) and this time it seems that they defeated Rome in battle and killed the provincial governor. The Emperor Commodus sent a punitive expedition which beat back the invaders once again and allowed him to take the title 'Britannicus'. There were further invasions in 197 when the tribes vented their fury on the hated Wall by burning all its habitable places and levelling it in parts.[11] The following year the Romans negotiated a peace, paid off the tribes and began to rebuild their defences. In 209 the Emperor Septimus Severus personally led an expedition to Scotland to reduce the tribes but after a successful campaign he

[11] Sheppard S. Frere, *Britannia* (1967).

died at York in 211. His son and heir Caracalla finally attempted what seems like a new policy. In return for peace he withdrew his forces from southern Scotland and began the long process of creating a buffer zone between Hadrian's Wall and Antonine's. It was this crucible which would forge the great P-Celtic kingdoms of Dark Ages Scotland, and which would ultimately produce the brilliant fighting machine led by Arthur against both old and new enemies.

6

AFTER ROME

After the death of Severus in AD 211 and the creation of the buffer
zone by Caracalla, Roman historians were much less interested in
southern Scotland. For most of the third century there was little
trouble from the north; it seems to have been a period of consolidation. The Romanized Votadini quietly survived and prospered,
despite a direct frontier with the warlike Selgovae. And on the
Clyde the Damnonii held on to their fertile lands, despite pressure
from the north and the Novantes and Selgovae in the south.

The Romans remained watchful. They reinforced five outpost
forts north of Hadrian's Wall: at High Rochester and Risingham on
Dere Street in the east, and at Bewcastle, Birrens and Netherby
in the west. Cohorts called *exploratores* were based at these camps.
Netherby is described in a Roman road map as Castra Exploratorum.
They were detachments of mounted scouts who patrolled the
Southern Uplands alert for trouble and able to report it back
quickly to the commander of the Wall. There was also a unit of
spearmen, the Raeti Gaesati from the Tyrol, based at Risingham.

The medieval ruins of Jedburgh Abbey contain two memories of
these frontier years. Trimmed down to serve as building stones, the
old abbey walls contain two Roman altars: one is for the Raeti

Gaesati and the other for a cavalry cohort, the Vardulli, based at Rochester. There is a plentiful supply of good stone in Jedburgh and these altars will not have been brought any distance.[1] The meeting of the Jed Water and the River Teviot had some strategic significance and it looks as though patrols met there and maintained a presence permanent enough to see altars put up. Jedburgh lies on the fringe of the territory of the Votadini and it looks as though it was a point of regular contact with Rome in the third century. In such a peaceful time, few problems would have been reported to the scouts of their Roman allies.

The Votadini must have been nervous though. They had welcomed Agricola and become consistent clients of Rome throughout the occupation and beyond. Their neighbours had been equally consistently hostile and with the Brigantes and Novantae had inflicted defeat and damage on the greatest fighting machine that the world had ever seen. And yet not only did the Votadini maintain their boundaries after the Roman evacuation, they seem to have thrived. By the beginning of the fourth century they had extended their territory west and north of the Forth, holding a substantial part of Fife.

The only realistic explanation for this is a military one. No amount of Roman statecraft in the second century had subdued the hill tribes of the north; only force had worked and even then for limited periods. The Votadini clearly learned much from the Voconti and the Sarmatians: the skills they acquired on the parade ground and in the riding school at Trimontium had earned them vigorous independence from their warlike neighbours. They had become a dominating military power.

Some of the lessons were also logistical. It looks as though Trimontium was occupied in the early part of the third century by soldiers who had their families living with them. These were veterans who had decided to settle in the territory of the Votadini

[1] RCAHMS, *Roxburghshire* (1956).

and it seems likely that the fighting skills of these men stiffened the tribal forces needed to check the Selgovae. They had to maintain the fort for the same reasons that Agricola first built it, as a point of containment at the mouth of Selgovan valleys. And also the Votadini would have wanted to be near their great sacred site at Eildon Hill North. The Military Road built with great labour was designed to deal with chariot-driving enemies approaching from the south-west. This was the Selgovan heartland of the Ettrick and Yarrow valleys. And at Carbantoritum or Carby Hill in Liddesdale, the Romans had had to deal with the charge of the chariots of the hill men much earlier.

The containment strategy of the Romans was extended further south to a place called Yeavering, near Wooler in north Northumberland. This was an important location. The Votadini maintained a large hill fort on Yeavering Bell that dominates the mouth of the College valley which winds up to the slopes of Cheviot itself and into the territory of the Brigantes; and also the Bowmont valley which offers a direct route through the foothills to the ridge country above Kelso and its crossing of the River Tweed. Yeavering was built in an ancient landscape of standing stones, abandoned villages and forts, and its name is old too: P-Celtic from Ad Gefrin, or Goathill. The bell looks east out over the flatlands to the North Sea to the island now called Lindisfarne but known to the P-Celts as Medcaut. It was the first landfall of Anglian pirates in the fifth century.

Archaeology shows decline at Trimontium and at some time in the third century the Votadini abandoned it, although there is evidence that the area to the west of Newstead village was inhabited by people who were still using Roman currency into the third and fourth centuries. Both it and Eildon Hill North depended on the fertile farmlands to the east for supply, and the fort was close to the border with the Selgovae. Prudence persuaded the Votadini to move their centre further downriver to somewhere smaller in scale, more easily defensible and a place where they could corral and pasture their warhorses in safety. As I hope to show, at some point in the third century they came to an old settlement on the Tweed where they built and fortified a stronghold perfectly suited to their military needs.

At the same time the Selgovae were changing. Names as ever suggest this, and a number of scraps of evidence, documentary, archaeological and toponymic, can be combined into a clear pattern. Two tribal groups had been a source of endless trouble to Britannia and its governors: the Caledonii and the Maeatae north of the Forth and Clyde, and the Selgovae, Novantes and Brigantes on either side of Hadrian's Wall. In the third century it seems that these groups combined so that the hill country from the Highlands down to the Peak District bristled with enemies who became generally known to southern contemporary writers as the Picts.

Like Pretani this is held to be a name derived from body painting or body decoration. The Picts were 'the painted people'. While this seems a little too easy a connection, there are few alternative derivations on offer. The incidence of the place-name prefix 'Pit' or 'Pet' broadly falls in with the northern areas of Scotland thought to be inhabited by the Picts, and there is a similarity between the terms – 'Pit' and 'Pict'. But their language is lost to us. They were illiterate and left no inscriptions that can be safely deciphered. However, St Columba's biographer Adomnan[2] remembers that the Q-Celtic-speaking saint needed an interpreter when he visited the court of the Pictish King Brude near Inverness sometime after 574. The likelihood is that they spoke a dialect of P-Celtic understandable to their southern neighbours, but not to Q-Celts.

In 296 the usurper Emperor Allectus removed part of the British garrison to support his ambitions in Europe. This was a signal to the Picts, now consolidating north of the Votadini and Damnonii, to assemble raiding parties. For the first time history records the appearance alongside them of a new people: the Scots of Dalriada.

---

[2] A.O. and M.O. Anderson, *Adomnan's Life of St Columba* (1961).

The combined force reached as far south as the great Roman fort at Chester, before the empire struck back and retrieved northern Britannia once more.

It seems likely that the Picts and Scots did not invade the province with any thought of conquest. They sought to destroy or weaken their hated oppressors, and most important to plunder their goods and livestock. They also avoided pitched battles with Roman legions and mostly waited for opportunities like Allectus's withdrawal to diminish the garrison of Hadrian's Wall and empty the forts which controlled and policed the roads of Britannia.

They also had to avoid the waxing kingdoms of the Damnonii on the Clyde and the Votadini in the east. I believe that they did this, and inflicted raids in the far south hundreds of miles from the Highlands of Scotland, by forming an alliance with those other implacable enemies of Rome, the Selgovae and the Brigantes. There are pieces of evidence that can be brought together to make a clearer picture.

Names first. Immediately to the south of Edinburgh lie the Pentland Hills. Rising steeply to 1,600 feet the range tails south-west into the heart of Selgovae territory. Pentland is derived from 'Pictland'. It is the same name that the Norse called the barrier sea between the Orkneys and Caithness: 'Pettaland-fjord', the Pictland Firth, the Pentland Firth.[3]

There is also a good deal of archaeological evidence for Pictish influence and immigration to the Southern Uplands. On the Borthwick Water near Hawick there is a beautiful Pictish symbol stone of a sort generally only found far to the north. It is carved with the image of a fish and is not something that could have been imported, dropped or even moved. It must have been erected by a group of people who understood its beauty, a group of Pictish settlers.[4]

[3] W.J. Watson, *The Celtic Placenames of Scotland* (1926).
[4] RCAHMS, *Roxburghshire* (1956).

In the Pentland Hills there is at Castlelaw Fort an example of Pictish domestic architecture. It is a souterrain or underground chamber, a place probably used for food or grain storage. There is another nearby at the village of Crichton and, most significantly, two examples south of the old Roman fort of Trimontium. One of them is built with stones from buildings in the settlement and must therefore postdate both Roman occupation and Votadinian control. They were probably built in the fourth century.

In addition there are ten forts of what is known as the nuclear design distributed throughout the Selgovan hills.[5] Again in the north the Picts built in exactly the same way all over their territory. One of the most elaborate of these is a stone-walled structure on Carby Hill. And even more characteristic, and expensive, is the Torwoodlee Broch just outside Galashiels. Brochs are towers (in shape not unlike a miniature cooling tower at a steelworks) of immense thickness which are far more typical of the Highlands and Hebrides, but clearly a powerful man found himself in the valley of the Gala Water and his way of showing prestige was to have a broch built. Since this was destroyed in the second century AD, probably by the Romans, it is unlikely that this man was a Pict, more likely a Selgovan chief who had had contact with Pictish allies, and had seen a northern broch. There is also evidence of two other brochs on the Gala Water, at Bow Castle and Crosslee. And there is a much larger stone-built hill fort at the Rink between Selkirk and Galashiels; about ten times the size of a broch, it uses the same dry-stone techniques and has a wall thickness of about thirteen feet. It is similar to the fort on Carby Hill in Roxburghshire. The sixteenth-century spelling of the name is Langrinck which is related to the derivation of the old county town of Lanark, which in turn is from *lanerc* for a cleared area. This place name has a distribution in Scotland almost exclusively in Pictish territory. Telling connections.

5 RCAHMS, *Peebleshire* (1967), *Selkirkshire* (1957).

Two more notices are important. Ninian is the first named Christian of Scottish record, and he flourished between 360 and 432. Almost exactly 300 years later Bede wrote in his *Historia Ecclesiastica* that Ninian had converted the southern Picts long before Columba had preached to the northern Picts.[6] These two groups lived either side of the central Highland massif, explained Bede. 'The southern Picts who live on this side of the mountains' were the object of Ninian's mission when he founded the white church of Candida Casa at Whithorn in Galloway. This must mean that Bede thought of the Novantae, the Selgovae and perhaps their allies the Brigantes as 'the southern Picts'. If they were not, then Ninian founded his church a very long way from the people he hoped would populate it.

The other glimpse of the Picts in the Southern Uplands is on a Victorian map which insists that the Catrail, the defensive or demarcating earthwork separating the Selgovan hills from the Anglian flatlands, was properly called 'The Picts Work Ditch'. Meaning that it was made by them.[7]

There is a final word on this from Gildas, the sixth-century writer who bemoaned the state of his country in *On the Fall of Britain*.[8] He explains that the Picts, the greatest enemies of Britain, had penetrated right up to the Roman wall by taking over the lands of the native peoples. Since the Picts were already very close to the Antonine Wall, Gildas must mean Hadrian's and the conquest of the lands of the Selgovae. Alliance or conquest, it is difficult to tell.

However, it is clear that for logistical reasons the Picts, the Selgovae and the Brigantes would have found it advantageous to combine. Not only were they more powerful, gaining access to the spine of Britain, from the Highlands to the Peak District, unhampered by the Damnonii or the Votadini, and the remaining Roman garrisons of Lancashire and Yorkshire, the Picts' alliance also

---

[6] Bede, *Ecclesiatical History of the English People* (Penguin, 1955).

[7] Ordnance Survey, *Kelso and Melrose* (1896).

[8] Gildas, *De Excidio et Conquestu Britanniae* (Phillimore, 1978).

allowed them to raid far into the south of rich Britannia. The classical historian Ammianus reports Pictish war-bands attacking London. The Romans found them difficult, elusive opponents and later writers such as Bede and the *Anglo-Saxon Chronicle* compilers called them the scourge of Britain, its greatest enemies. Later I will show that Arthur fought a brilliant campaign against the Picts and on five occasions brought them down from their hills to battle and defeated them.

7

THE KINGDOMS
OF THE MIGHTY

One of the most baffling and, to the sensitive, most offensive phrases in British culture is 'the Home Counties'. Home for whom? Certainly not for the great majority of the population of these islands whose addresses are not to be found in Surrey, Sussex, Middlesex or Essex. But perhaps we in the provinces who can never feel entirely at home should be more understanding. Because this is not about postcodes but rather the ancient origins of the shaping of attitudes and, crucially, assumptions.

The lands of the South, Middle and East Saxons are called 'home' by us all principally because they surrounded London but also because they signify the defeat of the P-Celts in the south and because, after a time, the Saxons who lived there began to write their own particular version of history, like all winners. And it is the version that has survived to define and focus English and therefore British identity. Despite the fact that Angles, Frisians, Jutes and Franks also invaded this island, it is significant that only the Saxons penetrated the Celtic lexicon. These words came quickly to mean all Germanic invaders but their original derivation is plain: 'Sais' in Welsh, 'Saoz' in Breton, 'Saws' in Cornish, 'Sasanach' in Irish, 'Sasunnaich' in Scots Gaelic and 'Sostynagh' in Manx. The language not only of general capitulation but also of acceptance.

Even now it is immensely difficult to wrench the mind-set of historians and their readers away from the south, almost impossible to convince them that the centre of defining action in Britain could be elsewhere. Both the *Anglo-Saxon Chronicle* and Bede's *Historia* had as a part of their purpose the legitimation of the Saxon kings of Wessex and the Angle kings of Northumbria, and broadly the conquest of most of England. Their patrons became the heroes of their histories, their enemies barely mentioned. Because the fifth and sixth centuries in Britain went almost completely unreported by contemporaries, these later versions of what happened in that time have come to be believed. They are not untrue, but they are not the whole truth.

Taking all of that together it is easy to see why the P-Celtic kingdoms of southern Scotland have been virtually forgotten. Of their names, Rheged, Manau and Gododdin resonate little; only Strathclyde is recognized because it was the name of a Scottish local authority. And yet these four offered the only serious initial resistance to the invasions of the Germanic tribes in the fifth and sixth centuries. Disciplined by their Roman allies, hammered by war into four warrior kingdoms, Gododdin, Manau, Strathclyde and Rheged resisted the Picts in the north and the Scots in the west. They were the crucible for the origins of Welsh language and literature; the poetry of Taliesin has come down to us; and in 'The Gododdin' they left the earliest piece of European literature in a vernacular language. With Ninian at Whithorn a century before Augustine arrived in Kent, Patrick the son of a Rheged nobleman converting pagans in Ireland, Kentigern a bishop in Glasgow and the ancient Celtic monastery at Melrose, the four kingdoms also kept the faith.

And this was no brief flicker. There were Strathclyde kings at Dumbarton for a thousand years. In 1018 King Owain the Bald fought alongside his Q-Celtic overlord Malcolm II MacMalcolm at the Battle of Carham on the River Tweed. As the Scottish host fought the Northumbrians to establish the river as the south-east frontier, the Strathclyde king was killed in the midst of the battle on the wide riverbank. He was the last of his ancient dynasty, of a tribe described by Tacitus in 80, the end of the Damnonian line. After Owain, the Gaelic-speaking MacMalcolms would tolerate no more Strathclyde kings.

In the fifth and sixth centuries the four kingdoms were the last light in the west before Britain sank into its Dark Age. And none shone brighter among them than Arthur, their great leader of battles, who held back the darkness long enough to keep us British.

Rheged was the largest of the kingdoms, running from an old fort that remembers the name, Dunragit, in the western end of Galloway near Stranraer all the way east to Dumfries, Carlisle and south through Cumbria, Lancashire and down to an industrial town that also carries the name of the old kingdom. Rochdale was first recorded as Recedham in the Domesday Book of 1086. At its zenith Rheged compassed all the territory of the Novantes in Galloway, the lands of the Carvetii around Carlisle and the Eden valley, the hill country of the western Brigantes in Cumbria and Lancashire. With the exception of the Carvetii, these tribes noted by Tacitus had been hostile to Rome, but as time wore on they came to learn from their enemies at close quarters. The mouth of the Solway and the western end of Hadrian's Wall was one of the most intensively militarized zones in the Roman Empire. And at Ribchester, Bremetenacum Veteranorum, where the Sarmatian Cavalry of the third century had been granted land, Rheged incorporated a tradition of military horsemanship not surpassed in Britain.

After the imperial government left Britannia to protect itself in 410, there is a historical belief that anarchy gradually took hold, civil institutions withered and towns were abandoned. In fact in the heart of Rheged where the kingdom hinged south on Carlisle, Roman civic life carried on much as before. By 369 the status of the town had been elevated to one of Britannia's five provincial capitals.[1] The Roman site was large, enclosing seventy acres. And in the twelfth century the reliable medieval historian William of Malmesbury noted an arched building of great antiquity still standing. It carried a Latin inscription to Mars and Venus.[2] When Roman buildings in Carlisle fell into disrepair in the fifth and sixth centuries they were rebuilt in a classical style, but in wood. The town was an important road meeting and the old straight ways were kept in repair, while Carlisle's aqueduct was still in use in 685.

St Patrick was not an Irishman. He was a P-Celt with an original name of Sucat. Around 400 an Irish raider chieftain named Milchu beached his boat on the Carlisle shore of the Solway and went inland for plunder and slaves or hostages. He abducted Sucat, who later escaped to Gaul where he joined a Christian community and took the Latin name Patricius. He did much in Ireland that is famous but the important thing here is his *Confessio* or autobiography written around 450. In it he describes the kingdoms of Rheged and Strathclyde as peaceful, organized places where taxes were still raised, courts of law functioned and in a letter to Ceretic, King of Strathclyde, Patrick addresses him as 'fellow citizen'.

It is very likely that the saint was describing only what he knew in Carlisle rather than generalizing about the new Celtic kingdoms. However it is clear that order was maintained in the Romanized north, that the rulers of Rheged, Strathclyde, Manau and Gododdin saw themselves as the inheritors of the empire, not its destroyers. There is a toponymic reference to Patrick a few miles from Carlisle: it is the town of Aspatria which means 'Patrick's Ash Tree'.

Rheged was linked as much by sea as by land, arranged, as it was, around the Solway Firth and Morecambe Bay. It was an enclosed sea, easy to navigate and with the Isle of Man in its centre, it must have been difficult to sail far out of sight of land in good

[1] Sheppard S. Frere, *Britannia* (1967).
[2] Michael Wood, *In Search of the Dark Ages* (1981).

weather. Although no sources mention fleets or sea battles and naval archaeology is non-existent for this period, the men of Rheged would have been seafarers. When the Scots of Irish Dal Riata left the Antrim coast first to raid and then to settle, they could on a clear day see the white beaches of Galloway. But they sailed instead to the mists and rocks of Argyll. Not by choice, I believe, but because Rheged resisted them successfully.

Seabourne commerce was alive in that time. Excavations at the royal centre of Rheged, the Mote of Mark near Dalbeattie, have turned up expensive glassware from the Rhineland and also pottery from Bordeaux, hinting at a wine trade.[3] The Mote of Mark also has another, more fanciful connection. In the later Arthurian legend, Tristan went on his tragic journey to find Isolde for his uncle King Mark of Damnonia, making him King of Cornwall. Perhaps, and not for the first time, Dumnonia and Damnonia became confused.

In any event there is much more certainty about another tale. All the dynastic lists for Rheged name a man called Coel Hen as a progenitor. His name is often sung by schoolchildren. *Hen* is the P-Celtic or Welsh word for old, and whether or not Old King Cole was merry, or liked fiddle music is not recorded anywhere except in a nursery rhyme. Perhaps the song is a distant reverberation of his power, for Coel Hen was the last British king to rule both sides of the Pennines and all of Rheged, even up to the Ayrshire coast where the district of Kyle remembers him.

In the middle of northern Rheged lay Whithorn, an unusual name because it is an Anglicization of a Latin place-name, Candida Casa. It means 'White House' and refers to the rare construction of a stone building, a new church. Bede wrote that the southern Picts had been converted by a bishop who was born in Britain but trained in Rome. His name was Nynia, more recognizable as

---

[3] Stewart Ross, *Ancient Scotland* (1991).

Ninian, and he was the son of an aristocratic P-Celtic family, possibly, like Patrick, from Carlisle.[4]

Some time between 366 and 384 Ninian travelled to Rome, where he was received by Pope Damasus I, consecrated bishop and then sent into the tutelage of St Martin of Tours, the Apostle of the Franks. Ninian came home, probably as Bishop of Carlisle, to evangelize the southern Picts. That is why he built Candida Casa, as an outpost close to the heathens. If the term 'Pict' had historically been understood to cover Novantes, Selgovae and Brigantes then the location makes sense.

There are traces of Ninian all over south-west Scotland. He founded churches, abbeys, monasteries and nunneries and according to his medieval biographer he also made an effort to convert the northern Picts, travelling through Angus and Aberdeenshire as far as the Cromarty Firth.

St David of Wales, or Dewi Sant, journeyed to Whithorn for instruction before he returned to Christianize north Wales. By the time Ninian died in 432, Rheged was becoming a Christian kingdom, and much of Celtic Britain had been touched by his mission. Archaeological evidence is scant for this period but it is surely significant that three Christian gravestones have been found in the valleys of the Southern Uplands. All have Latin names inscribed on them and together they make possible a reasonable conjecture: namely that the survival of the memory of Rome was linked to the spread of Christianity.

More than that, all this early Christian activity, uniquely early in Britain – more than a century before Augustine arrived in 592 to convert the south – speaks of consent and order. It could only take place in the context of a society run by a firm government, organized, sufficiently centralized and consistent, and relatively peaceful.

After the death of Coel Hen, Rheged split its southern territory into three portions: a kingdom based at York, another west of the

---

[4] Alfred P. Smyth, *Warlords and Holy Men, Scotland AD 800–1000* (1984).

Pennines and a third around Leeds. This last survived into the sixth century as the small British kingdom of Elmet. Its territory was approximately the same as an area of hill country which the Romans knew as Ladenses for the tribe who originally lived there. Ladenses is the P-Celtic ghost-name for Leeds, the central place of Elmet.[5] An interesting circle.

By 573 at the Battle of Arthuret, rival kings in Rheged were fighting and killing each other. But then, almost immediately after that, a king emerged who united all the lands of Coel and who ruled from Galloway in the west and down as far south as the Mersey. This was Urien of Rheged and the most successful of the P-Celtic kings in the north. He is well remembered because his bard was the great Taliesin and the poetry has survived.

> Urien of Echwyd most liberal of Christianmen
> Much do you give to men in this world
> As you gather, so you dispense
> Happy the Christian bards so long as you live ...
> Sovereign supreme ruler all highest
> The strangers' refuge, strong champion in battle.
> This the English know when they tell tales.
> Death was theirs, rage and grief are theirs
> Burned are their homes, bare are their bodies
> Till I am old and failing
> In the grim doom of death
> I shall have no delight
> If my lips praise not Urien.[6]

He united the four kingdoms and drove westwards to attack the Angles. The eighth-century chronicler Nennius wrote that:

---

[5] Andrew M. Currie, *Dictionary of British Placenames* (1994).
[6] Thomas Stephens, *The Literature of the Kymry* (1849).

Hussa reigned seven years. Four kings fought against him. Urien and Riderch Hen, and Gaullauc and Morcant. Theodoric fought bravely against the famous Urien and his sons. During that time sometimes the enemy, sometimes our countrymen were victorious, and Urien blockaded them for three days and three nights on the island of Metcaud [Lindisfarne].[7]

And then later Nennius added: 'But while he was on the expedition, Urien was assassinated, on the initiative of Morcant, from jealousy, because his military skill and generalship surpassed that of all the other kings.'

Although Urien was immediately succeeded by his son Owain who inflicted more defeats on the Angles, deploying his cavalry brilliantly, his achievements were short-lived. Owain died some time after 593. Rheged's power quickly diminished, and its famous name was not heard again in the poems and songs of the bards.

The name that endured and lives on even now is Strathclyde. Encompassing the largest local authority area in Britain, it includes the whole of the River Clyde basin and also broad swathes of the Highland areas which bound its penetrating firth and the long-fingered sea lochs that reach into the heart of the mountains. It is a hybrid P- and Q-Celtic name, which will seem appropriate once its story unfolds. The first element comes from the Gaelic *strath* for a 'wide valley' and the second P-Celtic river name Clyde from the root *clouta* called by Roman cartographers Clota, which means 'the cleansing one'. The original name of the tribe described by Tacitus, the Damnonii, did survive but not in the name of the kingdom.

The limits of the kingdom of Strathclyde were tighter than most of the modern local authority. Place-names mark them. At the head of Loch Lomond where the road climbs away north up towards Crianlarich, there is a place in the pass known to the Q-Celts as

---

[7] Nennius, *Historia Brittonum*, in John Morris, *The Age of Arthur* (1973).

Clach nam Breatain, or 'The Stone of the Britons'. It marks a geo-graphical, linguistic and political boundary, probably a battle-site and a place where messengers, embassies or kings met to talk. And yet there is nothing now to mark the site, one of the hinge-points of Dark Ages Scotland. Only the windswept crags, the tussocky grass and mounds of road grit waiting for the winter.

To the west the wide Firth of Clyde bounded Strathclyde and kept the Scots of Dalriada in their sea kingdom in Argyll. The Galloway Hills separated it from western Rheged and in the east there must have been a political settlement with the P-Celtic kings of Manau and Gododdin because, aside from Hart Hill and the protection offered by Flanders Moss, the frontier was not well guarded by geography. None the less the Damnonians of Strathclyde were the least accessible of the four kingdoms of the north – from the south. The Romans penetrated to the upper Clyde valley as far as Crawford, but their objective was to encircle the Selgovae, not subdue the Damnonii. There are relatively few Roman camps or roads in the west, suggesting that like their Votadinian neighbours, these tribesmen brokered an arrangement with Agricola which allowed the imperial army to concentrate on the east coast and their Caledonian enemies. The men who came to be known as the Picts would have been a threat to the green fields of the Clyde and compliance no doubt brought political gain.

Strathclyde never fell to the Angles. It was first and last a Celtic kingdom which understood itself in P-Celtic and finally in Q-Celtic before its memory faded in the eleventh century. As such it became the creator, receiver and preserver of traditions which will inform much of what follows. It endured centuries longer than the Gododdin and developed a powerful P-Celtic culture which, as I will show, politics pushed south to Wales at the end of the ninth century. Strathclyde absorbed the stories of the Gododdin, of Rheged and of Manau and of their Q-Celtic neighbours and pro-duced a Welsh-language version of Dark Ages Scotland which was later mistaken for a recital of events far to the south.

Riderch Hael is the first Damnonian king to assume recognizable historical shape. He reigned at about the same time as Urien of Rheged and was as vigorous in establishing his borders. But before these men begin to appear like conquerors whose armies redrew the map and coloured it deeply, it is important to remember that very small numbers were involved. There is a definition in the *Anglo-Saxon Chronicle* which may not have applied only to them.[8] Up to thirty men was a war-band or a raiding party and anything over that was understood as an army. Battles between powerful kings may have been fought between two groups of fifty warriors. These men certainly went on short campaigns in the summer fighting season but they sought plunder rather than territory. Lacking the organization and the resources to do more than lift what was valuable and removable, they could hold power over river valleys and ranges of hills but would not have seen geography as valuable in itself. Fighting was the core of the culture of the professional warriors who dominated the P-Celtic kingdoms of the north. They travelled far on their tough ponies and fought battles often very distant from their bases but their thoughts rarely strayed from what they would bring home – glory as well as plunder. They were raiders, not conquerors, and it is of more than passing significance that the words 'raiding' and 'riding' are etymologically very close indeed, and they also connect to a word that came originally from the Scottish Border: reiving.

When other war-bands arrived to compete with the aristocracy of the P-Celts, then it is proper to characterize warfare as political rather than simply economic. Urien drove the Angles across the Tweed down to Lindisfarne because he wanted to discourage them and not because he was embarking on the conquest of Northumbria.

There is another determinant matter here. To say that the kingdom of Rheged extended across the Tweed and into the north of England would be a misunderstanding. The power of Urien,

---

[8] *Anglo-Saxon Chronicle* (ed. and trans. Michael Swanton) (1996).

Top The site of the lost city of Roxburgh is now used for point-to-point horse racing and the jumps and pavilions are from a recent meeting. Behind them is the low plateau on which the city stood, and to its left is the castlemount.

Above Beneath the roots of this old chestnut tree lie the ruins of a substantial wall which begins to run towards the River Tweed to the left. The line of the wall is cut abruptly by the line of the modern Selkirk to Kelso road, which is embanked by a course of large dressed stones. These stones may be the remainder of the defensive ramparts thrown up by Arthur's predecessors from the stronghold of Marchidun down to the river. The steep slopes of the fortress mound rise only ten yards from the right of the picture.

Above The castlemount seen from the south, with the River Teviot defending its flank. The run of the medieval walls can be seen to the left, while the site of the old city lies a hundred yards or so off to the right. The depth and width of the river, photographed in March, shows what a formidable obstacle it was, both to attackers and for horses kept out on the haughland in the winter, out of the campaigning season.

Facing page

Top This is from the eastern end of the Marchmound and it shows a single fragment of medieval masonry on top of the ditched mound of the Dark Ages fort. The modern road runs to the right, cutting off a second defensive ditch on its down slope.

Left From the western end this offers a powerful sense of how massive the mound is, and how the labour of thousands of man-hours has improved on what geology created. The River Teviot is glimpsed to the right, and the Tweed to the left.

Top An aerial survey of the Roxburgh site.

Above Calchvyndd in the winter sunshine. The old chalk hill is hidden now by the terraced gardens of the large houses on its top and obscured in summer by the trees on the river island in the foreground. The Tweed is wide and deep here as it joins the Teviot at the Junction Pool.

Facing page The massive ruins of Kelso Abbey seen from the modern town.

Right The Trimontium Stone commemorates the complex of Roman military and civic sites which once stood in the lee of Eildon Hill North, whose flat summit dominates the area.

Below Taken near the time of the feast of Imbolc, in early March, this photograph shows Eildon Hill North in its setting of fertile farmland.

Top This is marked on the map as Scott's View since the sight of the three Eildon Hills watching over his beloved Borderland moved Sir Walter Scott to write so much about his native place. It is said that when his horses drew Scott's funeral carriage past the View, they stopped out of ancient habit. I hope that is true.

Above The Yarrow Stone, set on a hillside above the site of the Battle of the Wood of Celidon. The trees are mostly gone now, but the inscription on the stone remembers the clash of war in that place 1500 years ago.

The Hawick Horse. With its triumphant Border warrior bearing a raided English flag, it carries the enigmatic town motto, 'Teribus Ye Teriodin'. Or 'Tir Y Bas, Y Tir Y Odin' – 'The Land of Death, and the Land of Odin', a long echo of the Ride of the Dead.

King of Rheged, did temporarily encompass Northumbria but that is not the same thing. Urien's skill as a general meant success for his warriors whose loyalty and obligation was personal to him as long as they continued to collect the spoils of war. Rheged belonged, in a tangible sense, to Urien and to his son Owain. When they died there was no sense that Rheged would produce an heir or that an internecine process would produce a capable heir. Rheged was Urien's personal possession and when he failed, it declined.

The resilience of Strathclyde has much to do with this way of thinking. The Damnonian kings were great generals who in turn defeated all comers for close on 400 years. When the kingdom of the Gododdin collapsed in the mid seventh century, the Scots of Dalriada threatened to move east into the area around Stirling. Owen of Strathclyde led his war-band to Strathcarron where he caught the Scots, destroyed their small army and slew their king Domnall Brecc.

Forty years later another ambitious king came to grief, this time indirectly at the hands of the men of Strathclyde. In addition to war, their statecraft extended to diplomacy, dynastic marriage and what may have been peaceful coups d'état. Owen's brother was known to history as Bridei son of Bili and a man the Irish annalists confirm as 'the son of the King of Dumbarton'. The army of the Picts, Strathclyde's northern neighbours, was destroyed in 672 by Ecgfrith, the Angle King of Northumbria. In the aftermath, Bridei became at some point King of the Picts. No doubt bolstered and guided by his fellow Damnonians, he drew Northumbrians across the Forth and Fife and at Dunnichen Moss in 685 he utterly annihilated them. Anglian power was pushed far to the south over the Lammermuir Hills and down into the Tweed basin.

In the eighth century Oengus, son of Fergus, became one of the most powerful Pictish kings in history. He defeated the Scots of Dalriada and threatened Strathclyde to the south. Once again the Damnonians defeated their enemies and in 750 Oengus was killed and the Picts retreated.

Time and again Strathclyde won in crucial battles. Almost 900 years of power and then cultural occupation beyond that is a history without parallel in the British Isles. And yet the achievement of the Strathclyde Britons has been almost forgotten. Few remember that they named the Clyde or that Glasgow is their P-Celtic name of 'Green Hollow'.

The end came in 889. For more than a century the western seaboard of all Europe had been terrorized by the Vikings. They killed, stole and destroyed first and then in classic pattern began to settle. Kingdoms were made in the Orkneys, Manx and Dublin. They sailed up the Solway Firth into the heart of Rheged and saw the Clochmabenstane on the flat land near Gretna. The Vikings remembered it and began to talk of the 'Sul vath fjord' or the 'Fiord of the Pillar Ford' or the Solway Firth. Its northern shore with its sea lochs and natural harbours was a place they often raided and then settled. While the Vikings took western Rheged and swallowed Northumbria, the Damnonians held the Clyde and were not defeated.

But in 870 a fateful alliance was created. Olaf, overlord of the Irish and Scottish Vikings, joined his considerable forces with those of Ivar, who had defeated the Angles of Northumbria and East Anglia.

Perhaps as a precaution the Strathclyde kings had moved their centre from the green and indefensible hollow of Glasgow down the Clyde to the ancient fortress of Alcluid or the Rock of Dumbarton. Best seen from the opposite, western shore of the Firth of Clyde, it is a dominating place, a near-vertical rock climbing sheer out of the water on one side and offering a cliff-face to the landward. Alcluid was one of the most powerful fortresses in Britain.

When Ivar and Olaf sailed their huge fleet of 200 longships up the Clyde estuary, they knew that the Damnonians had defied attacks for 900 years but they were determined to take the rock. After a four-month siege – something unprecedented in Dark Ages warfare – Alcluid fell and with it the ancient kingdom of Strathclyde.

Viking occupation was short-lived and after 889 the Scots began to exert overlordship on the Clyde. The integrity of the old kingdom remained, those who worked the land still spoke P-Celtic and still worshipped Christ in the same way, but the Q-Celtic kings of Alba began to confer Strathclyde's kingship on their eldest sons. Rather in the way that the heir to the throne is nowadays made Prince of Wales, the Scots kings kept the title for their sons or important clients and also retained the old territory of the Damnonii for their sustenance as great noblemen. This arrangement lasted well into the early medieval period when King Owain of Strathclyde was killed fighting alongside Malcolm II MacMalcolm at the Battle of Carham. After that it fell out of use, although its remnant of northern Cumbria was held into the twelfth century by the heir to the Scottish throne. Before he became king in 1128 David I, founder of Kelso Abbey, was Prince of Cumbria.

After the mortal blow of the fall of Alcluid in 870, the kingship of Strathclyde lingered on in the shape of Eochaid son of Rhun. He was expelled in 889 and for the following year there is an entry in the Welsh *Chronicle of the Princes* which says: 'The men of Strathclyde, those that refused to unite with the English, had to depart from their country, and to go to Gwynedd.'

Leaving aside the confusion over the word 'English' (the Vikings had conquered Northumbria by 890) and remembering how little precision the Celtic languages of Britain showed when referring to Anglo-Saxons, this passage is unequivocal. It attaches events and dates to a clear migration from P-Celtic Scotland to Wales. There can be no doubt that the Damnonians took their stories south across the Irish Sea with them. They spoke a cousin language and tales of the glory of Strathclyde, the Gododdin and Manau and their defeat of the English, their resistance and their tenacity, slipped easily into the mainstream of orally transmitted songs, poems and stories. At the time of Rhodri Mawr when Wales was resurgent, there can have been no harm in recounting the tales of the victories of our cousins. They were almost our victories. They were our victories! We can defeat the English! The fact that the Scots greet an Irish or Welsh sporting victory over the English at anything as second only to a Scottish one should not be wondered at. And nor is the appropriation of Arthur. In 890 the men of Strathclyde sailed away with the memory of him from the Clyde and brought him to north Wales, where the 'Men of the North' became over time the 'Men of North Wales'.

However, the reputation of one of the Men of the North stayed where it began. St Kentigern was the apostle of Strathclyde and his name is a P-Celtic one, similar to Vortigern although a different sort of man altogether. It is a title from Ceann Tighearna or 'Chief Leader' or perhaps 'High Priest', or perhaps Ceann Tighe for 'Head of the Family'. He is also known as Mungo, a Q-Celtic familiar meaning 'Dear Friend', which survives in modern Scotland as a Christian name.

His church has also survived as Glasgow Cathedral, albeit in medieval form and his remains are said to be buried beneath. But it is a fanciful story that ties Kentigern as close to the city as any piece of substantiated history. At the court of King Riderch there was scandal. The queen was having an affair with a young nobleman and the king was anxious to expose the truth of it. He gave his wife a valuable ring which she in turn had given to her lover. The king noticed it on the lover's hand, removed it when he was sleeping, pitched it into the River Clyde where it was swallowed by a salmon. Riderch then challenged his wife to produce it. The distressed woman sought help from Kentigern who dispatched one of his monks to the river to start fishing. Miraculously, the monk caught the very salmon that had swallowed the queen's ring, thus saving the queen's reputation.

Nonsense, of course, but the kind of nonsense that is remembered. And which passes into heraldry. Glasgow still sports a salmon and a ring on its coat of arms.

While the origins of that tale are obscure, Kentigern's are less so. He was from Gododdin and his mother was described as a princess named Teneu who lived at Traprain Law, the centre of the northern Gododdin before the court moved to Edinburgh. Kentigern was educated by St Serf who was a very early British saint based at Culross on the southern shore of Fife near Dunfermline. Serf's cult was best known in Manau and it shows Christianity and its spread as a P-Celtic matter in southern Scotland.

After he joined the court of Riderch Hael in Glasgow, Kentigern is said to have travelled to north Wales to the place visited by Dewi Sant after he had left Whithorn. There are other stories about Kentigern which can serve to fill out a picture of him but for the sake of clarity and the direction of this narrative only one more tale needs to be told. It is a labyrinthine connection but worth making for all that. Even allowing for the licence of poets and the elasticity of date, it seems very likely that the saint Kentigern knew a pagan bard called Myrddin, the man known to the world as Merlin.

8

PART SEEN,
PART IMAGINED

There is an ancient streak of wildness in us all, a part of us that remains irrational, needs to remember instinct, reject reason, ignore consequence. Because what we believe, however illogical, shapes what we have done, history is surely part seen and part imagined. In order to understand the acts of ancient men and women, particularly in a pre-literate age, it is necessary to find some sense of their emotional lives, to understand how romance, love and magic worked on their minds.

Here I want to turn to a figure whose role as counsellor, teacher and magician seemed at first to exist only in the fables concocted by Geoffrey of Monmouth and his medieval imitators. Compared with Arthur, Merlin appeared an infinitely more mythic figure. And yet there is far more direct documentary evidence for his existence in the Dark Ages than for Arthur. There are three main sources of reliable information which can be pleached together to bear some weight.

Firstly, most of what is known about the career of St Kentigern comes from a biography compiled by a Cumbrian monk called Jocelyn in the thirteenth century.[1] He understood P-Celtic and relates well a sense of the kingdoms of Strathclyde, Gododdin and

[1] Jocelyn, *Life of Kentigern* (ed. J. Pinkerton) (1789).

118

Rheged. He uses material from the ninth century which has the ring of common sense to frame a coherent narrative of events that took place in the sixth century. Kentigern was active in Strathclyde between about 570 and his death in 612. The fact that he established a church as far south as Hoddam, near Ecclefechan in Dumfriesshire, has allowed historians to plot the expansion of the kingdom of his patron Riderch of the Clyde. In a passage of routine hagiographic propaganda, Jocelyn relates the story of a meeting, in a wood, between St Kentigern and a naked, hairy madman. Called Lailoken, he told the saint that he had been driven wild by the slaughter of a bloody battle fought nearby between the Liddel Water and a place known as Carwannok. After the battle Lailoken had fled into the forest. Later he reappeared to attend one of Kentigern's masses, possibly at Hoddam, where he interrupted by shouting out wild prophecies. And then, as the wild man senses the approach of his own death, he asks that Kentigern accept him into the Church.

Jocelyn's purpose in relating all this is transparent. In the sixth century all the P-Celtic kingdoms had converted but it is wrong to imagine that this happened comprehensively or quickly. While Ninian, Columba, Kentigern and others adopted a strategy of targeting the royal family and the top slices of society for conversion, it is likely that Celtic beliefs lingered for a long time among ordinary people and in remote places. Lailoken sounds like a Druid who lived a hermitic existence 'in the woods'. There are other versions of this story but its essence is clear, as is its relationship to an entirely other group of sources.

But before looking through the window into the sixth century which these offer, it is necessary to draw out a historical blind. Ever anxious to Latinize P-Celtic names, Geoffrey of Monmouth stumbled on a problem with Myrddin. If he had simply hardened the 'dd' to 'd' and added the suffix 'us' to give us Merdinus, his readers would have laughed at him. Merdinus means 'Shitty One'. And so Merlin was born, out of necessity rather than literary taste.

The sources that Geoffrey drew on were known collectively as the *Prophecies of Myrddin* and when he reworked them into his *Vita Merlini* in 1135, he added so much new and fanciful material that the legend of the Great Enchanter quickly overlaid his historical Celtic origins.[2] When the later accretions are scraped away and the work of Myrddin reduced as close to its sixth-century original as it is possible to get, the picture becomes much clearer, even though the primary sources are poetic rather than a set of prose reports.

There are five poems in all: 'Appletrees', 'Greetings', 'The Dialogue of Myrddin and Taliesin', 'A Fugitive Poem of Myrddin in his Grave' and 'A Dialogue Between Myrddin and his Sister Gwenddydd'. Mostly they contain prophecies, either general, cryptic, or specific. But studded through each of them are fragments of a real narrative with named people, places and incidents which can be found well established elsewhere in other sources.

Broadly the story of Myrddin runs like this. In 573 a bloody battle was fought at a place called Arthuret, between Longtown and Carlisle. Two sub-kings of Rheged opposed each other: the Christian King of York, Peredur, and the pagan King of Carlisle, Gwenddollau. From the king lists of the Old North, Gwenddollau ap Ceido appears to have had a considerable pedigree which places him sixth in descent from Old King Cole. And his memory is preserved in the name of the village of Corwhinley near Longtown. It is from Caer Wenddolau or 'Gwenddollau's Fort'. More pungent tradition places this king squarely in the old religion. Bards sing of princes travelling far to attend the 'balefire of Gwenddollau' or his cremation at Arthuret and he is also named as one of the pagan 'Bull Protectors of Britain'.

Peredur was also a P-Celt and an heir of Coel Hen, and internecine fights like this cannot have been uncommon as the old British kingdoms fragmented. Gwenddollau was defeated and killed in what sounds like a particularly savage encounter. His bard,

[2] R.J. Stewart and John Matthews (eds.), *Merlin Through the Ages* (1995).

Myrddin, was driven insane by the great slaughter and he fled from the field into the Wood of Celidon whose fringes lay near at hand. He became a madman ('mirth' originally denoted 'insane laughter' and it seems to have some relation to the name Myrddin) and began a long exile in the wild wood living on fruit and the occasional gifts of visitors. He was at the mercy of the weather – 'snow to my knees, ice in my beard' – and prey to his own imaginings. One of his fears seems however to have been real enough.

> I slept alone in the Woods of Celyddon
> Shield on shoulder, sword on thigh[3]

Because Myrddin fears not Peredur of York but Riderch, King of Strathclyde who is 'a lover of monks, a hater of bards'.

There are many more references which pin these poems to the sixth century and the connecting figure of Riderch as well as the great similarity between the poems and the stories Jocelyn tells of Kentigern which mean that Lailoken and Myrddin are very likely identical.

For the times these narratives represent an unusually rich store of historical material and they make Merlin's actual existence more acceptable than almost every other figure of the period. And more, they confirm him as one of the Gwyr Y Gogledd (the Men of the North). Seeking refuge in the Wood of Caledon, hiding from Christian kings, in the centre of the old territory of the Selgovae, Merlin is also emphatically a pagan. Perhaps the last of the Druids, surviving in a remote refuge among the tribe that was almost certainly, according to archaeology, the last in southern Scotland to convert. There is even, on the Ordnance Survey, high up on Hart Fell in the middle of the Great Wood, from whose slopes spring the Clyde, the Tweed and the Annan, a place marked as Merlin's Cave.[4] Perhaps it was there, in the whistling, snell winds of the

3 R.J. Stewart and John Matthews, *op. cit.*

4 Nikolai Tolstoy, *The Quest for Merlin* (1985).

121

seasons, that he searched the sky for portents: Merlin's observatory.

The historical Merlin lived sixty years after Arthur perished at the Battle of Camlann and there can have been no actual connection between them. But it is remarkable that these two men lived so close in place and time.

There is another source to buttress these literary sources: tradition and toponymy. Between Hart Fell and the town of Peebles lies the hamlet of Stobo. Its church is one of the oldest in Scotland; part of its fabric is Norman but the dedication is much older. Outshot from the body of the modern kirk is the North Aisle Chapel which was reconstructed in 1928 out of the ruins of a fifteenth-century mortuary chantry which in turn was built on the foundations of a seventh-century cell dedicated to the cult of St Kentigern. It is one of a clutch of dedications to the saint in the Selgovan hills.

Layers of tradition are sandwiched at Stobo between layers of archaeology. The name Stobo is derived from an Anglian word for 'a holy place', which means that the tradition of Kentigern was still alive when the Germanic invaders penetrated the upper Tweed, probably in the eighth century. That memory endured through the Middle Ages, the Reformation and right up to 1928 when the restorers inserted a stained-glass window into the wall of the North Aisle Chapel. There are two figures in it: a tonsured man wearing the brown habit of the Franciscans stands with his hand raised in benediction over a kneeling man who is long-haired, half-naked and wearing an animal skin. Under the monk is written the name Kentigern, and under the wild man Myrddin. More confirmation, albeit in a tradition, that Lailoken and Merlin were the same man.

However the location of this church and its modern window are what is important to the next part of this puzzle. Across the road from Stobo Kirk is a farm called Easter Dawyck, another straightforward Anglian or Old English place name meaning 'Crow Farm'. There are other English names in the area, but as the road bridges the young Tweed at a farm known as Altarstone, it is as though an invisible toponymic frontier has been crossed. English names cease and the landscape is named in P-Celtic. A group of ghost names that remember Merlin.

At their centre lies Drumelzier. That is a Q-Celtic name directly concocted from the much earlier P-Celtic Dunmedler.[5] Allowing for a metathetical confusion of consonants (common enough in Celtic names), it means 'The Dun of Myrddin', or 'Merlin's Fort'. While the hamlet and its kirk lie on the banks of the river, 400 yards up a steep hill stands Tinnis Castle. This is from P-Celtic Dinas, which now means a 'city' in modern Welsh, but in those days it was for a focal stronghold. To the north, less than a mile away across the river valley, is Dreva Craig, another large fort notable for its chevaux-de-frise defences. Designed to frustrate both infantry and cavalry charges, large boulders have been rolled and set in front of the ditches at Dreva. The name is also P-Celtic from *tref* for 'settlement'. Below the forts, on the flood plain of the Tweed, there is a standing stone and tucked under roadside trees just beyond the farm of the same name is the Altarstone. This is old, and if it is remembered nowadays as a place of sacrifice, then that tradition will have been even fresher in the sixth century.

Guarding the south-west, on Rachan Hill is another fort, completing the circle of lookouts and defences around Dunmedler's fertile flatlands where the Tweed is joined by its tributary the Biggar Water.

As often, modern names remember ancient association: the largest house in Drumelzier is called Merlindale and it is reached by Merlindale Bridge. But there is an older tale which has been repeated for centuries about the little hamlet.

> When Tweed and Pausyl meet at Merlin's grave
> Scotland and England shall one monarch have.

Quoted by Walter Scott in 1807 when it was already at least 400

---

[5] Mike Darton, *The Dictionary of Place-names in Scotland* (1994).

years old, this probably dates back to Thomas the Rhymer who in turn attributes it to Merlin.

Before dealing with the substance of this, I want to pin this place on the modern map. Pausyl is the same word as Possil in Glasgow and it is P-Celtic for 'settlement', but it is not noted anywhere on the Ordnance Survey. Flowing through the hamlet is the Drumelzier Burn, but knowledgeable local people not only remember its original name was Powsail but also that in the last century it was diverted into the Tweed at a point 500 yards upstream from its original outfall. If the Pausyl and the Tweed still met in the same place, the junction would be very near a standing stone which is clearly visible on the flood plain. Which would confirm another local tradition: that the old stone marks Merlin's grave.

Now there are lots of traditions about lots of things which confirm nothing more than fertile imagination. However this is different. In his *Life of St Kentigern* Jocelyn completes the saint's Christian triumph over Myrddin by noting that he claimed to be near death when he was graciously admitted to the church. More than that, he predicted the method of his own dispatch and its place. Jocelyn writes that Myrddin expected 'a triple death' and, by the banks of the Tweed, that is exactly what happened. Caught by shepherds, he was stoned and beaten before slipping into the river to be impaled on fishermen's stakes while simultaneously drowning. However impossibly theatrical, or unlikely that might sound, it is the where and not the how that counts.

Finally there is the provenance of the prophecies. By quoting the ancient couplet that grand old unionist Walter Scott was looking for local agreement with the Union of the Crowns in 1603. Since 'Scotland' and 'England' are concepts which postdate Myrddin by many centuries, how can these prophecies relate to how he thought?

Here is the linking passage, the last stanza from the poem 'Greetings'.

But I predict that after many things
With one bridge on the Taw
And another on the Tywi
There will be an end to war.

While this feels like a general plea for unity and peace of some sort, it is most likely, given Myrddin's experience at Arthuret, to mean to encourage P-Celtic unity against the common enemies to the east and north. And the bridges suggest, in the original Old Welsh, bridges of human bodies, not of wood. The rivers are very hard to place but if Myrddin made these prophecies and he lived on the Tweed and he held to the Druidic belief that water-meetings were magically powerful, then he may have meant the junction of Tweed and Teviot at Kelso.

Back upstream there is an important historical nugget to be found in all of this prophecy, toponymy and hagiography. Given the presence of both men in Drumelzier and Stobo, and remembering the highly partial slant Jocelyn would have given the meeting of Kentigern and Myrddin, I think it likely that the saint would have had to suffer interruption to his sermons. A powerful Druid in exile, whose prophecies have come down to us, rode two miles to Stobo from Tinnis Castle and harangued Kentigern as he attempted to say mass to his new converts. Paganism would have died hard in the Border hills and a line from 'Appletrees' might remember the enmity between Merlin and Kentigern: '*I am hated by Riderch's strongest scion.*'

What is certain is that Christian tradition, written down by Jocelyn, gave Merlin a uniquely savage death and that in itself may be a memory of great hatred.

My point is a simple one. In arguing that the P-Celtic kingdoms of southern Scotland saw the genesis of Arthur, it cannot be insignificant that the same place also gave birth to the legends of Merlin. Although they can never have met, it was no cultural accident that Geoffrey of Monmouth and later writers put them together. They were both Men of the North, two figures whose shadows are cast worldwide, who form a bipolar national myth of order and wildness, of reason and magic. They came from the same time and the same place, somewhere described happily by its natives as obscure: the Scottish Border country.

9

THE MEN OF THE GREAT WOOD

Shortest-lived, furthest east, the P-Celtic kingdom of Gododdin is the keystone to this story. Shortest-lived because it lay to the east, exposed to the Germanic invaders from continental Europe, the fourth Welsh kingdom of Scotland is named differently from the other three. Gododdin is the clear onomastic descendant of Votadini and this description of a people lived on in the style 'Y Gododdin' or 'The Gododdin'.[1] A tribe rather than a place like Rheged, Strathclyde or Manau.

They held three strongholds, each on impregnable hilltops. Traprain Law in East Lothian is a solitary crag with a flat top, standing tall in the midst of rolling cornfields. Archaeologists have found quantities of Roman coins and a remarkable horde of silver from Gaul which was beaten, ready for smelting. Perhaps a tribute. Across the Tweed to the south sits Yeavering Bell, another hilltop fortress near the confluence of the Rivers Glen and Till. A strange name, P-Celtic, which comes from Ad Gefrin meaning 'Goat Hill'.

The third Gododdin stronghold was Eildon Hill North, near Melrose and in the centre of the Scottish Border country. There

[1] W.J. Watson, *The Celtic Placenames of Scotland* (1926).

are traces of more than 300 huts on Eildon, an easy name meaning 'old fort'. At its foot, hard by the Tweed and Dere Street, was the busy Roman garrison of Trimontium. Counting its soldiers and auxiliaries and the local tradesmen who settle around it in a township and the traffic passing through, Trimontium (there are three Eildon Hills, side by side) was the nearest thing to a Roman city in Scotland with perhaps as many as 5,000 inhabitants.

The Gododdin were different from the other three kingdoms in another way. They wrote their own epitaph. Traditionally composed in Din Eidyn, or Edinburgh, by a man called Aneirin, there is a long poem 'The Gododdin' which describes the preparations for a battle thought to have been fought at Catterick in AD 600.[2] The imagery is pungent: warriors feasting for a year in the hall of King Mynyddawg of Edinburgh, tales of impossible valour, the hyperbole of battle and the bloody carnage of failure. Weighed down as they are by the glut of gory deeds, the values of these men are easy to miss. Loyalty, constancy and unwavering bravery are what the Gododdin admire. Against the background of the Christian struggle of the Men of the North against the pagan forces of Anglo-Saxon darkness, the Gododdin are heroic figures. Golden torcs around their necks, jewelled brooches clasping their woollen cloaks as they sit in the circle of firelight reciting tales of glory, inciting themselves to greater fame. Comrades bonded in battle, dependent on each other, the Gododdin show an early version of chivalry, a word based on the French word *cheval* for a horse and giving an under-meaning of 'the code of the horsemen'. And if Aneirin is to be taken literally, they practised what they extolled. At Catterick, all the Gododdin save one warrior were slaughtered by the Angles.

Because 'The Gododdin' is a transcribed and later version of an oral work, mistakes and anachronistic additions have certainly been made, but the sense of it and the drive of the thing come out all in a piece. It is authentic, give or take a bit of lexical quibbling.

[2] K.H. Jackson, *The Gododdin: The Oldest Scottish Poem* (1969).

'The Gododdin' survives in two compilations both included in the late thirteenth-century *Book of Aneirin*. The A version is longer and better organized but the B version uses older spelling forms and is probably the earlier and less corrupted rendition. Although each version contains verses that do not appear in the other, the content is basically the same, as is the style. Here is a flavour of the great poem.

Wearing a brooch, in the front rank, bearing weapons in battle, a mighty man in the fight before his death-day, a champion in the charge in the van of the armies; there fell five times fifty before his blades, of the men of Deira and Bernicia a hundred score fell and were destroyed in a single hour. He would sooner the wolves had his flesh than go to his own wedding, he would rather be prey for ravens than go to the altar; he would sooner his blood flowed to the ground than get due burial, making return for his mead and the hosts in the hall. Hyfeidd the Tall shall be honoured as long as there is a minstrel ...

The men went to Catraeth, swift was their army, the pale mead was their feast, and it was their poison; three hundred men battling according to plan, and after the glad war-cry there was silence. Though they went to the churches to do penance, the inescapable meeting with death overtook them ...

The retinue of Gododdin on rough-maned horses like swans,
With their harness drawn tight,
And attacking the troop in the van of the host,
Defending the woods and the mead of Eidyn.

The men went to Catraeth with the dawn, their high courage shortened their lives. They drank the sweet yellow ensnaring mead, for a year many a bard made merry. Red were their swords (may the blades never be cleansed), and white shields and square-pointed spear-heads before the retinue of Mynyddawg the Luxurious ...

A Gododdin warrior

The men went to Catraeth, they were renowned, wine and mead from gold cups was their drink for a year, in accordance with the honoured custom. Three men and three score and three hundred, wearing gold necklets, of all that hastened out after the choice drink none escaped but three, through feats of sword-play – the two war-dogs of Aeron, and stubborn Cynon; and I too, streaming with blood, by grace of my brilliant poetry …

The men hastened out, they galloped together; short-lived were they, drunk over the clarified mead, the retinue of Mynyddawg, famous in stress of battle; their lives were payment for their feast of mead. Caradawg and Madawg, Pyll and Ieuan, Gwgawn and Gwiawn, Gwynn and Cynfan, Peredur of the steel weapons, Gwawrddur and Aeddan, charging forward in battle among broken shields; and though they were slain they slew, none returned to his lands.

The men went to Catraeth in column, raising the war-cry, a force with steeds and blue armour and shields, javelins aloft and keen lances, and bright mail-coats and swords. He led, he burst through the armies, and there fell five times fifty before his blades – Rhufawn the Tall, who gave gold to the altar and gifts and fine presents to the minstrel …

It is grief to me that after the toil of battle they suffered the agony of death in torment, and a second heavy grief it is to me to have seen our men falling headlong; and continual moaning it is, and anguish, after the fiery men lying in the clodded earth – Rhufawn and Gwgawn, Gwiawn and Gwlyged, men of most manly station, strong in strife; after the battle, may their souls get welcome in the land of Heaven, the dwelling-place of plenty …

In the older B version there is a stanza that is pivotal for my own narrative. It is written in praise of one of Mynyddawg's greatest cavalry warriors, Gwawrddur, who fell in the slaughter at Catterick. But despite his valour he suffers by comparison.

He struck before the three hundred bravest
He would slay both middle and flank
He was suited to the forefront of a most generous host
He would give gifts from a herd of horses in winter
He would feed black ravens on the wall
of a fortress, though he were not Arthur
Among the strong ones in battle
In the van, an alder-palisade was Gwawrddur

This is the earliest, the first reference to Arthur. The poem was composed in Edinburgh around 600, and tells an epic story of the Gododdin in battle against the Angle invaders of north-east England. There is other, reliable evidence to show that Catterick was a historical event that certainly took place, and not something that lived only in the imagination of the bard Taliesin. The reference pins Arthur in time and in place. He lived before 600 since the reference and comparison to Gwawrddur is a memory – this man who fell at Catterick was a brave warrior, but he was not so brave as our kinsman, the hero Arthur. That is the sense of the stanza. And it is a crucial and convincing piece of evidence for Arthur as a battle leader of the Gododdin.

The mention of Arthur is not in a poetic sense dissonant. Nor is it illogical. If the interpolation was later and had a deliberate purpose behind it, then that can only have been to build the fame and importance of Arthur at some point after his legend had begun to develop. And yet there is no other reference to him in 'The Gododdin' and no attempt to elaborate or puff the mention of him and that is made. It is a natural and unfussy use of a name which by 600 had become a byword for valour among the Men of the North. Everyone knew who Arthur was and there was no need to explain or qualify.

In the *Book of Taliesin* there are other praise poems which paint general pictures of martial glory but which, unlike 'The Gododdin' do not relate to any historical event. In *Kanu y Meirch* or 'The

Poem of the Horses', Gwawrddur's mount is compared to 'Arthur's horse, boldly bestowing pain' and in a later stanza Taliesin admires a grey mare 'Llamrei, full valuable, wide nostrilled and powerful'.[3] In medieval Arthurian romance Llamrei was Arthur's charger. But these verses are only useful in understanding something of the tone of P-Celtic warrior culture; they do not offer much sense of how these people thought about the world, or, if Arthur was one of them, much idea of the sort of man he was.

Better to come at this from another direction. Another poem attributed to Taliesin opens a different way of thinking. '*Kat Goddeu*' was 'The Battle of the Trees', a shape-shifting poem concerning armies of trees, their hierarchy, their characteristics and their prowess. It is a mystical work, much of whose meaning is lost to us, but in its recital of tree lore and magic it opens a door to the ancient world of Glamoury, the forgotten Celtic Green World. The modern word 'glamour' meaning simply 'charm, allure, attractiveness, beauty' was originally much more interesting. It comes from an old Scots word which was certainly in use in the Borders as late as the 1960s when my grandmother used 'glammer' to mean a spell or the power to enchant. More, she used 'glamoury' (perhaps Scots orthographers would spell it 'glamourie' but I never saw the word written down) to mean magic in general, but neither in a good or bad sense. Perhaps that neutrality was what allowed 'glamour' to come to be attached in a positive way to beautiful women and their charms.

At all events the ancient meaning remembered in my grand-mother's usage was, more or less, natural magic or the magic of the natural world. More than the deeds of warriors and the clatter of battle, the Glamoury tells much about how the P-Celts dealt with the world they found around them every day.

But before I take a path into the Great Wood, it is important constantly to remember to walk on the right side of New Age daft-

---

[3] K.H. Jackson, *The Gododdin: The Oldest Scottish Poem* (1996).

ness and quaint tradition and pin the picture of the Gododdin to facts, events and sensible comparison.

The poem's title '*Kat Goddeu*' is a clear link with the Gododdin themselves. Goddeu also occurs in the poem as a proper noun – 'The Wood' or more likely 'The Great Wood'. Accepting at least that Taliesin was the bard of the King of Edinburgh, of the man who was chief of the northern Gododdin in 600, then it is reasonable to see 'The Great Wood' as co-terminus with 'Coed Celyddon' the vast forest of southern Scotland where Merlin took refuge after the disastrous battle at Arthuret in 573. Which in turn allows Goddeu to enter Gododdin and produce a more pulled-out meaning of 'The Men of the Great Wood'.

As far as it goes that definition is interesting but not detailed enough to add colour. What was the Great Wood like? How did Arthur and his kinsmen and women think about their world?

Before describing such remnants of the world of the Glamoury that can still be seen, some simple bits of physical evidence. Pollen archaeologists and dendrochronologists reckon that 1,500 years ago mean seasonal temperatures may have been as much as four to six degrees warmer. Not necessarily sunnier, but warmer. This sort of weather allowed vegetation of all sorts, but particularly trees, to seed more successfully and to grow and thrive in places now too inhospitable. Hardwoods thrived at altitudes up to 2,000 feet and in a density virtually unknown to us now, after many centuries of felling, clearing and cultivation.[4] The point is a simple one. The Great Wood was a phenomenon of natural power. Although large areas had been cleared or were no more than scrubland, parts of it were dark and hard to penetrate. It could reproduce itself without the intervention of people in any part of its life process. Tall trees were literally monumental to the Celts, the biggest living organisms in the world whose top canopies reached for their sky gods and whose roots penetrated deep into the earth and the Otherworld. It

[4] T.C. Smout (ed.), *Scottish Woodland History* (1997).

is not an overstatement to compare the Glamoury with the way in which nineteenth- and twentieth-century Europeans reacted to the jungles of Central Africa and South America. Fantastic beasts, lost cities and civilizations, apemen, the sense of the jungle's power, the danger and mystery of it, the heart of darkness. There was something of all of that in the way that the Celts thought about the Great Wood, the Goddeu.

It was beneficent as well as dangerous. Bears, wolves and wild boar are all gone now but the Celts knew them, feared them and respected them. The Welsh translation of Arthur can be read as 'Bear Man'. But the Celts used the woods widely as a source of hunted meat, of fruit and berries, of vegetables and, crucially, as their materia medica – something whose history is not lost and which will open a store of ancient knowledge when I come to deal with it presently.

As ever place-names remember the Great Wood and sometimes allow a sense of its edges. Dalkeith, just south of Edinburgh, is P-Celtic Dol Coedd or 'Field by the Wood'. Nearby is Penicuik or Pen y Cog, the 'Hill of the Cuckoo'. Then to the east Pencaitland or Pen Coed Lann, this time 'At the top of the field enclosed by the wood'.[5] There are many more but these three give some sense of the northern limits of the wood.

Individual trees also conferred names to places and in particular it is cheering to see that the Glamoury of the oak tree was strong enough to ensure that the Celtic root planted in England survived. *Darroch* is the Q-Celtic word for oak and *Derwen* the P-Celtic. They share *dar* as a common root and it is in Dartford in Kent, Dartmoor and Dartmouth in Devon, Darwen in Lancashire and less surprisingly in Derwentwater in Celtic Cumbria.

The story of York is extraordinary and shows the tenacity of these ancient tree names. It is first recorded in 150 as Eborakon and then Eboracum which came from the P-Celtic personal name

[5] W.J. Watson, *The Celtic Placenames of Scotland* (1926).

Eburos which in turn came from the word *iubhar* (best preserved in Scots Gaelic) which means 'yew tree'. The Angles who fought at Catterick against the Gododdin had already taken the city, but they did not understand its Latinized name. They twisted it into Eofor Wic Ceaster: 'A Wild Boar Homestead at the former Roman Army Camp'. Approximately. Then they boiled it down to Eoforwic which the Danish Vikings modified to Jorvik which appeared as York in the thirteenth century. The persistence of *iubhar* in the first part of the name is remarkable and it shows that the Glamoury has long fingers, reaching all the way to Manhattan Island.

The Celtic languages carry much in the way of attitude inside them. All languages do that, but without the labour of learning them it is difficult to understand how those attitudes work on the world that words describe. Although the P- and Q-Celts were not literate people, in the sense of writing down their languages, they did become influenced by the determined and consistent literacy of the Romans, whose Latin inscriptions, carved on stone, were placed where all could see them: on public buildings, on wayside tombs and on the insignia of the legions.

By the fourth century the Q-Celts began to develop an alphabet somewhat influenced by Latin, but emphatically Celtic in its application. Taking its name from the Irish God Ogma, the Ogham script is not an abstract like the Latin alphabet which children still learn today, where symbols representing sounds are followed in a sequence of twenty-six. The Q-Celts based Ogham script on trees.[6] Taking a long vertical line to represent the trunk, each letter or twig (the Irish word *fleasc* has both meanings) stands for each of the eighteen letters of the Gaelic alphabet, depending on its position and orientation. Some letters are straight lines or twigs at right angles, others are diagonal, and still more penetrate through the trunk to show both sides. And even more concretely each letter is represented by a different tree in the forest. Rather in the way that

---

[6] Yvonne Aburron, *The Enchanted Forest* (1993).

children recite A for Apple, B for Ball and C for Cat, the Q-Celts remembered their Ogham by the initial letters of the trees they saw around them. Their alphabet looked like this:

B	beith	birch	**M**	muin	vine
L	luis	rowan	**G**	gort	ivy
F	fearn	alder	**R**	ruis	elder
S	suil	willow	**A**	ailm	elm
N	nuin	ash	**O**	onn	gorse
H	l'uath	hawthorn	**U**	iubhar	yew
D	darroch	oak	**E**	eadha	green
T	teine	whin	**I**	iogh	yew
C	coll	hazel	**P**	beith bhog	soft birch

This, for consistency, is an old Scottish Gaelic version of the Ogham and it is almost identical with the Irish Gaelic list. The yew and the birch appear twice to cope with minor differences and the appearance of the vine as a tree or shrub is interesting since it seems to support the notion that the weather was warmer 1,500 years ago when the Ogham came into use.

The script only appears now on stones for the mundane reason that they have survived. It is almost certain that the most common vehicles for Ogham were either sticks, wooden stakes in the ground or living trees. All that has been coherently translated from the stones are a series of names and their locations suggest strongly that they were used as boundary markers.

There are 332 Ogham stones in Ireland, 40 in Wales, 8 in England, 2 in southern Scotland and 27 in the north of Scotland.

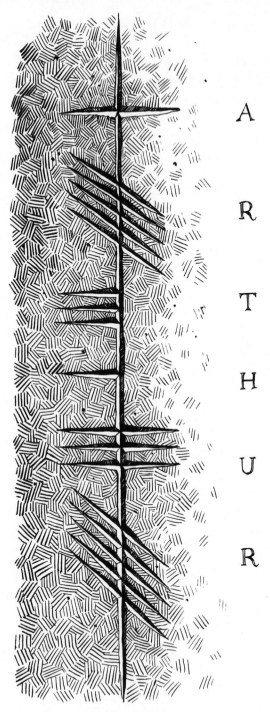

A
R
T
H
U
R

Ogham script

This last group are inscribed with a Pictish version of the alphabet which has proved impossible to decode.

Even though there are no surviving Ogham stones in P-Celtic, there are remnants of an adaptation of the script in what Welsh scholars call Coel bren. It means, somewhat tautologically, 'wood sticks'. And the names of trees in P-Celtic largely bear the same initial letters as their counterparts in Q-Celtic: *derwen* is for oak, *bedw* for birch, *collen* for hazel and so on. I think it likely that Ogham was carved on trees in the Great Wood in southern Scotland even though nothing has survived. If stones denoting boundaries were placed in the clearings, the riversides and the hill-tops, those who invaded or took control of the land would have removed them as a trace of former ownership. Where Oghams do survive, in Ireland, Wales and northern Scotland, no new people gained power for centuries and land remained in the hands of people who understood the stones.

The significance of this alphabet is to show clearly one of the ways in which Celts began to develop the idea that nature could have relative value and be considered in a hierarchy. More particularly, the uses of trees described in this letter-system allow a window into everyday life. Here are some examples of tree knowledge that follow the Ogham order.

Birch – their leaves make a tea which relieves rheumatism and breaks down bladder stones. In Scotland it is still believed that bad luck follows the felling of birches.

Rowan – everyday hand tools were made of this wood as were pegs to hold parts of implements together. The power of the tree to protect is the reason why it was found in farmyards and near houses, and in the eighteenth and nineteenth centuries when country people crowded into tenements in cities, they red-leaded their doorsteps to represent the berries of the rowan.

Alder – Gwawrddur was 'an alder palisade' for Taliesin because the P-Celts made their shields from this hard wood. Because it lasts a long time in water before rotting, alder was also used to make jetties and serve as piles for crannogs.

Willow – willow withies are still used for basketwork and archaeologists can show that the Celts coppiced the trees to produce more wands.

Ash – made spear shafts. In Merlin's poem 'Appletrees' there is a line: 'The Saesons will be slaughtered by our ashen spears'.

Oak – ships were made of 'hearts of oak' and more than any tree they were venerated. *Darroch* became associated with strength and nobility. A modern Gaelic poet uses the hierarchy of animals to describe it: 'salmon of trees, eagle of trees'. Druids were called 'oak-knowers' and groves of the trees were sacred. It hosted the mistletoe which Druids believed was an aid to fertility; we still kiss under it at Christmas. In Scotland people swore 'by oak and ash and thorn' and women hugged oak trees hoping for easier labour pains.

Tree lore is almost lost to us now but there is in the Ogham a genuine memory of what the Great Wood meant to the P- and Q-Celts and a fleeting sense of how they thought about it.

In 1823 William Cobbett went on his rural rides in Surrey and Sussex where he heard an entertaining echo of that past. He met an old man who claimed that when hazelnuts, beechnuts and others were plentiful it had an effect on young people. 'A great nut year was a great bastard year,' he told Cobbett and furthermore he could support his view by looking at parish records. He was only repeating tree lore, as was the old saying: 'When elder leaves are as big as a mouse's ear, women are in season.' Doubtful nowadays.

A good deal more likely is the survival of a very old wood-burning poem which had its origins in Devon and has now been pleasingly rewritten in English.

> Oak logs will warm you well,
> That are old and dry;
> Logs of pine will sweetly smell
> But the sparks will fly

Birch logs will burn too fast,
Chestnut scarce at all;
Hawthorn logs are good to last –
Cut them in the fall.

Holly logs will burn like wax,
You may burn them green;
Elm logs like to smouldering flax,
No flame to be seen.

Beech logs for winter time,
Yew logs as well;
Green elder logs it is a crime
For any man to sell.

Pear logs and apple logs,
They will scent your room,
Cherry logs across the dogs
Smell like flower of broom.

Ash logs smooth and grey,
Burn them green or old,
Buy up all that come your way
Worth their weight in gold.

Since we no longer depend on the natural world to warm us, these characteristics are forgotten.

To most of us now, as urban dwellers, the seasons mean little more than the length of the days and the outside temperature. Shelter is all around us and warmth is rarely something we have to work to create. The Glamoury is nothing more now than a collection of explanations of phrases and words, if that. But the plants, animals and seasons of Britain were forces of great power felt by the Celtic peoples of Britain in a way that has almost but not quite outrun living memory. An old Catholic priest from South Uist told me once that he bitterly regretted that children no longer went barefoot. From the feast of St Bride (Imbolc) on 1 February he wore no shoes and he said he could feel the ground come alive through the soles of his feet. And at Hallowe'en he could feel that the earth was ready to die. He spoke to me in Gaelic, because he believed that English had not the means of carrying these ideas. They just sounded daft, he said, looking away out of his kitchen window.

South Uist may be an unlikely place to look for Arthur but I am certain that in the chapel house on the machair I heard some sense of how his people thought about the world.

The tiny speech community of Scottish Gaels has also preserved something else which will colour a picture of all Celtic Britain and supply an elusive insight into the lives of those who are always ignored by early history: ordinary people.

A body of ancient medical practice has survived in Gaelic in the Highlands which is now sadly unique, but which once healed and helped sick people all over Britain and western Europe.[7] Described no longer as the Glamoury but demeaned by the name folk medicine, it was all but eradicated by the witch-hunts of the sixteenth and seventeenth centuries. The appalling punishments meted out by the Church to women who were guilty of nothing more than a knowledge of ancient herbal recipes for the relief of pain drove this body of lore first underground and then to extinction. Although the witch-hunters brought their terror very near to the edge of the Gaidhealtachd – in 1590 Agnes Sampson from the town of Keith was burned at the stake for alleviating labour pains for one of her pregnant neighbours – they never penetrated the glens and sea lochs to any great degree. Remoteness saved the Gaelic medical tradition and so did the obvious fact that it was not carried on in English. While women, and some men, were horribly tortured and burned by the agents of both Catholic and Protestant

[7] Mary Beith, *Healing Threads* (1995).

Churches all over western Europe, the Gaelic healers of the Highlands of Scotland quietly continued to use medicines they found growing around them to cure and console the sick and the old.

By its nature Celtic medicine was a tradition; a combination of long experience and observation with a necessary faith nourished by need and the example of others. Because a natural or herbal cure had a history of working, patients were more disposed to believe in its efficacy, to want it to ease pain or correct malfunction. Which in turn went a long way to ensure that it did.

Credibility was further buttressed by formality. Far from being a mere collection of remedies arrived at by centuries of trial and error, Celtic medicine was seen as the conventional wisdom. In other words the people of the Scottish Gaidhealtachd did not see it as 'folk medicine' or 'alternative medicine' or something inferior to what was practised in the Lowlands, it was simply medicine and all that there was.

Central to the survival of Celtic medicine is a remarkable family. Far-famed throughout the Highlands and down the centuries since Somerled, the Lord of the Isles, was what became known as the Beaton family. Before the sixteenth century they called themselves the MacBeths. But in either guise it is clear that, as the focus of Celtic healing, their genealogy goes back further than conventional history can trace it.

The Beatons and other medical families became professional doctors with a close connection to the clans and particular clan chiefs. So important was their role that even when the Scottish kings suppressed the Lordship of the Isles, the patronage of the Beatons and others continued.

But it was royal patronage in medieval Scotland which established the family as pre-eminent. In the early fourteenth century Robert I Bruce was the patient of Patrick MacBeth, undoubtedly a renowned doctor but probably unable to do more than ease the discomfort of the old king's leprosy. David II employed Gilbert,

143

Patrick's son and while the king was held hostage in England between 1346 and 1357, there is evidence that his doctor was allowed to travel between Scotland and England. Probably he returned to see home and family but perhaps he also needed to replenish his store of natural remedies. At all events it is clear that the Scottish kings from Robert I down to Charles I employed members of the Beaton family to minister to them. Such was the prestige of Celtic medicine that even a renaissance monarch like Charles I, painted by Van Dyke and sculpted by Bernini, turned to the ancient traditions of the Glamoury for help when he was sick.

In the sixteenth and early seventeenth centuries, before the witch hunters chased the old traditions into the hills, manuscripts began to appear which codified good practice and sometimes showed how wide was the net of Gaelic learning, with translations of European and classical texts often included.[8] These were sometimes used as manuals and marginal jottings are common. They show doctors as purveyors of common sense, of good hygiene and also men who listened to their patients in a proper attempt at diagnosis. Washing, cleanliness in cooking and food handling are all coupled with more arcane medical advice, as well as sound social counselling. In one manuscript a doctor writes that it is better to cook peas or beans with a pinch of cumin since that prevents farting.

The most substantial Gaelic medical manuscript was compiled by Angus Beaton of Skye in 1612. In a remarkable echo of the Glamoury, he writes his name on page 302 in a version of the Ogham alphabet. Using a pair of consonants to stand together for vowels, he mimics the strokes of the ancient script. This was a doodling attempt at a code which begs a larger question about the use and origin of Ogham. Was it something understood only by the Beatons' Druidic ancestors? And was its use somehow sacred? All that can be said with any certainty is that both the Druids and the

---

[8] Mary Beith, *op. cit.*

Beatons (and other families) were groups in Celtic society who carried valued traditions of great knowledge, who were revered and who occupied roles that placed them close to political power. Perhaps the use of Ogham is a slender thread that binds them together across millennia.

Although the persecutions of the seventeenth century killed the old medicine in southern Scotland and severed a direct link with the P-Celts of the Great Wood, there are still some telling traces to be detected. The Romans brought medical knowledge which found its way into what survived in the Highlands, and these practices and ingredients can only have been absorbed in times of peace and settlement, which in turn must mean that they were exchanged with the P-Celts of southern Scotland after 80 and before the withdrawal of the legions two centuries later.

Hygiene was the clearest connection, and unlike their southern cousins, Gaelic doctors absorbed the common sense of cleanliness and its direct connection to good health from the Romans. They also introduced more plants into the Celtic materia medica. Many of these were already native to southern Scotland but the Romans understood how to use them in compiling cures.[9] The juniper berry is a good example. Traditionally the Ettrick Forest, as late as the nineteenth century, abounded with juniper bushes which were picked at the onset of winter and the berries sold at market. The Romans knew that they had a purgative quality, very useful in treating stomach ailments and the convulsions they sometimes caused. Another example is male fern, an everyday name for a plant much used by Roman cavalrymen. The Gaelic name is *marc raineach* and as 'horse fern' it says more about its medical history. Horses are very prone to develop worms and there is strong evidence that the Romans introduced its use to the Gododdin in the second century AD. The roots were first powdered and then infused in the horses' drinking water.

[9] Tess Darwin, *The Scots Herbal* (1996).

The names of herbs also show how closely linked the medicine of the Highlands was with the P-Celtic south. Thyme is a common herb and the Gaels used it as a flavouring and also made a decoction of it for people who slept badly and suffered nightmares. It has an interesting name in Gaelic: *leis mhic righ Bhreatainn* or 'the plant belonging to the King of the Britons' son'.

The origins of that are now lost but the link between medicine and diet was very close and looking through the herbals and lists of aphorisms and observations, it is possible to gather a good sense of what the Celts of southern Scotland ate, and thereby an idea of the everyday texture of their lives.

By and large they were vegetarians. They ate oatmeal porridge sometimes flavoured with seasonal berries: juniper, raspberries, wild strawberries, and sometimes they added hazelnuts and beechnuts. They made brose from barley and added pulses to it, usually peas or beans. Broth from kail and wild celery and vegetable stew were common dishes. Milk from cows, ewes and goats was a source of protein either drunk fresh or made into cheese or butter. Eggs from a variety of birds were eaten and fish netted or hooked from the lochs, rivers and seas. The P-Celts were loath to kill many domestic animals for meat and they depended on their skills as hunters to supply protein, particularly in wintertime. Here is a beautiful song from a mother to her child which was found bound into the A version of 'The Gododdin'. It is a uniquely homely piece which gives a clear sense of family life among the P-Celts of southern Scotland in the seventh century.

> Dinogad's speckled petticoat
> was made of skins of speckled stoat:
> whip whip whipalong
> eight times we'll sing the song.
> When your father hunted the land
> spear on shoulder club in hand
> thus his speedy dogs he'd teach

Giff Gaff catch her catch her fetch!
In his coracle he'd slay
fish as a lion does its prey.
When your father went to the moor
he'd bring back heads of stag, fawn, boar
the speckled grouse's head from the mountain
fishes' heads from the falls of Oak Fountain.
Whatever your father struck with his spear
wild pig wild cat fox from his lair
unless it had wings it would never get clear.

Silverweed grows wild now in hedge roots and on roadsides but both Celts and Romans ate it in quantity. Its roots, dried and roasted, are said to be nutty and taste like parsnips. Its usefulness is remembered in its Gaelic name, *an seachdamh aran* or 'the seventh bread', and the great collector of traditional poetry and music, Alexander Carmichael, wrote down a very old verse in praise of the silverweed.

Honey under ground,
Silverweed of spring
Honey and condiment
Whisked whey of summer.
Honey and fruitage
Carrot of autumn.
Honey and crunching
Nuts of winter

The Scots language occasionally remembered the effects of Celtic herbal medicine very obviously. Water pepper is called *lus an fhogair* in Gaelic, which means literally 'the plant which expels', and it was commonly used as a purgative. In Scots it is known still as hot arsmart.

More romantic is the tradition that love-making under the rowan tree was likely to bring pregnancy for a virgin and give her a male

147

child into the bargain. Since the Scots climate did not often allow couples to venture out of doors to find a discreetly placed rowan, housebuilders brought the wood inside. The old name for the crossbeam in a chimney breast is the 'rantree' and it allowed tradition to be served in fireside comfort.[10]

The Glamoury lasted a long time. In his *Tour of Scotland*, made in 1772, Thomas Pennant saw Highland midwives take a green stick from an ash tree and hold it over a fire so that the sap oozed into a cup, which they then gave to the newborn baby as its first drink of life. This is a lineal descendant of the Glamoury. The Celts believed that the ash was a powerful and protective tree; they used its branches for divination and its straight limbs for spear shafts. The Norsemen held that the ash was their World Tree, called Yggdrasil. In its top canopy, far from the sight of men was Asgard, the house of Valhalla. Around its trunk was Midgard, the world we see now, and below the soil among its roots was Niflhel or the World of the Dead. And below that was 'Hel' or the underworld.

The collector Alexander Carmichael published the *Carmina Gadelica* beginning in the early part of this century. It contains much that is beautiful and even more that is practical. There is a lyrical poem of great simplicity which also acts as a guide to where different tree species grow.

> Choose the willow of the streams,
> Choose the hazel of the rocks,
> Choose the alder of the marshes,
> Choose the birch of the waterfalls.
>
> Choose the ash of the shade,
> Choose the yew of resilience,
> Choose the elm of the brae,
> Choose the oak of the sun.[11]

[10] Sheila Livingstone, *Scottish Festivals* (1997).
[11] Tess Darwin, *The Scots Herbal* (1996).

As the Industrial Revolution emptied the landscape and people forgot their knowledge of the plants and animals around them, a country to town trade developed. Since organized cultivation began, surplus had always been exchanged or sold on market days, but what began to happen in the nineteenth century with the rapid growth of cities was different. Country knowledge, country skills and products, even country people came from another world, a place visited by city people but no longer understood by them. That is a gulf that has widened ever since, and its beginnings were noted by a nineteenth-century historian whose description of a wood fair already carries the seeds of division.

> The shortwood in the glens is worked into various useful articles, and disposed of in the low country. In the month of August there is a timber market held in Aberdeen for several days, which is of ancient origin, and to which the Highlanders bring ladders, harrows, tubs, pails, and many other articles; those who have nothing else, bring rods of hazel and other young wood, with sackfuls of aitnach or juniper and other mountain berries.

Where Celtic medicine, tree and plant lore, and a general affinity for the land survived, a sense of that ancient way of life also continued. Occasionally it was reported to the sophisticates of the city and the righteous of the Kirk as quaint at best, and outright pagan at worst. But for us these random glimpses offer an insight into life in Dark Ages Scotland.

It is known that Druids had supervised the ritual sacrifice of bulls both in pursuit of divination and also for votive purposes, sometimes on behalf of an important person, a king or a leader of some sort. There is no doubt that sacrifices of bulls conducted in exactly the same manner and for the same purposes were happening in the Highlands of Scotland as late as the 1670s, and possibly beyond.

The outraged elders of the presbytery of Applecross reported in 1658 that 'abominable and heathenish practices' were going on in the area. Men from Achnashellach had gathered at what sounds like an ancient holy place, the site of ruined buildings and a hollowed-out stone where 'they tryd the entreing of thair head'. They brought a bull with them, tethered it and then killed it in sacrifice. They walked sunwise around the site and attempted divination and prophecy by the hollowed-out stone.

Twenty years later, in 1678, the Dingwall presbytery noted another bull sacrifice, this time on the island Eilean Ma Ruibhe in Loch Maree. To this old and holy place Hector Mackenzie brought his two sons and a grandson and on the site of an ancient temple they sacrificed a bull to 'the god Mourie'. They killed the animal 'in one heathenish manner ... for the sake of his wife Cirstane's health'.

The old tradition died very hard and these reported incidents would have been only a part of what still went on in secret and remote locations.

Some communities had more confidence and did not trouble to keep their old ways out of the sight of the Kirk. At the old Celtic festival of Samhuinn, on the west side of the island of Lewis people gathered at the church of St Mulvay. Then one of the men took a jug of ale and waded through the breakers into the Atlantic where he stopped, and with the crowd on the beach, he chanted verses now lost to us which were intended to invoke the sea-god Seonaidh. Then he poured the ale into the sea to encourage the god to wash ashore a good harvest of seaweed so that the fields would be well fertilized. After he had regained the beach, the crowd returned to the church, put out the altar candle and began a night of singing, dancing and drinking. The Kirk eventually suppressed this festival but even after the ritual was stopped the crowd still gathered on the beach to chant and invoke the sea-god Briannuil, asking him to blow a north wind so that the seaweed was washed ashore. So complete is the triumph of Presbyterianism that Gaelic dictionaries now list Briannuil as a synonym for Satan.[12]

---

[12] Edward Dwelly, *The Illustrated Gaelic–English Dictionary* (reprinted 1994).

Some Druidic traditions escaped censure because they were either innocuous or misunderstood, or both. On the Black Isle near the village of Munlochy is what is now called the Clootie Well. Instead of the more common Celtic habit of throwing objects of value into water in return for the granting of a wish, the Clootie accepts just that: cloots or rags are tied to the bushes either side of the well. And local residents have observed groups of young girls drinking the water and then tying their knickers on the bushes.

This habit has spread throughout the western world. At air bases in Britain the wives of pilots flying missions to Iraq during the Gulf War tied rags on the wire-netting fences around the perimeter, and the country and western standard 'Tie a Yellow Ribbon round the Old Oak Tree' combines at least two Druidic traditions.

This may seem a long way from the Men of the Great Wood, the Gododdin, and certainly the survival and understanding of these ancient memories tells us little of their politics and their military history. But it does help an understanding of how they thought about the world, what they believed and what, in that revealing phrase, was second nature to them.

10

THE GENERALS

Whatever his rank it is clear from historical sources that Arthur was no king. None of the genealogies of British or P-Celtic kingdoms lists him as an ancestor who ruled before the Anglo-Saxon or Q-Celtic takeover. In no contemporary or near-contemporary account is there mention of a King Arthur. Instead he is called *dux bellorum* or the 'leader of battles', a title more reminiscent of Roman military terminology than anything royal or hereditary. Elsewhere he is styled 'Artorius miles' or 'Arthur the soldier'. It was Geoffrey of Monmouth who anointed him king in 1135, a title that none of his contemporaries would have attached to him. Because Arthur was a professional soldier, a man who was appointed to lead a cavalry army on behalf of a coalition of kings; in modern parlance he was a general. Others had done a similar job before Arthur and to understand his role fully it is necessary to brush in some of the background.

Britannia was valuable. The imperial authorities exerted themselves greatly to protect the province throughout its occupation, particularly from incursion from the north. Emperors led legionary armies against the tribes of Caledonia and later spent much effort in dealing with seaborne attacks from the east. Septimus Severus died at York and a century later in 306 Constantine II was proclaimed emperor in the legionary fortress. More troops were stationed in Britannia than in any other province, even though its sea defences were more secure than the long land frontier on the Rhine–Danube line. That meant in turn that many imperial usurpers chose to raise rebellion in Britannia, backed by its wealth and remote enough from Rome to allow time to build a power base.

In the fourth century the continental empire was under constant pressure from barbarian attacks and the instability this caused led to much faction fighting between imperial candidates. And the focus of Roman power was shifting slowly but inexorably to the east and the new capital at Constantinople.

While there was general decline and fragmentation in the west, the process was slower and less dramatic in Britannia. Communications remained good while the extensive network of paved roads was maintained. It was much much easier to travel from, say, London to Edinburgh in 400 than it was in 1600. In the countryside, villas survived and thrived. Archaeologists digging at Hucclecote in Gloucestershire and Great Casterton in Rutland have found new mosaic floors laid at the end of the fourth century. While it grew increasingly difficult to retain slaves and other bonded agricultural workers, the fertile flatlands of Britannia continued to support organized villa-farms well beyond 400.

At Wroxeter, near Shrewsbury, the great basilica fell into disuse around 350 but archaeologists have found evidence of a remarkable new structure which was built over the levelled rubble of the hall. A new municipal centre, rather like a modern shopping mall, was constructed in a classical mode, except that it was not built out of stone but of timber.

During the first half of the fourth century the province enjoyed some relief from the raids of the Picts and the Saxons and political peace also seems to have reigned. Britannia basked in unprecedented prosperity. But its ripeness inevitably attracted unwanted attention. In 342 there was trouble, so severe that the Emperor Constans arrived the following January or February. Although details are scant, it seems that the Picts had mounted a heavy raid down through the old territory of the Selgovae and had burned the outpost forts north of Hadrian's Wall at High Rochester, Bewcastle and Risingham. The patrol groups known as the Areani were involved in some unspecified action or other but the only concrete decision made by Constans was one of policy. The substantial fort at High Rochester or Bremenium, which lay on Dere Street in the territory of the Gododdin, was abandoned. Since frontier security was of paramount importance to the emperor, this must have involved a judgement about the military capabilities of the Gododdin. He and his advisors took the view that it was better to leave defence in the hands of warriors who knew the Picts, who had been their eastern neighbours for at least a century, whose lives and land lay beside their line of advance, and whose intelligence about the movement of these hill tribes must have been second to none. Constans' judgement is important for this narrative. The Picts had been the curse of Britannia for generations; imperial forces had struggled to contain them. In 343 the Gododdin were entrusted with the task of subduing the Picts.

At first they failed, spectacularly. In 350 the usurper Magnentius, a Spaniard who had risen through the ranks of the Roman army, removed troops from Britannia to support his imperial ambitions on the continent. After his death in 353, a sinister official named Paul arrived in Britannia to organize reprisals against the usurper's supporters. Nicknamed 'Catena' or 'the Chain', he further depleted the military and civil infrastructure in his purges.

After 360, raids from the north became more frequent. The Gododdin seem to have been powerless to prevent the Picts from descending on Britannia intent on destruction and plunder. Once over the Wall there seems to have been little to prevent their bloody sprees.

And then in 367 a remarkable event took place. In what the Romans called the Barbarian Conspiracy, the tribes of the north, the Scots in the west and the Franks and Saxons in Europe attacked the provinces of Britannia and Gaul simultaneously. Co-ordinated in some unknown fashion, these raids were the most devastating yet to be visited on the south.

It seems that the Roman frontier patrols, the Areani, had been bribed by the Pictish chieftains both to supply intelligence and to fail to report the massing of the northern host in the Selgovan hills. The Gododdin may have taken the prudent course and done nothing.

Perhaps they and the treacherous Areani were intimidated by the first appearance of a new people, the far northern allies of the Picts. Their savagery was appalling and St Jerome claims in a memoir to have seen them commit cannibalism in Gaul. They were the Atecotti. The name is P-Celtic and it means 'the Old Peoples'.[1] They came from Caithness and Sutherland and the Western Isles. St Columba's biographer Adomnan remembers an incident in Skye when the saint met an old man who spoke a language that was neither P- or Q-Celtic, but must have come from the north. There are Ogham stones inscribed in a language where it is possible to make out personal names but the rest is utterly unintelligible to us. Perhaps the Atecotti were a remnant of the Old Peoples who, driven far to the north, make a brief and bloody appearance in history as the most savage and feared elements in the Barbarian Conspiracy.

Having bypassed the Gododdin and the forces of Strathclyde, the Picts, Scots and Atecotti burst through Hadrian's Wall and then, at some point, they destroyed what remained of the imperial field army. That victory allowed bands of warriors to roam at will in the province, burning, slaughtering and plundering as they made their bloody progress south. It must have been terrifying. Many

[1] John Morris, *The Age of Arthur* (1973).

soldiers in the provincial forces deserted, slaves took the cover of chaos as a chance to escape and join in the mayhem. The sole motivation of the northern tribes was plunder and destruction; they were raiders, not invaders.

Nevertheless the incursion provoked an immediate imperial reaction. By the spring of 368, at the start of the campaigning season, a man known to history as Count Theodosius arrived in Britannia with four regiments to expel the barbarians, clean up the mess and take measures to discourage a recurrence.

Theodosius acquired the seemingly anachronistic title of 'Count' because of a series of far-reaching changes made to military nomenclature in particular and to the Roman army in general. This process was begun in the early fourth century by the Emperor Diocletian who created the office of Dux, a Latin word which broadly means a mixture of 'leader' and 'commander'. Benito Mussolini adopted it in his self-conferred title of Il Duce and the rulers of Venice for the quasi-royal Doge. To the Romans it bore a more specific meaning of 'commander of frontier forces'.

These new titles, their chains of command and the units under their control were listed in a fascinating document called the *Notitia Dignitatum*.[2] Covering both the eastern and western empires, the extant version dates from around 395 but includes a good deal of earlier information. The army in Britannia is described in three sections, each under the control of a different officer.

First and most senior is the Dux Britanniarum, the Commander of the British. He had direct oversight of fourteen units, all but three of which were stationed to the east of the Pennines in Durham and Yorkshire. His headquarters was the old Army Command North at York, where the Sixth Legion had been based for nearly 200 years. Three units were of a new type: cavalry regiments which operated independently of infantry. In a signal defeat

---

[2] Sheppard S. Frere, *Britannia* (1967).

near the city of Adrianople in what is now Bulgaria, the Emperor Valens had seen his infantry-based legions destroyed by the heavy cavalry of the Sarmation Alans. That had a profound effect on Roman strategy and led directly to the promotion of mounted units as a strike force in their own right.

The second part of the forces under the command of the Dux was the entire garrison of Hadrian's Wall. The *Notitia Dignitatum* of 395 lists each fort and its occupants in perfect sequence but, given the large withdrawals of troops in the late fourth century, this must be out of date and an aspiration rather than a fact.

The regional forces, the *comitatenses* of Britain, were under the leadership of the Comes Litoris Saxonici, the Count of the Saxon Shore. Based in the south, his title was his job – to deal with the landings of raiders from across the North Sea and the English Channel. But it is clear that in 367 when the storm of the Barbarian Conspiracy burst on Britain, the count had no regional army at his disposal, only a scatter of frontier troops stationed in shore forts.

The Comes Britanniarum was in charge of six cavalry units and three infantry regiments. This small force, about 6,000 men, was in essence Britannia's field army, whose role was to deal with invasion or rebellion. Again, contemporary Roman historians make no mention of this army when the Picts, Scots and Atecotti raided the province in 367.

In all, at its full complement, the Roman garrison of Britannia should have numbered around 25,000 men in the fourth century. It is highly unlikely that it ever reached that figure. In 402 the Roman general Stilicho the Vandal withdrew a large part of the garrison for the defence of Italy against Alaric and the Visigoths. In 407 Constantine III pulled out most of the skeleton forces that Stilicho had left.

It is difficult to tell what the strength of the garrison of Britannia was in 367. However the actions of Count Theodosius the following year offer some retrospective sense of the disaster that had overtaken the province. Nectaridus, the Count of the Saxon Shore, had been killed and his small force defeated and disintegrated. A man with a German name, probably a professional soldier from the Rhineland, Fullofaudes, had been Dux Britanniarum and was captured by the Picts.[3] Many of his soldiers had simply run away and bands of deserters had formed in the countryside.

When Theodosius landed with four regiments of regular troops at Richborough, he made straight for London so that he could use the provincial capital and the road system that radiated from it to begin the work of re-establishing order. Instead of an invading army of Picts, Scots and Atecotti, Theodosius came across small bands of warriors who had overwintered in the south and had carried on harrying and wasting villas and towns. These were easy to pick off and once he had captured or killed those who did not flee in front of his forces, he issued an amnesty to all deserters. This allowed Theodosius to use experienced men in re-creating the three army commands of the province and to regarrison Hadrian's Wall.

Because of their treachery and probably because he did not have the manpower to spare, Theodosius abolished the Areani and also did not reoccupy any of the outpost forts north of the Wall. That necessitated an extension of the frontier policy initiated thirty years before by the Emperor Constans. In essence Theodosius took three of the four original tribal groupings which had grown into the kingdoms of Strathclyde, Gododdin and Rheged as a political, cultural and military base and set professional soldiers in charge of modest cavalry forces as prefects over them.

This is a vital step in the narrative and it needs to be shown clearly what happened. The northern genealogies provide the first and most important piece of evidence. Around 370 a man called Quintilius Clemens is named as the ruler of Strathclyde.[4] He is styled in the Roman fashion with nomen and cognomen, or family and personal names in the correct order. Antonius Donatus at the same time assumed command of forces in south-west Scotland,

---

[3] John Morris, *op. cit.*

[4] John Morris, *op. cit.*

perhaps stretching as far east as Selkirk and south to Carlisle. These were the marches of the embryonic kingdom of Rheged. Catellius Decianus was given authority over the northern Gododdin, that is the Lothians and the place that became known as Manau-Gododdin, around Stirling in the west. His centre was most likely Traprain Law. South of the Lammermuirs were the southern Gododdin whose territory comprised the Tweed basin and the flatlands of modern Northumberland, perhaps down as far as the wall itself. Their commander was a man called Paternus Pesrut, which translates as 'Paternus of the Red Cloak'. This is a description of a serving Roman officer.

Their names, their territories and their coincidence in time show that these men were not native kings flattered by fancy Roman titles or names. They were professional soldiers planted by Theodosius in a buffer zone between the Roman walls with a clear brief to prevent a recurrence of what happened in 367.

There is no doubt that these appointments formed a consistent part of imperial policy. Two years later in North Africa, Theodosius faced very similar problems. This time his solutions were recorded by two written sources. First the Roman historian Ammianus: 'He sent men experienced in persuasion to the surrounding tribes...to entice them to an alliance, now by fear, now by bribes, sometimes by promising pardon for their impudence.' And then he 'put reliable prefects in charge of the peoples he encountered'. Corroboration is supplied by St Augustine of Hippo:[5] 'A few years ago a small number of barbarian peoples were pacified and attached to the Roman frontier, so that they no longer had their own kings, but were ruled by prefects appointed by the Roman Empire.'

Now, even more corroboration is available from recent archaeological work around Traprain Law, the capital of the northern Gododdin. Very significant numbers of fourth-century coins have

---

[5] Augustine of Hippo, *The Anti-Pelagian Treatises* (ed. F.W. Bright) (1880).

been found recently in this place and another location. These are not silver or gold coins but small copper pieces only of value in a money economy, the sort of currency that was used by soldiers and accepted in return for goods and services. A full explanation of the greater significance of these finds belongs later in this story but suffice it to say for the moment that they show significant late fourth-century Roman activity in southern Scotland.

Count Theodosius was a thorough soldier, not only able to defeat the enemies of the empire but also to analyse the implications of victory. The experience of Roman military planners had been that any defeat of barbarians was temporary. After a time more of them came. Theodosius knew that and when he placed his prefects in charge of the nascent intramural kingdoms, he made longer-term recommendations in his report to Rome. Ammianus tells us that he 'protected the frontier with lookouts and garrisons, recovering a province that had yielded to enemy control, so restoring it that, as his report advised, it should have a legitimate governor, and be henceforth styled "Valentia".'

This last was a familiar piece of flattery; the joint emperors at the time were Valens and Valentinian. But more interesting is the creation of a buffer province between the insurgent tribes of the north and the valuable province of Britannia in the south. The correct location of Valentia is important at this point and Roman sources are disappointing in that they assume that a reader will know. Given the appointment of the prefects and given that Theodosius would have wanted to motivate the soldiers stationed between the walls, I believe that Valentia incorporated the old occupied territory of the first and second centuries which lay between Antonine and Hadrian's walls. In this way he drew the young kingdoms into the empire, made the tribesmen citizens and gave them a stake in its survival and prosperity.

There is evidence to support this placing of Valentia. First the coins. The new discoveries of 539 Roman coins in the Borders are not hoards of gold and silver cached away during bad times. They are not the stuff of treasure. Almost all are bronze, around half an inch across and some have dates as late as 402. Of no use for bribery and with no value as trophies, these discoveries are of the small change of everyday use, the operation of a money economy in the Scottish Border country towards the end of the fourth century. These coins can only have arrived in the pouches of Roman soldiers and the money chests of their paymasters. Albeit in small numbers and in a new political arrangement, they show that the Romans were back in the Tweed basin for the last three decades of the fourth century. Long enough to have a military impact and long enough to reinforce the old traditions of warfare learned first by the Votadini at Trimontium on the parade ground and in the riding school.

The tradition of re-Romanization lasted into the memory of St Patrick. He had reason to denounce his fellow P-Celts and in particular the new kingdom of Strathclyde established by the prefect Quintilius Ciemens. Patrick attacked his successor Coroticus saying that the behaviour of his soldiers was to be condemned. It meant that they were 'not citizens of the Holy Romans, but of the devil, living in the enemy ways of the barbarians'.[6]

More telling is a later memory of the citizens. In his barren attack on the inadequacies of the mid sixth-century values of Britain, the Welsh monk Gildas gave the soldiers of the resistance forces an interesting name. He called them *cives* or 'the citizens'.[7] It is a close lexical cousin to the Romano-British vulgate term *combrogi* which has a looser meaning of 'fellow countrymen'.[8] The P-Celts of Britannia came to call themselves the Cumber and the map is studded with place names that incorporate the word. Comberton, Cumberlow and many others lie in the south-east of England, showing that the Anglo-Saxons did not sweep the humbler sorts of native Britons off the land and drive them relentlessly westwards.

[6] John Morris, *op. cit.*

[7] Gildas, *De Excidio et Conquestu Brittaniae* (Phillimore, 1978).

[8] John Morris, *op. cit.*

The most obvious survival of the name is in the old county of Cumberland which is now incorporated in the larger unit and older form of Cumbria. Historians record that P-Celtic or Old Welsh was spoken in the Eden valley around Carlisle until the early 1500s and in the Lakeland fells it persisted even longer, into the nineteenth century when shepherds in Langdale were known to have used Welsh numbers to account for their flocks.[9]

But it is in the Welsh word for Wales that the name has endured most vividly. '*Cymry am beth!*' or 'Wales for ever!' is what the passionate roar from the terraces of Cardiff Arms Park, and while not eternal, Cymry is a very old name indeed. And a remarkable remnant of Britannia, a small Celtic nation on the edge of Europe that calls itself the Citizens.

It was also what the armies of the generals began to call themselves in the early sixth century. Against the barbarians Arthur led the Cymry, the soldiers of the citizens, the last phase of organized resistance to the hordes of invaders who had occupied all of the Western Roman Empire by 500.

Cymry is powerful in this story of names, not only because of the romance of the thing but also because it rings such a clear note down 1,500 years of experience. It tells us how these men saw themselves, the army of the citizens, heroic in the teeth of relentless barbarian advance. The keepers of light against the onrush of darkness, Christians against pagans, knowledge and order against savagery, ignorance and greed. Perhaps we understand the spirit of the army of the Cymry in our hearts. Without knowing any facts, we instinctively stand with them, even though they lost and even though history has almost forgotten them.

Arthur's campaigns, however, will be better understood in a careful context clearly set out. The prefects of southern Scotland are remembered by the northern genealogies as the founders of dynasties and their names were rendered in P-Celtic style. Cinhil

[9] N.K. Chadwick, *The Celts* (1970).

for Quintilius, Cluim for Clemens, Padarn for Paternus and Anhun Dunawd for Antonius Donatus. However there is another name entangled with the men in the king lists which also shows a Roman pedigree. He was Macsen Wledig, and his story will take us a step nearer to Arthur.[10]

The victory of Count Theodosius was so complete that the *Notitia Dignitatum* later records four regiments of Atecotti fighting in Europe in imperial service. So complete that in 370 the prosperity of Britannia had risen to new heights.

However, there was trouble of a different sort in Rome itself. The army, volatile at the best of times, had begun to resent the privileges granted by the young Emperor Gratian to his barbarian bodyguard. Discontent spread like a cancer through the provincial commands until in 383 the army in Britannia proclaimed a new emperor, a man unconnected with the Roman nobility, a usurper. He was a Spaniard who had fought against the Picts, Scots and Atecotti with Count Theodosius fifteen years before. His name, Magnus Maximus, was bent into Macsen Wledig by the P-Celts who supported him. It simply means 'Macsen the General' and it was the first use of Wledig, or Guledig, as a title for a military commander in Britain.

Gaul deserted the Emperor Gratian without bloodshed and Macsen moved quickly to consolidate his control across the Channel. He welded together a field army out of parts of the British garrison and thereby dangerously weakened the province's defences, particularly in Wales where he probably removed the remnants of the Twentieth Legion from the fortress at Chester. This allowed the gradual penetration of invaders from Ireland into the Lleyn peninsula in the north and Pembrokeshire in the south.

Macsen quickly pulled the provinces of the western empire under his banner and within a year Africa, Spain, Gaul, Germany, Italy and Britain acknowledged his imperium. At his instigation the

---

[10] Sheppard S. Frere, *Britannia* (1967).

mint at London, now named Augusta, began once more to produce gold and silver coins, sufficient of which have survived to suggest considerable numbers were cast.

Macsen's co-emperor in the east, the legitimate Theodosius I, tolerated the usurper for four years until in the Balkans their armies clashed in 388. The battle went against Macsen and he was beheaded some days later.

This episode is important to this story in a number of ways. When Macsen was defeated there is evidence, again from the *Notitia*, that he had recruited native British forces and that after his defeat they retreated into Gaul and settled in Armorica.[11] The town name of Bretteville remembers this. These men began a tradition of British settlement which continued into the eighth century, established the P-Celtic language which, as Breton, is still spoken in the area of north-west France now called Bretagne, or Brittany, or Little Britain.

The early British king-lists gave Macsen a founding role in Wales and his prowess is recorded in an early Welsh tale preserved in the collection of stories known as the *Mabinogion*.[12] 'The Dream of Macsen' contains much romance and also several accurate historical facts. More pointedly, he was also installed as the founder of the northern dynasty of Rheged, one of the kingdoms of southern Scotland most successful in the sixth century in dealing with the Anglo-Saxon invasions. This is less surprising when the settlement of P-Celtic soldiers in Armorica is taken into account. Because of the lack of a tradition of arms in the south, it is highly likely that he led cavalry warriors from the Gododdin, Rheged and Strathclyde in his European campaigns.

This tradition is seated in historical reality. In 384 Macsen returned to Britannia from Gaul to lead the P-Celts of the north against the Picts and Scots.[13] His campaign was successful and his

[11] John Morris, *op. cit.*

[12] Lady Charlotte Guest (ed.), *The Mabinogion* (1906).

[13] John Morris, *op. cit.*

victory enduring. From around this period a new kingdom based in the Forth valley and on the fortress on Stirling Castle rock came into being. Called Manau or Manau Gododdin, its creation signalled a new policy of aggressive counter-invasion into the territory of the Picts.

The name itself is difficult to parse. It may be related to the derivation of the Isle of Man and the Welsh name for Anglesey, Ynys Mon, which are both connected to the name of the Celtic god of the sea Mannan or Manannan mac lir in the Irish version.[14] However that may be, it is a derivation offering little enlightenment. The place-names of the area are much more helpful. In his *Ecclesiastical History of the English People*, written around 730, Bede described P-Celtic Scotland in a rapid sketch: 'In the middle of the eastern estuary [the Forth] stands the City of Guidi.'[15] Bede was usually precise in his Latin and by *urbs* he meant a substantial settlement and not a few huts on an island. Guidi sounds very much like a reference to Goddeu or Gododdin. The River Forth is tidal at Stirling and the town was almost surrounded by a waterlogged moss until modern times. Urbs Guidi was Bede's name for Stirling. P-Celtic names survive in the area at Polmaise, 'the settlement on the plain' and at Gogar, meaning 'a height' or 'a small hill'. But they are more precise in the east where toponymy strongly suggests the boundary of the new kingdom, a frontier with the Pictish tribes of Fife and the north.

The first clue is in the old Scottish county town of Clackmannan. Extending no more than a few square miles Clackmannanshire was by far Scotland's smallest county and that in itself implies an ancient survival, an echo of the P-Celtic kingdom of Manau. Clackmannan is partly a Q-Celtic name which pulls out into Clach na Manan.[16] With Manau taking a genitive case by adding a final 'n' it means simply 'the Stone of Manau'.

---

[14] W.J. Watson, *The Celtic Placenames of Scotland* (1926).

[15] Bede, *Ecclesiastical History of the English People* (Penguin, 1955).

[16] W.J. Watson, *op. cit.*

Like the marker of the northern bounds of the kingdom of Strathclyde at Clach nam Breatainn, I believe that Clackmannan sits on a frontier. The only difference is that the stone itself has survived. It stands next to the medieval tolbooth in the centre of the little town, a rough, unhewn rock people call simply 'the stone'.

A few miles north lies the steep-sided range of hills known as the Ochils and between them and Clackmannan are two more P-Celtic names that help to define the old kingdom. The Powis Burn runs south from the hills and empties into the upper estuary of the Firth of Forth. It is a name like the Welsh local authority Powys and it has the same derivation. From the Latin *pagenses* it means 'provincial land' or more precisely 'frontier land' which, as the easternmost part of Wales, Powys most certainly is.[17] The Powis Burn strongly suggests the eastern mark of Manau, but more confirmation is available 800 feet above it.

The hill that glowers over the coastal plain and its settlements has an odd name. Dumyat is P-Celtic and it means 'the fort of the Miathi'. Nearby is Myot Hill which shares the derivation.[18] Both come from Miathi, or Maeatae which was an alternative name for the Picts, probably a sub-tribe based in the Ochil Hills and the up-country to the north of them. Clackmannan, Powis Burn and Dumyat are only eight miles apart. The names remember a frontier, a place where ancient enemies stood off from each other. And also a place conquered, probably during Macsen's campaign of 384, and held by the powerful kingdom of the Gododdin. Their military skills, their ability to mobilize quickly and their political confidence allowed them to occupy and settle flat land with few natural defensive points, overlooked by the Pictish Ochil Hills and hemmed in by the Firth of Forth in the south. The kingdom of Manau lay at the navel of Scotland, holding the land bridge to the Highlands in the north and the fertile grasslands of the south. Able to see the night-time fires of their enemies in the hills and knowing

[17] Andrew Currie, *Dictionary of British Placenames* (1994).
[18] A.P. Smyth, *Warlords and Holy Men, AD 80–1000* (1984).

that they could break any peace treaty in a moment, the P-Celts held Manau by force of arms. It was their own buffer state between the Picts and their own southern heartlands. Between the battles of Macsen in 384 and the time of Arthur a hundred years later, the military kingdom of Manau grew in power and in prestige.

For ten years after the execution of Macsen the wealthy south of Britannia was peaceful. But in 396 there is evidence of renewed Pictish raiding. It seems that they sailed out of their east coast harbours in Fife, the Tay, the Angus coast and the Moray Firth, bypassed the P-Celtic kingdoms of Scotland and struck at the less defended towns and villas of the south. The Roman historian Ammianus records a Pictish raid on London at this time. What is striking is the strategy of the Picts. They had always had a naval capability but their audacity in attacking London and its hinterland with a force limited in size by sea travel is interesting. It showed how vulnerable the south had become after Macsen evacuated most of its garrison in 383.

In Rome the government of the young Emperor Honorius was managed by a general known to us as Stilicho the Vandal. He launched an expedition to restore imperial order in Britain in 396–8 but could not scrape together more forces to deter future Pictish raids. In fact the armies of Alaric posed such a serious threat to the security of Italy in 401 that Stilicho was forced to withdraw even more soldiers across the Channel.

In 406–7 three usurper emperors were proclaimed by what remained of the army in Britain and the last of these, Constantine III, seems to have been a capable soldier. In December 406 a severe winter froze the Rhine and allowed hordes of barbarians to cross. Vandals, Alans and Sueves poured into northern Gaul and Constantine realized that he had to act. Creating an expeditionary force out of the army in Britain, he crossed the Channel and, linking with imperial forces on the continent, he defeated the barbarian armies and regained northern Gaul. However Britain had virtually no garrison left and from the time of Constantine's campaign imperial control of Britannia ceased, and was never re-established.

Severance was made formal in a letter from the Emperor Honorius to the cities of Britain in 410 when he advised them to look to their own defences.[19] This was most likely a response to an appeal for help but it is probable that with the breakdown of central government (why else was Honorius writing to the cities?) and the removal of imperial protection, Britannia broke into factions. The contemporary historian Zosimus records something more aggressive, close to rebellion:

> The barbarians across the Rhine attacked everywhere with all their power, and brought the inhabitants of Britain and some of the nations of Gaul to the point of revolting from Roman rule and living on their own, no longer obedient to Roman laws. The Britons took up arms and, braving danger for their own independence, freed their cities from the barbarians threatening them; and all Armorica and the other provinces of Gaul copied the British example and freed themselves in the same way, expelling their Roman governors and establishing their own administration as best they could.

To some in Britannia there was no reason to think Honorius's letter a final act. The province had been Roman for close on 400 years and there had been periods of difficulty and hiatus before. But the completeness of Roman withdrawal is underlined by the fact that the emperor wrote to the cities of Britain, and not to the Dux Britanniarum or to either of the Comes. Most probably he could not since the substance of these commands no longer existed. All the soldiers had gone.

When the Roman imperium ceased, the new P-Celtic kingdoms of the north emerged quickly and with vigour. Based on the old

---

[19] Sheppard S. Frere, *Britannia* (1967).

territory of the dissident Brigantes, the area ruled by Coel Hen formed itself in Yorkshire and across the Pennines to Lancashire. Immortalized as Old King Cole, he enjoyed great prestige and was installed near the top of most northern genealogies.[20] His name was Roman in its derivation, either Coelestius or Coelius and since his kingdom is largely coincident with that assigned by the *Notitia Dignitatum* to the Dux Britanniarum, Cole Hen may de facto have been the last to hold any semblance of that office. On his death the lands of Coel split into three P-Celtic kingdoms with Elmet lasting into the seventh century.

In the south little of a political nature seems to have happened at first. Routine raiding took place but it is not until 425 that some sense of an independent Britain emerged. A man called Vortigern, not a personal name as most historians assert but a P-Celtic title still in currency in Q-Celtic as Mhor Tighearna or 'great leader', appeared as a ruler of some sort in south-eastern Britain. He did not style himself Dux or even Imperator but rather took a British title and, taken together with Zosimus's report of rebellion and expulsion, it is reasonable to see the Vortigern as leader of a British party.

The eighth-century English monk Bede[21] begins his history in 449 with the Vortigern's invitation of a group of Anglo-Saxons led by Hengist and Hrosa to England and particularly to Kent where for mercenary services rendered, he allowed them to settle on the Isle of Thanet (a P-Celtic name meaning 'the shining island') in the Thames estuary. Because Bede was writing a winner's history of England which he dedicated to his patron the Angle King of Northumbria, he was interested in the origins of the Anglo-Saxon conquest of Britannia and he lit upon the first organized settlement of warriors who came to stay and fight for a living rather than simply plunder and return home across the North Sea. Allowing

[20] John Morris, *The Age of Arthur* (1973).
[21] Bede, *op. cit.*

for his Anglo-Saxon bias, Bede is generally accurate and scrupulous in what he says. For that reason most historians accept his version and focus on the fortunes of Hengist, Hrosa and their descendants' conquest of the south. Consequently they often miss something that Bede repeats several times and something that was at the centre of the Vortigern's concerns. He brought the Saxon mercenaries to the south-east because the seaborne attacks of the Picts were becoming intolerable and after the Roman evacuation he had no troops to put into the field against them. And more, there had been no tradition of arms in the south for centuries.[22] Roman law forbad the bearing of weapons and in part the letters to and from Honorius were a clear legal statement that those old prohibitions could no longer obtain. But what should be emphasized here is that it was the Picts, the Miathi and others who were seen as the most powerful threat to Britannia. So dangerous that the Vortigern was willing to permit Anglo-Saxons to settle in order to protect the riches of the south. For much of the fifth century Britannia's enemies descended upon it from the north, not from across the North Sea.

Although the Vortigern was an important figure, he was not central. He did not guide British strategy, he was not the focus of British power. That lay in the north with the armies of the Cymry. A remarkable series of events that took place around 425 showed the military planners of the Gododdin directing efforts to preserve the integrity of Britannia.

Hardened by generations of campaigning, led by Macsen on his European adventure, able to take and hold territory right up to the mountain borders of Pictland, the Gododdin and their P-Celtic neighbours were the only coherent philo-Roman fighting force of any real substance in Britannia after 410. They did not depend on mercenary help, they knew their enemies and in 425 they took responsibility for security far from their own kingdoms. History

---

[22] John Wacker, *Roman Britain* (1980).

has failed to take sufficient notice of them because their fate was not at first bound up with the Anglo-Saxons and they were not active in the south-east. And no historian wrote about them. Much of their tradition became entangled with the heroic literature of Dark Ages Wales and disconnected from its true origins in the kingdoms of the mighty between the Roman walls.

When Macsen removed the Twentieth Legion from Chester and much of Britannia's Welsh garrison in 383, he left a gap in the province's defences which was exploited by the Q-Celtic tribes of Ireland. The Scots, as they should properly be called, invaded and settled the coast from Anglesey down to Pembroke. Some time around 425 the Gododdin acted decisively to prevent Wales falling into the hands of the Scots. The eighth-century monk Nennius includes this document: 'Cunedag, ancestor of Mailcunus, came with his eight sons from the north, from the district called Manau Guotodin, CXLVI years before Mailcunus reigned, and expelled the Irish ... With enormous slaughter, so that they never came back to live there again.'[23]

Like the Vortigern, Cunedda is not a personal name but rather a P-Celtic military term meaning 'good leader'. All memory of this extraordinary man is condensed into the modern spelling of his title, the popular Christian name: Kenneth. In the Welsh documents the British rank attached to Macsen is also conferred on Cunedda to make him, somewhat tautologously, Cunedda Guledig or Good Leader and General. This implies posthumous promotion by people who had forgotten the original meaning of the first name. But it may also betray a trace of ancient propaganda. Even in 425 perception was important and the notion of a man whose whole personal identity is overtaken by his function and reputation cannot have been unhelpful in the progress of his campaigns. It is always more impressive to hear news of the advance of the army of the Great Leader, the General, than simply to be told that it was led

---

[23] Nennius, *Historia Brittonum*, in John Morris, *The Age of Arthur* (1973).

by someone called Kenneth. The title Guledig was beginning to bear significance in post-Roman Britain.

The Welsh genealogies have much to say about Cunedda.[24] Fragments of hard information are repeated often enough to be trusted. He was the son of Aeternus and the grandson of Paternus Pesrut, the Roman officer with the red cloak set in authority over the southern Gododdin.[25] This is vital continuity. It seems likely that Cunedda was a title given to this soldier. Both his father and grandfather had traditional Roman names with nomen and cognomen in the correct order. Also the genealogies name one of his sons as Caraticus and a grandson as Marianus.[26] Unlike the Vortigern Cunedda did not lead an anti-Roman faction which preferred British titles, he was a third-generation professional Roman soldier who led an army of P-Celtic speakers who addressed him in their own language.

Nennius originates Cunedda from Manau-Guotodin which may be a conflation of two territories into one linked entity, rather like the way in which different countries like Austria and Hungary were linked in the phrase Austro-Hungarian Empire. In addition it may also be a reference to a campaign against the Picts in Manau.[27] The Gododdin successfully maintained their northern redoubt around Stirling for many generations and Cunedda will have learned his battle craft in the hardest school possible, against the Picts, the scourge of Britain, those whom the might of imperial Rome could not subdue. Too much cannot be made of this. Bede constantly refers to the fifth-century depredations of these tribes and for that period the Gododdin and Strathclyde lived cheek by jowl with them, more than surviving, as Cunedda showed. That can only have been possible because the traditions of Trimontium thrived, the cavalry skills and tactics of such as the Sarmatians were

[24] Thomas Stephens, *The Literature of the Kymry* (1849).

[25] John Morris, *op. cit.*

[26] Nennius, *op. cit.*

[27] John Morris, *op. cit.*

learned, because Paternus Pesrut developed a military structure that was flexible and deadly, and because, in sum, the P-Celtic kingdoms of the north had become, after centuries of grinding conflict with the Picts, the toughest and furthest-reaching fighting machine in fifth-century Britain. Cunedda's expedition to Wales shows that.

Before he went south, there is evidence that Cunedda campaigned in Manau. A late poem remembers: 'Splendid he was in battle, with his nine hundred horse, Cunedda ... the Lion ... the son of Aeternus.[28] This is followed by two lines whose literal meaning is obscure but which say fairly clearly that he fought against enemies in the north-east of England. By the early fifth century Anglian pirates had attacked the Northumbrian coast, later setting up bases on Lindisfarne and at Bamburgh. It may be that raiders had ventured up the Tweed or the Tyne and Cunedda mobilized his cavalry to deal with them, using either Yeavering or another horse fort on the Tweed.

When he marshalled his war-band to ride south to Wales, Cunedda's cavalry was given a P-Celtic name. The Gosgordd is obscure now and applied only to the ceremonies of the annual Eistedfodd where the bardic retinue is so named. But some of its ancient sense still sticks to a Q-Celtic word *casgairan* which means 'the slayers' or 'the conquerors'.[29] In Welsh heroic poetry the Gosgordd consisted of 300 horsemen, a direct borrowing from Roman models where an *ala* of cavalry attached to a legion was of exactly the same size.[30]

There is also mention in the poems of 'Gosgordd Mur' or 'the Cavalry of the Wall', meaning the Roman wall, more likely Antonine than Hadrian given the Gododdin's occupation of Manau. This is described as a large force and as in the lines

---

[28] John Morris, *op. cit.*

[29] Edward Dwelly, *The Illustrated Gaelic-English Dictionary* (reprinted 1994).

[30] Karen Dixon, *Roman Cavalry* (1994).

celebrating Cunedda's prowess, it may have been as many as 900 or three *alae*.

Taking account of the need for spare mounts, the Gosgordd Mur may have been a thousand strong. Cavalry only campaigns when the grass grows and a force of that size would have required much logistical management, and, for the times, a huge commitment of resources in men and materials which must have depleted the power of the P-Celtic kingdoms. So why did they do it?

Some historians believe that a central post-imperial power, based in London or the south-east, perhaps the Vortigern, ordered the Men of the North to send a force to rescue Wales from the Scots. There is no evidence or tradition for this and in any case it is extremely unlikely. Even in their pomp the Romans could not deal with the tribes of the north, and what is on record is the Vortigern's lack of military clout. He needed to import Saxon mercenaries to put substance behind his rule. Moreover Wales is more quickly and more easily reinforced from England than Scotland. It is nearer and much easier geographical going than the long ride over the Cheviots and down the Lancashire coast to Chester and then along the north Welsh coast to the Lleyn peninsula. The fact is that even if the Vortigern represented some sort of pan-British authority and even if he wanted to drive the Scots out of Wales, he simply did not have the military means to do it. He depended on ultimately unreliable Saxon mercenaries who were famously ferocious fighters but they were almost all foot soldiers, with poor body armour and little or no equipment of the sort needed for a long march and a long campaign far from base. And more to the point, if the Vortigern did not have forces of the quality of the P-Celtic kingdoms, why should they pay the slightest bit of attention to him or the south-east and its problems? In an age where military hitting power was virtually all that mattered, the notion of a weakened leader dictating strategy to a superior force based 400 miles to the north makes no sort of sense at all. Cunedda went to Wales because he and the military planners of the Gododdin made a decision to do so. That historical fact by itself makes the north the centre of British power after Rome.

Cunedda's campaign must have been a tremendous exercise needing much forethought and precise execution. Given the experience and training of his grandfather and father, he probably travelled south on Roman roads and to overnight safely he would have used old cavalry forts such as the Ribchester base of the Sarmatians and certainly the great legionary fortress at Chester. These places could cope with large numbers of men and horses, had water supplies and defences which were serviceable even as late as 425. The expedition is more reminiscent of the statecraft of the immediate Roman past than the small-scale, relatively primitive sort of warfare of Dark Ages Britain.

Cunedda changed the history of Wales. He came with his cavalrymen not only to expel the Scots from the coastal regions but also to settle and stay. He founded a dynasty which endured for eight centuries only ending with the defeat of Llewellyn the Great by Edward I in 1282/3. Cunedda left his name on Gwynedd, and his son Caraticus on Cardigan or better Ceredigion and his grandson Marianus is remembered in Merioneth. An Irish tribe, the Deisi, seem to have clung on to Pembroke but the victory in the north was emphatic. Tradition pointed to the ruined and deserted huts of the Irish for generations after Cunedda's victory.[31] More telling, the expedition is the only example of a lasting British victory; the Scots were expelled from Wales and did not return. Elsewhere and for the rest of the century the story is one of containment and then, later, of ultimate defeat.

The P-Celtic kingdoms sent Cunedda's expedition to rescue Wales because they could afford to spare the manpower to do it and because opportunities for the ambitions of the Good Leader and his troopers were limited by the Picts in the north and powerful P-Celtic neighbours in Strathclyde and Rheged. Macsen was

[31] Gwyn A. Williams, *Excalibur* (1994).

able to persuade the cavalry of the four kingdoms to follow him to Europe for the same reason. That speaks of great strength in the north, but also something of the sense of themselves that the Cymry had by 425. Cunedda led an army of the citizens to help his fellow countrymen in extremis. In that period there had been raids on Britain from several quarters but no one had yet settled as the Scots did in west Wales. When the south needed the help of the Kingdoms of the Mighty at the end of the fifth century, they rode down the Roman roads to fight for them.

The transplantation of such a large number of Gododdin warriors to Wales began the transmission of the traditions of the P-Celtic kingdoms of southern Scotland.[32] Cunedda's men brought their stories and sowed them where they settled. Soon they grew away from Scotland and places that meant nothing in Wales were soon discarded and replaced with names that listeners knew. Even talk of 'the north' or 'Yr Hen Ogledd', the Old North, came to mean north Wales to some bards rather than southern Scotland. Dynasts like Cunedda's sons and grandsons cared more about the legitimization of their power in a new place rather than the geographical accuracy of the stories extolling their prowess. It is easy to see how the Old North was forgotten. And when the Welsh language died in Scotland, perhaps in the 1300s, there was no one left to remember. The only Welsh speakers lived in Wales and it is a natural assumption that stories told in Welsh must have happened there.

Cunedda was succeeded by a man with a Roman name, Germanianus, styled 'son of Coel Hen'.[33] He ruled over the southern Gododdin from Yeavering and another fortress on the River Tweed which will become very important to this narrative. His name implies some connection with barbarian mercenaries. There is a tradition of settlement by a small group of German warriors on

[32] N.K. Chadwick, *The Celts* (1970).
[33] John Morris, *op. cit.*

or near Hadrian's Wall – the place-name Dumfries, meaning 'the Fortress of the Frisians', is only the most striking example of this legacy – and as a prefect, Germanianus would not have hesitated to employ federate troops to protect the area he controlled.[34] Perhaps the great expedition to Wales had left a strategic gap.

The weakness of the south, which Cunedda's expedition underlined, is made pointed in a story first recorded by the Gaulish monk Constantius in the middle of the fifth century. He wrote a life of St Germanus, an early Bishop of Auxerre who visited Britain in 429 with Bishop Lupus of Troyes.[35] They had received a papal commission to deal with the growth of the Pelagian heresy in the former province. The British Catholic bishops had appealed to Pope Celestinus for help. The ideas of Pelagius were popular among the British aristocracy, partly because he was a P-Celt and possibly from Strathclyde. He had visited Rome some time around 400 and been appalled at the corruption and the laxity of moral standards in the city. He preached that strenuous personal efforts were needed to avoid sinful ways and find the road to individual salvation. It seems an unexceptionable view to us now but St Augustine was appalled by this insistence on the effectiveness of free will, and St Jerome became even more incensed and called Pelagius 'a fat hound weighed down by Scottish porridge'. The heretic was excommunicated twice, but despite such vociferous official disapproval his ideas found widespread favour among his countrymen. The Vortigern was probably a Pelagian, his beliefs making him a natural leader of a British, anti-Roman party.

It is therefore not surprising that Constantius does not mention the Vortigern in the account of Germanus and Lupus's visit of 429. However there is one nugget of information in the account which downplays the Vortigern's power by convincing implication. Constantius knew Bishop Lupus personally and he got from him the only first-hand account of a battle in fifth-century Britain.

34 Mike Darton, *The Dictionary of Place-names in Scotland* (1994).

35 Peter Beresford Ellis, *Celt and Saxon* (1993).

While he and Germanus were in Britain, the Saxons and Picts had formed an alliance and their army needed to be confronted. Before he became a priest, Germanus had had military experience. Therefore when he heard of the approaching danger, he

offered himself as commander. His light troops thoroughly explored the country through which the enemy's advance was expected; choosing a valley set among high hills, he drew up his army ... in ambush. As the enemy approached, he ordered the whole force to respond with a great shout when he cried out. The bishops cried out thrice together 'Alleluia'; the whole army replied with a single voice, and the great cry rebounded, shut in by the surrounding hills. The enemy column was terrified; the very frame of heaven and the rocks around seemed to threaten them ... They fled in all directions ... many drowning in the river they had to cross ... The bishops won a bloodless victory, gained by faith, not by the might of men.

Although it contains strong doses of myth and propaganda, that is an account of a real battle. In his *Historia Ecclesiastica* Bede repeats the story in an embellished form which has the bishops set up a baptism centre in the camp of the British army to equip the soldiers spiritually, and in general he awards more credit for the victory to the Almighty than Constantius does.[36]

A number of important points need to be drawn from this. First and most obvious, there was little military organization in the south in 429, certainly no central or national authority based on London. Even if the Vortigern did rule from there, he was powerless to prevent a visiting Gaulish bishop from leading a British army. Even if the reason for the non-involvement of central authority was the Pelagian/Catholic divide, no military clout existed to prevent Germanus from taking charge. It sounds as though individual

---

[36] Bede, *op. cit.*

districts and towns, perhaps with some local organization still intact, took what responsibility they could for their own security. Since the evacuation of the last of the provincial garrison in 407 there had been no regular troops to speak of except the Vortigern's Saxon mercenaries. And by 429 some of them or some of their kinsmen had combined with the Picts to raid in the south.

In order to inflate the magnitude of the military miracle, Bede's account emphasizes how demoralized the southern British were in the face of Pictish aggression and before Germanus buckled a sword-belt around his surplice. The most striking thing about the description of what became known as the Alleluia Victory is how much tactical information it contains. Germanus clearly knew what he was doing. Like a professional soldier he first sent out mounted scouts to locate the enemy and then conjecture their line of advance. Then, according to Bede, he set his 'untried troops' to face the enemy on the floor of a steep-sided valley across whose mouth flowed a river of some size. Drawn in by the sight of inexperienced and possibly ill-armed troops, no doubt quaking in their boots, the Pictish/Saxon column marched into the trap set by Germanus. Ambushed, the enemy fled and many were drowned attempting to cross the river behind them.

Now, if all that British forces did was to shout 'Alleluia', then it is unlikely that such a rout would have ensued. But the mention of light troops, or auxiliaries, implies at least some cavalry and they probably turned the Picts and Saxons and drove them into the water. This is the first incidence of what would become a familiar British tactic towards the end of the fifth century.

The location of the Alleluia Victory is important since it would offer a sense of where the south was vulnerable and how far inland the Picts would penetrate. The logic of the prelude to the battle is that Germanus found himself at a town where he was engaged in the business of conversion or diplomacy. And since raiders targeted towns as the most concentrated source of plunder, that would make sense from both sides. Germanus landed on the south coast of England and several large Roman towns lay in that area: Winchester, Silchester, Cirencester or Bath. However in the case of the first three the geography does not fit; the landscape is too flat. But if the Picts and Saxons were moving from the east to the west and using the old Roman roads, then Bath would have been a likely target. The town is still approached from the west through a relatively steep-sided valley and the River Avon is close at hand.

Whatever the precise location of the Alleluia Victory, it shows that there was little more than local organization in the south. Any combination of Pict and Saxon was highly dangerous and memories of the Barbarian Conspiracy of 367 would not have faded. Therefore if a central authority had existed then it would most certainly have engaged with this threat. And the fact that a visiting cleric, on another mission altogether, had to take command of such forces as there were does not say much for British organization of any sort. In that context it is significant that nineteen years previously the Emperor Honorius had written to the cities of Britain telling them to look to their own defence. He had no one else to write to. And when the historian Zosimus writes of the end of Roman power in the West: 'The Britons took up arms and ... freed their cities from the barbarians threatening them,' he again mentions only the local authorities. Finally, the incident shows how casually vulnerable the south was in the early 400s. Its conquest was only a matter of time.

The end began slowly. The *Anglo-Saxon Chronicle* is precisely that, a propagandizing account of the gradual takeover and eventual triumph of the Angles, Saxons and others. It only represents their point of view and says little about the British. But occasionally the record is clear-eyed:

Vortigern invited the Angle race here and they then came here to
Britain in three ships at the place Ebba's Creek. The king
Vortigern gave them land in the south-east of this land on
condition that they fought against the Picts. They then fought

against the Picts and had victory wheresoever they came. Then they sent to Angeln, ordered [them] to send more help and ordered them to tell of the worthlessness of the Britons and of the excellence of the land. They then at once sent here a larger troop to help the other. These men came from three tribes of Germany: from the Old Saxons, from the Angles, from the Jutes.[37]

Early events are concentrated in the south-east, mainly Kent, and it may be that the Vortigern exerted his authority in that area. Perhaps he was King of London and Kent. However the picture of increasing Anglo-Saxon settlement and their realization that southern Britain was theirs for the taking is difficult to mistake. It is also significant that in the south of England for the first four decades of the fifth century the principal problem is unequivocally Pictish raiding. In 442 that changed for ever. The leader of the Saxons was a man called Hengist, a nickname meaning 'the Stallion', and he began to make demands for goods and food which he knew were unlikely to be met. Writing around 540 the British priest Gildas paints a vivid picture of what happened:

The barbarians ... were not slow to put their threats into action. The fire of righteous vengeance, kindled by the sins of the past, blazed from sea to sea, its fuel prepared by the arms of the impious in the east. Once lit, it did not die down. When it had wasted town and country in that area, it burned up almost the whole surface of the island, until its red and savage tongue licked the western ocean...

All the greater towns fell to the enemy's battering rams; all their inhabitants, bishops, priests and people, were mown down together, while swords flashed and flames crackled. Horrible it was to see the foundation stones of towers and high walls thrown down bottom upward in the squares, mixing with holy altars and

[37] *Anglo-Saxon Chronicle* (ed. and trans. Michael Swanton) (1996).

fragments of human bodies, as though they were covered with a purple crust of clotted blood, as in some fantastic wine-press.
There was no burial save in the ruins of the houses, or in the bellies of the beasts and birds.[38]

Hengist's warriors tore through the south with appalling ferocity and even though they suffered reverses, the revolt of 442 began a process that turned southern Britannia into England. Resistance was patchy and leadership lacking.

Both Bede and the *Anglo-Saxon Chronicle* record an effect of the revolt. In 443, after a year of destruction and slaughter, the cities of Britain sent an appeal to 'Aetius, thrice Consul'.[39] Addressing him formally by his Roman title, they begged him to send help – but not against the Saxons. The *Chronicle* states bluntly that they requested help against the Picts and Bede implies the same thing.

Aetius was the military ruler of a large part of Gaul. After the barbarian crossing of the frozen Rhine in 406, and the chaos their incursions caused, he carried on the work of Constantine III in maintaining a robust central authority. Here is part of the text of the letter: 'To Aetius, thrice Consul, come the groans of the Britons … the barbarians drive us into the sea, and the sea drives us back to the barbarians. Between these, two deadly alternatives confront us, drowning or slaughter.'

Aetius could send no help, but the letter shows how powerful and persistent the sense of empire was, and how great the desperation of the beleaguered Britons. In addition they may have thought Honorius's letter of 410 no more than a temporary measure. Why should the emperor abandon the valuable province of Britannia for ever?

Natural disasters compounded the situation. Plague swept through southern Britain in 446 and around the same time there is evidence that sea levels rose and coastal towns experienced

---

[38] Gildas, *De Excidio et Conquestu Britanniae*, in John Morris, *op. cit.*
[39] John Morris, *op. cit.*

tremendous flooding.[40] It is little wonder that by 460 there were reports of mass migration across the channel to Armorica (now Brittany), where in the 380s the British troops of the defeated Macsen had settled. Whole communities left in what sounds like an organized manner. A bishop 'of the British in Armorica' was recorded in the 460s. In addition 12,000 able-bodied men of military service age took ship, abandoning Britannia for the place that became known as Little Britain.

This mass migration does not seem so dramatic if it is understood in an imperial context. Because Britannia and Gaul were still reckoned to be part of the same Roman state, it was no more unlikely than moving from Leeds to Southampton might be now. Communities of Britons also sailed to settle in northern Spain where the episcopal see of Bretona was founded. In 527 a Bishop Mahiloc, a P-Celtic name, attended a church council. By the ninth century the Spanish British had become part of P-Celtic Galicia.

But this haemorrhage of the Cymry and so many of their young men signalled the loss of south-eastern Britain. Kent, Sussex, Middlesex and Essex are old county names that record the Saxon victory. By 461 the war in the south-east was over.

Gildas takes up the story again and his text contains an uncharacteristic note of hope:

After a time, when the cruel raiders returned to their home, God strengthened the survivors. Distraught citizens fled to them from different locations, as avidly as bees to the beehive when a storm is overhanging, and with all their hearts implored, 'burdening heaven with unnumbered prayers' [Aeneid ix, 24] that they might not be destroyed to the point of extermination. Their leader was a gentleman, Ambrosius Aurelianus, who perhaps alone of the Romans had survived the impact of such a tempest; truly his parents, who had worn the purple, were overcome in it. In our

[40] John Morris, *op cit*.

times his stock have degenerated greatly from their excellent grandfather. With him our people regained their strength, challenged the victors to battle and with the lord acceding the victory fell to us. From then on now our citizens, and then the enemies conquered; so on this people, as the Lord is accustomed, he could make trial of his latter day Israel to see whether it loves him or not.[41]

Ambrosius Aurelianus was obviously a man who saw himself as a Roman and his pedigree, according to Gildas, was imperial. He may have been a descendant of Macsen but more likely it simply meant that he was a well-connected aristocrat, and one of the few who had survived the Saxon revolt and the migrations to Brittany. Again Welsh sources attached the title Guledig and changed his nomen to Emrys, a name which has survived into modern Welsh usage. Although Gildas was clear that the fortunes of the Britons revived under Ambrosius Aurelianus, he gave no details of his victories or his campaigns. Of his military prowess all Gildas had to say was that he was a skilled cavalry commander, 'brave afoot, he was braver on horseback'. There is some ingenious place-name evidence which links towns and villages containing the element Ambros, such as Amesbury in Wiltshire, with places where he raised native army units.[42] If that attractive conjecture is correct then the distribution of sites surrounds the Saxon gains in Kent, Sussex, Middlesex and Essex. It is very convincing.

Ambrosius's status as a Roman-British aristocrat leading the resistance to the Saxon invaders symbolizes a tradition noted by Gildas that only the upper classes fled westwards. Ordinary people stayed on the land, hoping to continue farming a living from it. But towns began gradually to go out of existence, particularly in the areas that fell first to the rebels.

The historical near-silence about Ambrosius Aurelianus and the

[41] Gildas, *op. cit.* in John Morris, *op. cit.*
[42] John Morris, *op. cit.*

beginning of British resistance is frustrating, but not puzzling. As the winners of the war the Anglo-Saxons were unlikely to report the loss of a few battles. And as the barbarian armies overran Gaul, Spain and Italy in the second half of the fifth century, there were few on the continent who could or would record events in Britain. Communication was closing down and in the west the idea of the empire was dying. Only in Britain did its memory live on into the following century, kept alive by the exploits of a brilliant general. Successor as Guledig to Macsen, Cunedda and Ambrosius Aurelianus, Arthur stemmed the barbarian tide, made a peace that lasted fifty years, and allowed Britannia to shape itself into a Britain we recognize now.

FINDING ARTHUR

In the shadow-lands that lie between the brilliant lights of unarguable historical fact and the fleeting shapes of myth-history, which is only part seen and part imagined, we need to stare hard to make out the mighty form of Arthur. Properly concerned as we are between what is true and what is untrue, we sometimes miss the value of the half-truth. In this way historians have put to one side the legends and their power and given all their trust to the scraps and sketches of dependable literary and archaeological sources. And inevitably the results do not satisfy. The fifth and sixth centuries in Britain are not a good period to choose to study if certainty is what you seek.

It is better to look again at the stories we have told ourselves about Arthur, to try to sift out the utterly fanciful from the authentic, to lean but not to rely on the bits that ring of the common truths of folk memory. For that is what lies at the heart of the legends and myths of Arthur – a memory of a hero, a man whose battles, campaigns and adventures warmed the winter firesides of the Celts of Britain. They were the first underclass. Deprived of their history and thirsty for heroes, they kept alive the story of Arthur, adding, embellishing, outrageously exaggerating, but forgetting nothing.

Some of the truth of the man and what he did is embedded among the flighted finery of this fancy.

Geoffrey of Monmouth was a Welsh-speaking priest who lived in Oxford in the first half of the twelfth century. Without question he was a man of remarkable insight, imagination and enterprise. And yet because it is widely believed that all he did was to invent and decorate existing oral stories about Arthur, literary historians do not treat him as the serious and seminal figure he undoubtedly was. In order to create the first genuinely popular and widely influential publishing success before the invention of the portable printed book, Geoffrey drew widely on the P-Celtic tradition.[1] From poems such as 'Culhwch and Olwen' and collections of stories such as the *Mabinogion*, he took the basic elements of the Arthur story and welded them into a coherent and gloriously overblown narrative which he grandly titled *Historia Regum Britanniae* (*The History of the Kings of Britain*). Britain, mind, not England.

But before going on to deal with the *Historia*, it is worth remembering, and for this narrative vital to note, that it was not Geoffrey's first publication. Some years before he had collated an edition of *The Prophecies of Merlin*. P-Celtic stories about Merlin had survived into the twelfth century in Wales and although his retelling of these in print does bear unmistakable traces of Merlin's Scottish origins, Geoffrey locates him emphatically in the south. In fact he makes him King of Powys and insists that he came from Carmarthen. The geographical relocation of the Great Enchanter is a good precursor for what happened, much less obviously, to the story of Arthur.

As his source for the *Historia Regum Britanniae*, Geoffrey claimed that he used an old book given to him by a fellow ecclesiastic at Oxford, Walter the Archdeacon. This man was a genuine historical figure who died in 1151 and who possessed some academic

---

[1] Geoffrey of Monmouth, *The History of the Kings of Britain* (Penguin, 1966).

reputation. Allegedly he gave Geoffrey a book in 'the British tongue' which then formed the basis for the *Historia*.

Broadly the book deals with the history of Britain from the arrival of Brutus the Trojan, a sort of respectable, classical founding figure, up to and including the reign of Arthur. This was the story that Geoffrey really wanted to tell and he devotes the burden of the book to it. Merlin the Mage, he wrote, first appeared during the reign of Vortigern who was dethroned in favour of the rightful king Ambrosius Aurelianus. In turn he was succeeded by his brother Uther who became Arthur's father. On the latter's accession, the glorious passages of the *Historia* begin to flow. Arthur first rides into battle against the savage Picts and destroys them, before dealing similarly with the Saxons, and then in a curious episode, defeating Lucius, a procurator of the Roman Empire.

The *Historia* was wildly popular and, given the severe limitations of handwritten publishing, its influence was immediate and widespread. Geoffrey Gaimar and Robert Wace from Jersey both produced versions in Norman French. The first is lost to us now but Wace introduced the Round Table into the story. This is an important detail since it reminds us that the Arthurian oral tradition also existed, in a purer form, in Brittany, preserved by emigrants from Britannia as the province fell under the control of the Angles and Saxons. The Breton stories seeped into the French tradition and so when Geoffrey's *Historia* appeared it quickly triggered the medieval romances of Chrétien de Troyes who wrote *Lancelot, Erec et Enide, Yvain, Cligés* and *Perceval*. They are all P-Celtic stories with tinges of tell-tale British origins. For example, Yvain is almost certainly Owain, King of Rheged, still a hero to his descendants in the twelfth century. And *Perceval*, the francophone equivalent of Peredur, the winner at Arthuret and a near contemporary of Owain's, was the first of the Arthurian romances to tell the story of the Grail, itself a British tradition. In the thirteenth century in Germany, Wolfram von Eschenbach adapted, elaborated and transliterated *Perceval* into *Parzifal* and the Grail legend became profoundly influential in classical German literature.

In Britain the stories of Arthur attracted other, often extraneous, tales and by the fifteenth century when Thomas Malory sat down to write *Le Morte d'Arthur* there existed a formidable body of material. Malory's is a huge work which set the basis of the story as it is understood now.

Consumed by lust for Igraine, the wife of Gorlois, Duke of Cornwall, Uther persuaded Merlin to change his appearance to resemble her husband. After a night of passion, Arthur was conceived. The baby was then spirited away to the castle of Sir Ector where Arthur was brought up ignorant of his true parentage. After Uther's death there was no clear successor and Merlin thrust a sword into a block of stone saying that whoever pulled it out was the rightful king. Arthur did and Merlin proclaimed him Uther's heir, knowing the true story all along. When he had established himself on the throne by snuffing out substantial rebellion, Arthur married Guinevere. Camelot became a symbol of goodness and a magnet for manly virtue. While defeating the Roman Emperor Lucius and winning the purple for himself, Arthur returned to Camelot where Guinevere and Lancelot had begun a clandestine affair. During the quest for the Holy Grail, their adultery was exposed and Lancelot fled. Enraged and saddened, Arthur condemned Guinevere to death. Whereupon Lancelot rescued her and fled to Europe, pursued by Arthur who had foolishly left his son Mordred as regent (the boy had been the issue of incest with Morgan, whom Arthur did not realize was his sister). At length the evil and doubtless strange Mordred attempted to usurp the throne. Arthur returned to confront his son/nephew in battle on Salisbury Plain where he killed Mordred but was himself fatally wounded. Arthur was then laid in a boat bound for the Isle of Avalon. None saw him die and some said he was only sleeping and would one day return: Rex Quondam et Futurus, the Once and Future King.

The popularity of these stories never withered but in the nineteenth century they were extensively reworked and reintroduced to the Victorian public. William Morris wrote 'The Defence of Guinevere' and Lord Lytton produced a book-length poem, *King Arthur*, but most influential was Alfred Lord Tennyson's *The Idylls of the King*. It installed Arthur firmly in the romantic, chivalrous, wronged and passionate role where he lives today. The stories fired Tennyson's gifts and, just as Geoffrey of Monmouth had done seven centuries before, the *Idylls* made literature out of legend, an identity out of the myth-history of the past.

Geoffrey called his book *The History of the Kings of Britain* and tellingly subtitled it *The Matter of Britain*. Not England, or Scotland, or Ireland or Wales, but Britain. The book's pages spoke of an earlier, more decent, less tainted time when the whole island was united under a successful and upright king who gained his throne on merit and held it because he was virtuous. While it is easy to understand the attractions of a united, idyllic, British past to Victorian imperialists anxious to rule as much of the world as possible, it is also not surprising to hear less and less of the Celtic origins of these Edenic stories. Clothed in shining armour, in the gilded drapery of the Gothic revival, images of Arthur kept the medieval, chivalrous gloss of the High Middle Ages originally conferred by Monmouth, de Troyes, Malory and the others. Arthur the Warlord, the philo-Roman Guledig was almost submerged in a welter of borrowed grandeur.

And yet for the sharp-eyed, the sense of the original story persists. Arthur was fighting for the survival of Britain long before the ideas of England, Scotland and Wales were born. He was and remained famous as a war leader, a king in the later stories but also a courageous and canny general. The image of Arthur astride a snorting charger may be a medieval anachronism but the truth is not so very far away. Cunedda's Gosgordd and the swan-maned steeds of the Gododdin lacked only the scale of the heavy horses that charged at Agincourt bearing 400 pounds of man, weapons and armour. More particularly some of the names remain. Owain of Rheged lived on as Yvain long after his campaigns against the

Angles and the extent of his great kingdoms were all forgotten. His father Urien was completely absorbed into the stories and his real achievements and origins lost. He was made Arthur's contemporary, husband of Morgan Le Fay, King of Gore and much else. But if the traces of Gore are followed exhaustively in the legends, it becomes clear that it was thought of as a kingdom near Scotland, separated from it by the River Tember and like the Celtic Otherworld it could only be crossed by a bridge of swords. Just visible, through opaque myth, is a memory of the kingdom of Rheged.[2]

That there was a parallel, more rigorously historical appraisal of the Arthur stories in the twelfth century and before, there can be no doubt. Contemporaries laughed at Geoffrey of Monmouth because they knew something of the history of Britain after the Romans left. While Geraldus Cambrensis, a Welsh monk, made fun of the magical effects of the *Historia*, an earlier Norman-French historian, William of Malmesbury wrote these tantalizing sentences: 'This is that Arthur of whom modern Welsh fancy raves. Yet he plainly deserves to be remembered in genuine history rather than in the oblivion of silly fairy tales; for he long preserved his dying country.'[3]

Clearly William knew a good deal about Arthur but to our loss neither he nor his fellow clerics wrote down much of it. He baldly notes that Arthur aided the warrior Ambrosius Aurelianus in his fight against the invaders, and then attributes a victory at Mount Badon to Arthur. But there is another glimpse of a body of knowledge which is more pointed for this present rendition. The romances of Chrétien de Troyes showed the vigorous Breton traditions of Arthur at work. When the migrations from southern Britannia to Armorica began again in the mid sixth century as the Saxons raided and settled more of what became England, the

[2] Ronan Coghlan, *The Illustrated Encyclopaedia of Arthurian Legends* (1991).

[3] William of Malmesbury, *The Acts of the English Kings* (1947 edn).

exiled P-Celts brought fresh memories of their great leader. These remained relatively uncorrupted into the early Middle Ages because the dukedom of Brittany managed to play off Angevin against Capetian and retain a robust independence. The Arthur stories were important to a separate Breton identity and they did not make careless assumptions about his origins. Writing about something else in 1120 the chronicler Lambert de St Omer makes a passing reference: 'There is a palace of Arthur the Soldier, in Britain, in the land of the Picts, built with various and wondrous art, in which the deeds of all his acts and wars are seen to be sculpted.'[4]

This, taken together with William of Malmesbury's comments, allows a view in the twelfth century that Arthur was a soldier who led the armies of P-Celtic Britain against its enemies and delayed conquest for some time. And Lambert knew of a palace in Scotland where he commemorated his achievements: where else but his base and native place?

That a man with the name of Arthur caused buildings, if not palaces, to be built is not now in doubt. On 4 July 1998 a team of archaeologists from Glasgow University made an astonishing discovery. Excavating the Cornish hill fort and castle on the rocky peninsula of Tintagel they came upon an inscribed slate. Scratched with a knife were the words: '*Pater Coliavificit Artognou*', which translates into 'Artognou, father of a descendant of Col, has made this.'

The slate was discovered under debris which can be certainly dated to the early sixth century. It had been used as a drain-cover but before had served as some sort of inscribed plaque fixed to a small stone building on the sheltered eastern edge of the peninsula. Other material, such as fragments of the only known sixth-century glass flagon ever found in Britain, shows that Tintagel was a site of sophistication and importance with clear trading links with Europe

---

[4] John Morris, *The Age of Arthur* (1973).

and an economic base that allowed luxury goods to be acquired and used.

But the inscription holds precious information, allowing a number of observations. First and most obvious is that an important man with a name very like Arthur lived at or visited Tintagel at exactly the period when documentary sources say that a historical Arthur was alive. More, it is a unique Dark Ages example of an inscription which names an individual but which is not a memorial or a tomb. In other words Arthur was a sufficiently significant and famous man to cause plaques bearing his name to be erected while he lived. To date there has been no other discovery demonstrating prestige in such an emphatic way. The style both subtracts and adds. Arthur is given no title, not king or Guledig, nor a Roman rank, but rather his name is spelled in P-Celtic, meaning 'bear man' or 'like a bear' from the word *arth*. And to underline his native British status, the inscriber added 'father of a descendant of Col'. If that description is intended to add dignity and fame to the simple statement of Arthur's name then it can only refer to Coel Hen, the early fifth-century king of the north, a founder of the line of Rheged, perhaps the last Dux Britanniarum. And being 'the father of a descendant of Col' must mean that Arthur or Arthnou, as it should be pronounced, married a woman whose genealogy included Old King Cole, and whose child therefore became his direct descendant.

This clear link to the Old North does not, however, deal with the issue of a man with a name like Arthur causing a building to be raised in Tintagel. If he was based in the north, then why is hard archaeological fact emerging as far away from the Scottish Border country as it is possible to travel without leaving Britain?

The answer is simple, if a little convenient. If Arthur was a war leader whose success and expertise brought him to defend P-Celtic Britain wherever it was attacked then there is no doubt that he came south, either with his horse-warriors or on diplomatic business. Cunedda travelled a great distance to fight the Irish in

Wales and given good logistical planning there is no reason why Arthur could not have gone further. Moreover his victories also depended on political acumen. The P-Celtic kingdoms combined under the direction of a Guledig, pooling both soldiers and resources to contain common enemies. The kingdoms of the north had a tradition of alliance and there is a credible document from the Nennius collection which describes the campaigns of Urien of Rheged against the Northumbrian Angles in the 580s.

> Hussa reigned 7 years. Four kings fought against him, Urien and Riderch Hen [Strathclyde] and Guallauc [probably Manau] and Morcant [Gododdin]. Theodoric fought bravely against the famous Urien and his sons. During that time, sometimes the enemy, sometimes our countrymen were victorious, and Urien blockaded them for three days and three nights on the island of Metcaud [Lindisfarne].

But while he was on the expedition Urien was assassinated, on the initiative of Morcant, from jealousy, because his military skill and generalship surpassed that of all the other kings. Which shows both the dangers and advantages of alliance. In order to mount a siege, even only for three days, a Dark Ages force would have needed both greater organization than a war-band and also enough kit and supplies to maintain a siege by an army not on the move and foraging.

Arthur was in Tintagel not because of immediate military con-siderations – in the early sixth century Cornwall was far from the front line – but because he needed to secure the support of the man who controlled such a wealthy and well-connected place. And perhaps also because he wanted to persuade those not immediately threatened by Saxon advance that it was none the less in their best interests to contribute to the cost of resistance.

That the Arthur of Tintagel did not style himself a king is also significant. Urien's assassination signifies the extreme political difficulty of creating and sustaining alliance among ambitious and jealous British kings. These victories against the Angles were won in territory Morcant had lost. After victory there must have been a dispute over ownership and reoccupation so severe as to cause the death of the King of Rheged. As a professional soldier Arthur may have been able to avoid dynastic clashes of this fatal sort.

At all events the Tintagel discovery offers substantial underpinning for any account of a historical Arthur. And more than that it renews some faith in the power of folk memory. Stories of Arthur had wreathed the rocky peninsula for a long time, most of them dismissed as fantasy and no store at all set by their persistence. The Arthur Stone tells us that even the most confused and elaborate tales were ignited by a spark of truth somewhere in the darkness of the past.

Presently I want to turn to the best and hardest documentary evidence behind the stories of Arthur, and there to show that he was one of the Men of the North, a general who led the armies of the Cymry. But before doing so I want to reconsider what has gone before and draw together a context and a background against which the action that follows can be better seen.

Underpinning all that I am contending is the story of the Men of the North, the lost kingdoms of Britain, ignored and forgotten. Honed, trained, settled and horsed by the Roman cavalry, carrying the billowing Sarmatian dragon and, uncannily anachronistic in the style of Thomas Malory's knights of the Round Table, pointing the *contus*, the heavy lance, as their chargers thundered into a gallop, the horse warriors of the Cymry became the most feared native fighting force in Britain after Rome abandoned the province. Buffer kingdoms wedged between the demands of Roman discipline and the expediencies of imperial policy, with the stubborn Brigantes and Selgovae in their midst, and the savage, unpredictable Picts to the north, the P-Celtic kingdoms of southern Scotland were hammered on the anvil of war for generations, first surviving and then breaking out south to Wales and north into the lands of the Miathi, the southernmost tribe in the early Pictish federation.

As well as their weapons and methods, their most mystical cavalry traditions found a curious through-line in the romances of Chrétien de Troyes and Geoffrey of Monmouth. The powerful, magical and malign figure of Morgan, or Morgan le Fay, Arthur's sister and consort came from a Breton tradition which had derived the name from Modron,[5] which in turn came from the parade-ground goddesses of Trimontium, the Matres Campestres, who were sacred to cavalry troopers.

These equestrian skills and traditions also allowed the only securely recorded example of native British statecraft in the Dark Ages, of large-scale military activity more reminiscent of Roman strategy than anything contemporary, the expedition of Cunedda to rescue Wales. Sent by the planners of the Gododdin, accompanied by the Gosgordd of perhaps a thousand horse warriors, Cunedda struck back against the invaders of Britannia in a determined and decisive stroke, the only example where the P-Celts made permanent reconquest. And 150 years later Urien and Owain of Rheged led the still-vigorous armies of the Cymry in the defeat of the Northumbrian Angles, another rare British success also won from the Old North. These great generals represent the beginning and end of a long and traceable tradition of military dominance imposed from the Gododdin, Strathclyde and Rheged. Their most brilliant victor was Arthur, fighting and winning on several fronts, as I hope to show.

And a man remembered in the earliest war poetry of the native British, the earliest vernacular literature of the old Latin West. Arthur's name was a byword for bravery in 600 when Aneirin composed 'The Gododdin'. The first reference to Arthur in a dateable piece of literature is in a poem sung in Edinburgh among the Men of the North. Not in Wales, not in the west of England but in southern Scotland.[6]

[5] Ronan Coghlan, *op. cit.*

[6] Gwyn A. Williams, *Excalibur* (1994).

Even in the dying days of the empire in the west, emperors fought hard to hold the valuable province of Britannia. And when Magnus Maximus, or Macsen, launched his bid for the purple in 381, he went to considerable lengths to organize the northern frontiers. Having fought alongside Count Theodosius after the Barbarian Conspiracy, he already knew the Men of the North and to stiffen their ability to resist the incursions of the Picts he led the Gododdin armies into Manau and secured an aggressive frontier redoubt in the shadow of the hill fort of the Miathi. In this way he extended and strengthened the authority of Theodosius's prefects, the military governors of the kingdoms of southern Scotland. And because of the power of the Men of the North he could afford to reduce their numbers by leading them to Europe where he pursued his campaign to be recognized as a legitimate emperor.

The first of the generals were renamed and absorbed into the P-Celtic polities they endeavoured to direct. Particularly important was Paternus Pesrut, the man with the red cloak, the grandfather of Cunedda, and the first prefect of the southern Gododdin of the Tweed basin. New coin finds show Roman activity in southern Scotland extending into the early fifth century, 200 years after convention dates their military withdrawal.

Remembering the style of these prefects with nomen and cognomen, Antonius Donatus, Quintilius Clemens and so on and the way in which their names were softened into P-Celtic, it is easy to see how Artorius could become Arthur. In the centuries of Roman occupation several men called Artorius had served in the army in Britain but it was a rare name. And therefore it is difficult to imagine that it could have been an eighth- or ninth-century invention when memories of Rome had all but gone. Artorius translated into Arthur is the survival of a real person.

More substantial is the extraordinary way in which the landscape is named for Arthur. Over half of Britain and Brittany there are more than 2,000 places that commemorate him: hills, caves, rocks, streams, geological oddities; the gazetteer is huge. This must speak of a hero, of a real person whose achievement made an indelible mark on the memories of the ordinary people who walked and worked the land, even if no contemporary and few historians after him wrote down what he did.

Gildas's *De Excidio et Conquestu Britanniae* is the only account close to the time when Arthur lived and he does not mention him. But he does say that Britain enjoyed a 'time of present security' between 500 and 560. Which in turn clearly implies military success in stemming the invading tide. It was Arthur who did this in a long and widely spread campaign which culminated in a decisive victory around 500 at a place called Mount Badon.

Seventy years later the north was still British and still the focus of P-Celtic culture, the place where its defining stories were made and told. That is true of Arthur, and also of Merlin. It is more than a coincidental buttress to my argument to know that the two most colourful and powerful figures in the weave of British legend both came from southern Scotland and lived within two generations' reach of each other. It shows where the core was, where Britain was most emphatically Celtic with enough confidence to tell itself stories, to remember its heroes and prophets.

Also significant is a flurry of royal Arthurs at the end of the sixth century.[7] Four royal fathers named their sons Arthur and most prominent but unlikely was the Q-Celtic King Aedan MacGabrain of Dalriada. As Guledig he led an alliance of the kingdoms of the north against the Angles, losing at Degsastan in 603. Using the name as a sort of banner against the invaders, he named his son Arthur and rode into battle with him against his illustrious namesake's enemies.

The pattern made by all this evidence is sometimes difficult to follow, often only partial or allusive and always unsatisfactory. Thus far it is only possible to assert with confidence that Arthur existed and was a successful war leader in the British resistance to

---

[7] Gwyn A. Williams, *op. cit.*

their external enemies, and equally possible to assert that the P-Celtic kingdoms of the north provided a cultural, political and military focus of a power lacking in the civil society of the south of England. All the circumstances are right but the key linkage between the Men of the North and Arthur is only implied, not yet securely made.

The most solid, most reliable documentary evidence will do that if carefully considered. This material comprises three bits. First there are the *Annales Cambriae* or the *Annals of Wales* which historians also call the *Easter Tables*. Certainly compiled close to the time Arthur lived, they were transcribed much later, complete with radical errors of dating. Then there is Gildas. His *De Excidio et Conquestu Britanniae* or *The Ruin and Fall of Britain* is a bitter and arid review of the recent post-Roman past written in the middle of the sixth century. Disappointed, sometimes dismissive and snooty, Gildas offered an account short on names and facts and long on blame and complaint. And finally there is Nennius, a Welsh monk who wrote in the eighth century the *Historia Brittonum* or *The History of the British*, a ramshackle, disjointed collection of story and history. 'I have heaped together all that I found from the annals of the Romans, the writings of the holy fathers, and the traditions of our own old men,' runs his disarming preface. As good a recipe as any.

Buried under confusion and contradiction, the story of Arthur is in these documents and it can be found and assembled if the searcher brings the right compass. Looked at from the north, much of the mist clears and Gildas, Nennius and the *Easter Tables* can be set in a line to form a clear narrative.

Gildas first. There is a powerful tradition that he was a southern P-Celtic priest summoned to Ireland to help restore and regulate the running of monastic life.[8] *The Rule of Gildas* was likely written around 565 and it dealt with the quotidian issues of life in a

---

[8] John Morris, *op. cit.*

monastery, offering advice on how to resolve disputes, discipline the errant sensibly, and some words on the place of a monastery in the politics of the world beyond its walls. Gildas was clearly a literate and experienced man who understood something of the legacy of Rome and the loss of order and learning that followed its fall in the West. His letters and the *De Excidio et Conquestu Britanniae* (*The Ruin and Fall of Britain*) install him as part of the flickering remnant that preserved parts of the old world as it was overrun by the barbarians pouring out of the east.

This is Gildas's theme. He has much to say, in a self-consciously decorated style, about the general causes and effects of the invasion of Britain by the Anglo-Saxons, and maddeningly little about the detail of what happened. He is the source for the traditional story of the coming of the Germanic peoples whom the P-Celts called (and still call) the Sais or the Saxons. Their ultimate victory – which Gildas can clearly see coming – is to be a divine punishment. Because the British kings were slothful, sinful and incompetent, God would punish them by allowing the Sais to take their lands and extinguish such enlightenment as remained. But there were some heroes and, more important, some recognizable bits of history in Gildas's narrative. Around the year 460, after the Saxon revolt in the south and after the unsuccessful appeal to Aetius, the military commander in Gaul, there occurs this passage:

Meanwhile as the British feebly wandered, a dreadful and notorious famine gripped them, forcing many of them to give up without delay to their bloody plunders, merely to get a scrap of food to revive them. Not so others: they kept fighting back, basing themselves on the mountains, caves, heaths and thorny thickets. Their enemies had been plundering their land for many years; now for the first time they inflicted a massacre on them ... [With the Britons now on the offensive] the impudent Irish pirates returned home, though they were shortly to return, and for the first time the Picts in the far end of the island kept quiet from now on, though they occasionally carried out devastating raids of plunder. So in this period of truce the desolate people found their cruel scars healing over.[9]

This is the beginning of the resistance. The south had fallen and P-Celtic forces were regrouping in the 'mountains, caves, heaths and thorny thickets' of the north and west. The heirs of Cunedda and the warriors of the Gosgordd absorbed fleeing refugees from the south-east and turned back to face and defeat the barbarians. The cavalry of the Gododdin had ejected 'the impudent Irish pirates' and 'now inflicted a massacre' on the Sais. While 'for the first time' the Picts did not pose a continual and immediate threat to Britannia.

In this extract Gildas offers a neat summary of the status of the war for Britain in 460. The P-Celts had three lots of enemies, Picts, Irish and the Saxons, and their resistance came from the up-country of mountain, heath, cave and thicket. These were the places controlled and recolonized by the Men of the North. They were organized. They had cavalry forces previously deployed against the Irish and the Picts but not the Saxons. These last were foot soldiers, often poorly equipped and unlikely to have the tactical discipline to close ranks and stand their ground against the furious charge of Cunedda's Gosgordd. If they had turned, then Gildas was right to report a massacre.

There are traditions in Wales that Ambrosius Aurelianus was based there.[10] Dinas Emrys is 'the fort of Ambrosius' in the mountains of the north but unfortunately Gildas does not describe his campaigns or list his battles. But in the passage that names Ambrosius there is a notice of a great British victory. 'This lasted up until the year of the siege of Badon Hill, almost the most recent defeat of the rascals and certainly not the least. That was the year of

[9] Gildas, *De Excidio et Conquestu Britanniae*, in John Morris, *op. cit.*
[10] Ronan Coghlan, *op. cit.*

my birth; and as I know since then forty-four years and one month have already passed.'

Several bits of vital information and a clear set of attitudes are to be read from this passage. Taking together other sources about Gildas and when and how long he lived, it is possible to date the Battle of Badon Hill to 499 or 500. If he describes it as the 'most recent defeat' of the Saxons and it happened forty-four years before he wrote about it, then it sounds like a decisive victory which allowed more than forty years of peace to follow. Gildas says that the battle was 'a siege' and that it was fought on a hill. Now if it was the Cymry who were besieged on a flat-topped hill fort with their cavalry horses, then it would have needed a large Saxon army to surround it completely, and to feed themselves while doing it. A large army, a siege – this sounds like the culmination of a long campaign with much at stake at Badon.

And finally Gildas's attitude. To describe the Saxons he uses a Latin word *furciferes* which literally means 'fork-carriers'. This has nothing to do with their weaponry but is a demeaning term for a slave, someone who waits at table. Better translated as 'rascals', it shows how Gildas thought about the Saxons. Lower-class ruffians, irritants, perpetrators of great and destructive mischief, destroyers, almost completely beneath contempt if it were not for their military success against the querulous, corrupt kings of the British.

Badon was a famous battle. Pivotal in marking the successful end of a campaign of British resistance but also in recognizing the new frontier. By 500 half of what became England was lost. East of a line drawn from Southampton to Hull, the Germanic invaders controlled most of what had been the wealthiest and most intensively farmed and settled part of Britannia.[11]

The *Annals of Wales* also remembered Badon but before looking at the relevant entry, it is important to understand what these documents were. They had two functions: one historical and one

[11] James Campbell (ed.), *The Anglo-Saxons* (1982).

religious. In a tradition initiated in Ireland monastic chroniclers began to imitate Roman Christian forms by compiling tables of years which noted key events: the birth and death of Christ, the early papacy, the movement of saints and the process of conversion and so on. The Irish adapted this model and also mixed in parts of their pre-Christian history. The second function of the annals was as an aid in reckoning the date of the moveable feast of Easter. The most important festival in the Christian calendar needed precise plotting and complex methods were used in arriving at an agreed date. The years and dates were usually arranged in columns and often a manuscript would leave the right-hand side of the page blank so that scribes could write short notes of important events against any given year.

These Irish annals were transmitted first to Scotland where missionary exchange was frequent and activity was intense and well documented. The early Christian history of Britain has a northern focus with Ninian at Whithorn in Rheged almost a century before Augustine came to Canterbury, Kentigern at Glasgow in Strathclyde, Patrick from Carlisle in Rheged and other lesser figures elsewhere among the Men of the North. It is impossible to trace the mechanics of this sort of transmission or even the location of sender and receiver, but its context and what that allowed are clear enough. Christian Ireland and Christian Scotland were in regular contact both through the mighty figures of Columba and Patrick but also ultimately in sharing the distinctive practices and beliefs of what came to be known as Celtic Christianity.[12] By the early seventh century Irish and Scots monks found themselves in conflict with Rome ostensibly over the dating of Easter but actually a range of issues was at stake. At the Synod of Whitby in 635 the Celts lost the political battle and retreated to their island and Highland heartlands, and to the margins of temporal involvement.

But before that event, the Celtic Church was powerful and

---

[12] Alfred P. Smyth, *Warlords and Holy Men AD 80–1000* (1984).

traditions and stories from Ireland regularly found their way into P-Celtic history. The *Annals of Wales* for the fifth and sixth centuries are very largely transcriptions of Irish annals for the same period.[13] Likely compiled at first in the north, they include a few British notices which understandably deal with events known to the chroniclers and which seemed important to them.

In both versions of the *Annales Cambriae* the following is written against the year 499 or 500: 'The Battle of Badon, in which Arthur carried the Cross of Our Lord Jesus Christ for three days and three nights on his shield and the Britons were the victors.' This is extremely important. In a battle mentioned by the reticent Gildas, dated clearly by him to the same date, Arthur is unequivocally named as the leader of the British forces who won a decisive battle against the Saxons which allowed a long period of peace until the last quarter of the sixth century. More, the annalist adds a little to Gildas's account, saying that the battle lasted three days, a detail which fits well with the notion of a siege. And since this is a very rare corroboration between two sources in an age where there are very few pieces of documentary evidence of any sort, it allows us to be sure about the importance of Badon and its date of 499/500. And also surer about the reliability of both Gildas and the annalists.

There is another entry, which also appears in both versions of the *Annales Cambriae*: '516/517. The Battle of Camlann, in which Arthur and Medraut fell: and there was plague in Britain and Ireland.' This allows a little more flesh on the narrative. Not only is Arthur named again but the date of his death is given, as is that of another man, Medraut. And, very important, there is another location to add to Badon. Where Camlann and Badon were is clearly key to an understanding of the prosecution of the war and the career of the Guledig, Arthur.

The last piece of documentary evidence is the *Historia Brittonum* of Nennius, a Welsh-speaking monk writing in the middle of the

---

[13] John Morris, *op. cit.*

eighth century. It is a collection of documents honestly drawn from several sources and uncritically welded together into a rough and ready sequence of events.

Nennius opens with a long and colourful slice of myth-history, beginning, like a typical monastic chronicler, with Noah and the Flood. And then in a shift of tone detectable across thirteen centuries, he begins to write of post-Roman Britain.

This is known as the Independent Section and it deals with the deeds of the Roman British leader Vortigern, and his fateful encouragement of the Saxons' settlement in Kent. But the burden of the narrative centres on the supernatural powers of Ambrosius, a boy brought to Vortigern originally as a candidate for human sacrifice. The myth relates how the Britons had tried to build a new fortress but that its foundations always crumbled, toppling the walls. The blood of a 'fatherless' boy (an illegitimate child, one assumes) was needed to placate the gods and cement the founds. But the boy Ambrosius shows astonishing powers by telling the Vortigern to drain a pool which lies under his unsteady castle. When this is done, red and white dragons are found. They fight and the white is victorious – a prophecy, says the boy Ambrosius, of the eventual defeat of the British by the Saxons. A good source for the Red Dragon of Wales, and probably a memory of the Sarmatian *draconarius*. This is, reputable scholars contend, the first appearance of a version of Merlin and a tale that Geoffrey of Monmouth made much use of when he wrote his *Historia Regum Britanniae* four centuries later.

Nennius establishes the German invaders/settlers on the east coast of Britain and then relates how Aesc 'came from northern Britain and settled in Kent, whence came the Kings of Kent'. Even from these slight sentences, it is clear that the Angles and Saxons had created some organization and some control over the eastern English seaboard. From the later *Anglo-Saxon Chronicle*, the succession of Aesc in Kent can be sensibly dated at 468.

Then Nennius continues:

> Then Arthur fought against them in those days,
> with the Kings of the Britons, but he himself was
> the Leader of Battles.

The Dux Bellorum or the Guledig leading an alliance of British kings against those who would take their territory away from them. The clear statement in this sentence that Arthur is not a king is confirmed in another, more mythic part of the text where Arthur is described simply as *miles*, a soldier. He marshals his borrowed army against the Saxons, and Nennius follows his passage about Aesc with '*Arthur pugnabat contra illos*' with *illos* clearly meaning 'those people' or the Anglo-Saxons. However other sources are less clear. Gildas writes of 'three enemies' while the *Easter Tables* are silent, saying only that the Britons were victors. Since there is hard evidence for conflict on all sides – Cunedda fought the Irish/Scots in Wales, the Picts and Scots raided as far south as Chester in 361 and London in 396, and the Anglo-Saxons began arriving from the east a generation later – I think it reasonable to assert that *illos* would have applied to more than the kinsmen of Aesc, although, writing at three centuries' distance in Wales, Nennius had probably forgotten that. Invaders needed to be resisted wherever they came from and the P-Celtic kingdoms of southern Scotland had held out against pressure from all sides and sources.

The central passage in the *Historia Brittonum* is a sequential list of the locations of Arthur's victories and it is worth setting down here in full:

The first battle was at the mouth of a river which is called Glein. The second, third, fourth and fifth were beyond another river which is called Dubglas, in the district of Linnuis. The sixth battle was beyond the river which is called Bassus. The seventh battle was in the wood of Celidon, that is, Cat Coit Celidon. The eighth battle was in the stronghold of Guinnion, in which Arthur carried a likeness of Holy Mary Everlasting Virgin on his shield, and the heathens were turned in flight on that day and there was a great slaughter upon them because of the goodness of Our Lord Jesus Christ and the goodness of the Holy Virgin Mary his mother. The ninth battle happened in the city of the Legion. The tenth battle happened on the bank of a river which is called Tribruit. The eleventh battle was done on the hill which is called Agned. The twelfth battle was at Badon Hill in which Arthur destroyed 960 men in a single charge on one day, and no one rode down as many as he did by himself. And in all these battles he emerged as the victor.[14]

Despite the fact that it is set down in inelegant, imprecise and badly spelled Latin, perhaps 300 years after the events, this passage has the smit of authenticity about it. It reads right. Almost certainly derived from a bardic recital of the great deeds of Arthur, the original Welsh can be heard echoing behind Nennius's rough-edged prose. Celidon, Guinnion and Badon sound like the remnant of a rhyme scheme and the repetition of the Old Welsh 'Cat Coit Celidon' is a surviving alliterative fragment. It reads like the frame of a terrific campaign fought over a wide area of Britain, and most resounding of all it speaks of brilliant success. After years of defeat and retreat, Arthur led the British in a dazzling series of victories which stabilized the kingdoms of the Cymry and beat back the enemy for two generations.

Also this battle-list is the best evidence of what Arthur actually did, and, I will argue, convincing proof that he was not based in the south-west of England. Only one of the battle-sites could possibly have been located in the area where almost every historian places Arthur, and that is a highly conjectural thesis underpinned by circumstance with no toponymic evidence to back it. I want to show that Arthur's battles locate him, place him in his centre of power, the area he wanted most dearly to defend, where the enemy were

[14] Nennius, *Historia Brittonum*, in John Morris, *op. cit.*

most powerful. Not in Glastonbury, South Cadbury Hill or anywhere near, but in the Scottish Border country, the place he came from and had his base.

After the end of the battle-list, Nennius adds, 'in all these battles [Arthur] emerged forth as victor' and then stops the narrative. But from the *Easter Tables* it is known that there was a thirteenth battle at a place called Camlann where Arthur perished and which happened at least fifteen years after the final victory at Mount Badon. That makes ten names of places for thirteen battles, and, aside from the references to Christ and the Virgin Mary and a hint of military tactics, that is essentially all there is: ten names.

The first of Arthur's victories was won at the mouth of the River Glen, spelled Glein by Nennius. The meaning is straightforward: both P- and Q-Celtic in their respective versions of *glyn* and *gleann* mean a valley. Many valleys bear the name: Glencoe, Glenmore, Gleneagles but there are only two rivers called Glen. One rises near Grantham and flows for much of its course through the Fens of Lincolnshire before emptying into the River Welland near Spalding. In the fifth century much of this land was undrained and lay under seasonal water. Because it was flat – no glens. More likely as a derivation is the P-Celtic word *glan* for a bank or banking or riverbank. Subject to flooding, the Fen rivers are all heavily embanked to protect the fields lying around them. That spelling as well as the geography would disqualify the Lincolnshire River Glen from Nennius's list. That leaves the Northumberland River Glen as more likely, although before this begins to sound too emphatic, I have only a reasonable reading of geography and good dictionaries to support me. And what I have seen for myself.

The Glen runs into the Till which in turn is a major tributary of the Tweed, at that time firmly in the territory of the Gododdin. It flows out of the Cheviot Hills in one of the most beautiful valleys in Britain running hard by the fortress of Yeavering Bell. One of the key strongholds of the Gododdin, it is a flat-topped hill with seventeen acres enclosed behind the remains of a long palisade, and the compacted stone bases of 130 huts have been identified. As important as Traprain Law and Eildon Hill North, Yeavering Bell held the southern frontiers of the Gododdin. It lay only fifteen miles from Bamburgh, already a haven for Anglian pirates in Arthur's time, but it is much more likely that he fought a battle on the River Glen to protect his fortress from the embryonic kingdom of Deira. Based near York in eastern Yorkshire, the Angles were limited in expansion by their kinsmen's success to the south and so, when their numbers allowed it, they raided north into the lands of the Gwyr Y Gogledd.

Although Arthur stopped them on the flat ground by the River Glen (horse trials are still held on the banks of the river and close by is an ancient standing stone, known as the Battle Stone), the Angles eventually captured Yeavering Bell and built an extensive royal palace at its foot.[15] This was excavated forty years ago to reveal a long rectangular hall, several smaller halls, a pagan temple (later converted into a church when Paulinus baptized King Edwin of Northumbria in the River Glen) and a remarkable open-air auditorium or meeting place known as the Grandstand. Set out like a section through a Roman amphitheatre, it had seating for several hundred but room at its base for only a small dais where, presumably, the Anglian king sat. Not designed, therefore, for debate but rather as a place where the monarch literally laid down the law to a pre-literate aristocracy who all witnessed the same thing being said to them by the same man at the same time. Remarkable.

Without labouring the point, I think it much more likely that Arthur would choose to fight near an important fort, big enough to secure his cavalry, in the path of Anglian war-bands pushing northwards, on good ground of his own choosing, rather than splash around in the clatch and mire of the Lincolnshire fen.

There is another reason for believing that Glein is the River Glen in Northumberland. Because geography often dictates strategy and

[15] James Campbell, *op. cit.*

forces armies to meet at or near the same place, even separated by millennia, the case is strongly supported by a series of later conflicts. At the foot of Yeavering Bell in 1415 Robert Umfraville defeated Scottish raiders on their way south at what became known as the Battle of Geteryne (or Yeavering); and then in exactly the same place in 1465 a Yorkist force defeated Lancastrians in an important skirmish in the Wars of the Roses. Three miles away a disastrous battle at Flodden Field destroyed Scotland's fighting capability for two generations in 1513. And a mile to the east of Yeavering, Harry Hotspur defeated the Earl of Douglas at Humbleton Hill in 1402, his story ultimately finding its way into Shakespeare's *Henry IV, Part I*.

Two more points from this. Arthur was defending a Gododdin fortress at the Battle of Glein on ground that was flat and unobstructed, and, crucially, that was near a river. This last is a tactical theme which occurs throughout the Nennius list and it was the choice of a cavalry general commanding a small force of troopers who went against foot soldiers. Perhaps they surprised the Angles as they forded the river and splashing in on their horses turned them and rode them down along its banks or drove them into places where it was deep. A small mounted force could rout a much larger army of infantry in this way.

Parallels are available elsewhere. In Gaul military success against the Franks and Goths was due almost entirely to the brilliant use of small cavalry forces against overwhelming numbers of infantry. Around 471 an aristocrat called Ecdicius routed thousands of Goths near Clermont-Ferrand with, it was claimed in a contemporary source, only eighteen mounted warriors.[16] While the arithmetic is heroic, the principle is clear, and although Ecdicius seems to have fought only one campaign, the chronicler Sidonius described crowds dancing with joy at his spectacular success.

There is good evidence for sixth-century battles in Britain of this

---

[16] John Morris, *op. cit.*

sort, and given the Gaulish experience of the fifth century, I think it highly unlikely that Arthur fought differently from his children and grandchildren or his neighbours.

The other germane point is to draw a clear distinction between raiding and invading. Since Gildas and the *Annales Cambriae* date Badon Hill in 499/500, then Glein is likely some time in the decade before that, too early to talk of Anglian settlement in the Gododdin territory. But raiding had gone on for a long time before and could be catastrophically destructive. When Arthur drove the Angles into the river, he was dealing not with an invading army but a war-band after plunder.

The next four battles in Nennius's list were all fought in the same place; clearly a short campaign against the same enemy was prosecuted 'beyond another river which is called Dubglas, in the region of Linnuis'. Now this is problematic despite a double map reference: the name of the place and the area where it is situated.

Dubglas is P-Celtic for 'dark river' and gave us the modern surname Douglas. Logically the Ordnance Survey should be scoured for Rivers Douglas and indeed there are several candidates. However at first blush there seem to be none located in a region with anything like the name Linnuis. This has, incidentally, not deterred several laureated historians from insisting that Nennius must mean the area of Lindsey, part of present-day Lincolnshire even though no river bears or bore a name remotely like Douglas – generally accepted in any case to be a Scottish surname.[17] They are so fixated with Arthur's struggle to contain the Saxons in the south that they happily tolerate such an ill-fitting hypothesis.

However, if the campaign of four battles was not waged against invaders from across the North Sea but rather dealt with incursions from the north, from the Picts and the Scots, then the geography begins to fit the text much better. There is a River Douglas that flows into the Clyde near Lanark, there is even a village named

[17] Peter Beresford Ellis, *Celt and Saxon* (1993).

Douglas, and a Douglas Castle. And the infamous Douglas clan, at one time Scottish king-makers, and the opponents of Hotspur, originate from this bleak stretch of the Southern Uplands. Near the confluence of Douglas with Clyde there is the village of Drumalbin, a name which means the ridge of the Scots, perhaps a memory of a battle formation or a defensive position.

The value of this possibility is that it may identify a northern source for Arthur's enemies correctly but it cannot, by any ingenuity, be made to sit in a region by the name of Linnuis.

For that it is necessary to go further north, and also to look for a strategic context. Most famously William Wallace and then Robert Bruce understood the importance of Stirling and its castle as the key to the whole of the north of Scotland. It is easy to forget this nowadays when we are able to move freely virtually anywhere. For the Dark Ages and a thousand years afterwards, Scotland was cut in two by the Firth of Forth to the east and the great and treacherous bog-land called Flanders Moss which stretched westwards from Stirling to the lake of Menteith and the foot of the mountains around Ben Vrackie. The only safe road from south to north was dominated by the towering rock of Stirling Castle, and the bridge over the Forth.

This is where invaders had to funnel through if they wanted to gain the fertile south. And this is where Arthur halted them in a brilliant campaign. Names once again contain secrets.

Earlier I noted that the Gododdin's only modern onomastic survival was the Q-Celtic or Gaelic name for the Firth of Forth, Linn Giudain. Bede offers some help. Early in his *Ecclesiastical History of the English People* he notes how narrow the waist of Scotland is, lying between Alcluith in the west and Urbs Guidi in the east. Alcluith is Dumbarton Rock and the focal fortress of Strathclyde, and Urbs Guidi is Stirling, a western outpost of the Gododdin. Pronunciation of the first element of Linn Guidain begins to unlock this. In its Q-Celtic meaning of 'firth' 'Linn' is spoken with a 'u' suffix so that it sound approximately like 'Leenu'. I think that 'in the region of Linnuis' means in the area of the Firth of Forth. Dubglas or more correctly in P-Celtic Dubhglais for 'dark stream' is again made clearer in the version used in its cousin language, Gaelic. Because it meanders through a trackless area of peaty bog-land and takes a deep brown colour from it, the Gaels call the River Forth 'an Abhainn Dubh' or the 'Dark River'.[18]

Remembering how constant a threat they were to the south – the raids on London in the late fourth century showed how far they could reach – Arthur's war against the Picts was not only a local matter, an attempt to protect the Gododdin kingdom of Manau. It was also part of a clear policy designed to protect all of Britain from its enemies. Even in 540 Gildas describes the Picts as *'transmarini'* able to sail to whatever point of plunder looked promising. All the sources for the fifth century repeat that it was the Picts and not the Anglo-Saxons who posed the greater threat to Britannia. Bede, the *Anglo-Saxon Chronicle*, Gildas and such European commentaries as exist, often note the threat of the Picts. And when the Vortigern found himself in power in the south, he had immediately to deal with the problem of Pictish incursion and, fatally, he brought in Saxon mercenaries to guard against them. Even though the Angles, Saxons and other Germanic settlers posed increasing difficulties as the fifth century wore on, the fearsome reputation of the Picts, built up in Britannia over centuries, did not abate. In the 490s Arthur had to counter these ancient enemies and in four battles by the Dark River in the district of the Firth he quietened them.

And in the same way as at Glein, many battles have been fought in that place for similar strategic reasons. The Irish annals reported a Battle of Manau won by Aedan MacGabrain in 582 against the Picts, while in 711 the kings of Northumbria were pushing their power north and they defeated the Picts in the Battle of Manaw. Both Stirling Bridge in 1298 and Bannockburn in 1314 were fought nearby for the same compelling geographical reasons which brought Arthur's cavalry to the shores of the Firth of Forth.

[18] Iain Taylor, unpublished manuscript.

In attempting to decipher Nennius's list I have followed another assumption, not, I hope, a fanciful one: that the bardic or aural source for it originated with the Gwyr Y Gogledd, the composers of 'The Gododdin' and the focus of P-Celtic or Old Welsh language culture. If that is so, then it is more likely to be a recital of battles won where they lived, in southern Scotland. However that may be, it does not apply to the sixth victory, won 'beyond the river which is called Bassus'.

Neither the map nor any of the text offers much help with Bassus but my firm belief is that it was not in southern Scotland.[19] The only 'Bas' names are in England, such as Basingstoke, Bassenthwaite, or Basildon and all of these are early English, relating to personal names. In P- and Q-Celtic the prefix 'Bas' does exist and is a borrowing from Greek via Latin for *basilica* for a church. The name of the town of Paisley near Glasgow is P-Celtic and has this origin. However, there is nowhere on a map of Britannia in 490 to 500 which has both the prefix and any strategic significance. In Staffordshire there are three villages called Basford which all lie on the Hammerwich Water. That last is an English name and it may have replaced a River Bassus now remembered only in the villages. Nearby is Lichfield and the Roman settlement of Letocetum which was a crossing of two Roman roads, one running north-west to south-east, the other south-west to north-east. Both Saxon raiding parties and British cavalry used Roman roads, and even by the end of the fifth century they remained in good repair.

It is possible that Arthur fought a raiding party near a river in Staffordshire whose name has been lost. He had the mobility to strike quickly over long distances but if Nennius has the sequence of battles right, then it seems an unlikely thing. Cavalry can operate only in the spring, summer and early autumn and to move so far from his base and use up so much of a campaigning season in doing so, Arthur would have needed a good reason. Glein had a

---

[19] Peter Beresford Ellis, *op. cit.*

logic, as did the campaign against the Picts in Manau. The battle at the River Bassus was not remembered by any other historian and the landscape forgot it too. Either it was a skirmish fought on the way to something more important, or Nennius misplaces it. Or likely both.

By contrast the location of the seventh battle is much clearer. Unusually in the vast historiography of Arthur no historian, no matter how fixed their gaze is on events in the south, disagrees that 'the wood of Celidon, that is, Cat Coit Celidon' is in southern Scotland.[20] In the near-contemporary story of Myrddin, he fled from the Battle of Arthuret near Carlisle in 573 into the Wood of Caledon. It is the place now called the Ettrick Forest, to the west of the town of Selkirk.

The question here is not the location, but the enemy. Who fought against Arthur in that place? Not the Angles who were too few and too far east at that time. Of Gildas's list of the three enemies of Britannia, it can only have been the Picts. The Wood of Caledon is the heartland of the ancient tribe of the Selgovae. And remembering the scatter of Pictish remains that lie south of the Pentland Hills near Edinburgh it seems very likely that he had to go into battle against the old enemies of the Gododdin in combination with a Pictish force on the fringes of their territory.

Added to this conjecture is a rare piece of Dark Ages archaeology which definitely locates the site of a battle around 500. At Yarrow Kirk, eight miles west of Selkirk, hard by the river of the same place there is a standing stone bearing a remarkable description. Very weathered now and difficult to read, it carries these words:

Hic memoria perpetua
in loco insignisimi principes Nudi Dumnogeni.
Hic iacent in tumulo duo filii Liberalis.

[20] John Morris, *op. cit.*

Which translates as:

This is the everlasting memorial
In this place lie the most famous princes Nudus and Dumnogenus.
In this tomb lie the two sons of Liberalis.[21]

The immediate area around the Yarrow Stone also remembers
an ancient battle very clearly. To the north-west there is a marshy
area of haughland known as the Dead Lake and tradition holds that
it was a mass grave for warriors killed in the same action that
claimed Nudus and Dumnogenus. Near at hand is an old cottage
which still bears the name Warriors' Rest. But two more standing
stones in the immediate vicinity are much too old to relate to the
battle and it may be that the Yarrow Stone was a third, comman-
deered by the victor to commemorate his distinguished compatri-
ots. A few hundred yards to the south-west is a concentrated group
of four place-names with Nennius's 'Cat' in them: Catcraig looks
down on the battlefield while Catslackburn, Catslack Knowe and
Cat Holes lie on the lower ground nearby.

The terrain once again suits the operation of cavalry against foot
soldiers. There is flat ground, well drained, close to a river where
there is an old ford, no longer used now. Just as at Glein, a surprise
attack on a group of infantry could have caused panic, allowed little
concerted action and turned the enemy into fatal flight. But if
Arthur fought the Picts here then it did not all go well for his side.
There was a cavalry and chariot tradition among the Picts which
may have stiffened their resistance. Two P-Celtic princes, who
sound like Damnonians from Strathclyde, fell in the fray and warriors were buried in a place that people remembered. None the less
only victors erect memorials and Arthur's expedition into the
heartlands of the Selgovae achieved its objective.

The Battle of Celidon Wood is the only location in the Nennius

[21] RCAHMS, *Selkirkshire* (1957).

list that no one disputes. Just as in 'The Gododdin', an epic poem written in Edinburgh, Arthur has his earliest literary reference. Facts are extremely rare in all this and these may be the only two bits of documentary evidence that are universally accepted. And they put Arthur in his right place: a leader of battles, a cavalry general who led the coalition army of the P-Celtic kingdoms of the Old North, the Cymry.

More traditions require to be relied on if the eighth of Arthur's battles is to be correctly placed. There is precious little else to help with the phrase 'in the stronghold of Guinnion', except that Nennius adds that Arthur fought with 'a likeness of Holy Mary Everlasting Virgin, on his shield and the heathens were turned in flight on that day, and there was a great slaughter upon them, because of the goodness of our Lord Jesus Christ and the goodness of the Holy Virgin Mary, his mother.'[22]

Two bits of clarity to sit alongside the mystery of the place-name. First a fulsome piece of early Christian propaganda advertising the decisive intervention of Christ and (twice noted) the Virgin Mary. Not surprising, Nennius was a monk and proselytizing part of his early purpose. But why wait for the eighth battle to insert the message? Why not top and tail the whole glorious campaign with God and his Mother? There must have been a particular reason.

Fort or Castellum Guinnion implies a substantial fortification, perhaps a Roman camp or a hill fort and there are any number of candidates all over Britain, never mind the Borders. *Guinnion* sounds and is a P-Celtic or Old Welsh word. It means 'white place' or more anciently 'holy place'. This last will clearly fit better with the sudden appearance of the Virgin Mary on Arthur's shield. He was using Christian iconography to defend a holy place, probably associated closely with the twice-mentioned Virgin, and putting the pagans to flight.

[22] Peter Beresford Ellis, *op. cit.*

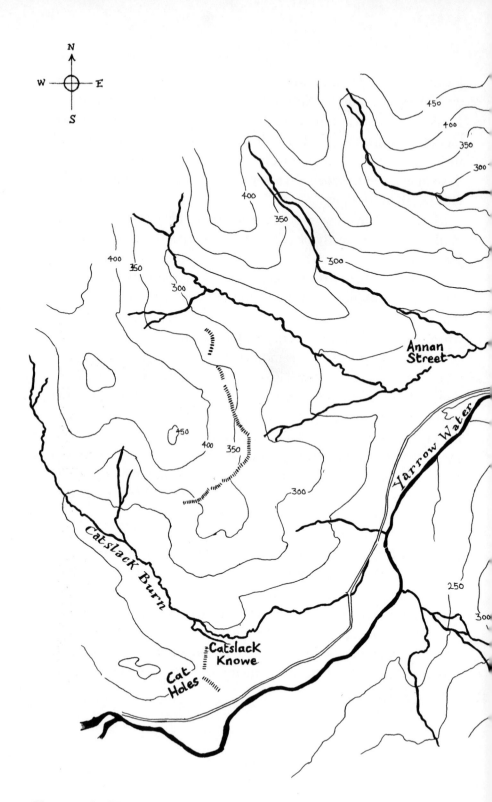

Yarrow, the Warriors' Rest and Annan Street

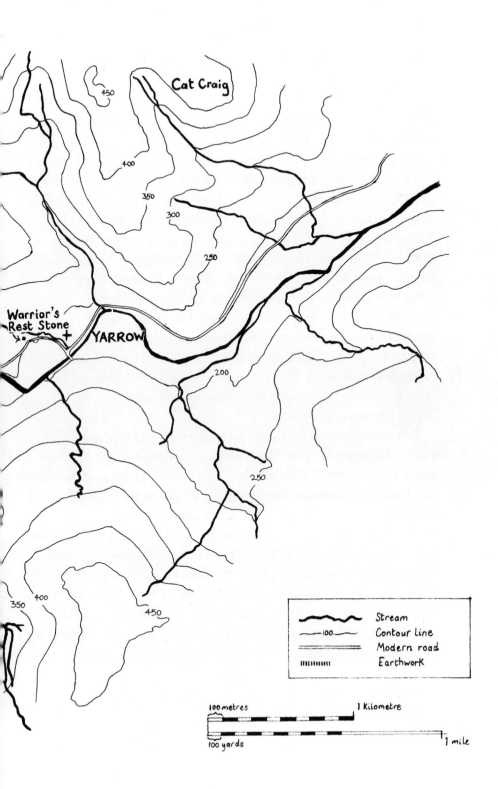

Cat Craig

450

400

350

300

250

Warrior's
Rest Stone

YARROW

200

250

350 400

450

	Stream
100	Contour line
	Modern road
	Earthwork

100 metres ——— 1 Kilometre

100 yards ——— 1 mile

This narrows the field dramatically, particularly if the pagans in question are Angles or Saxons rather than Picts or Scots (who had in any case been exposed to some missionary activity by this stage). Even further, if Nennius has the sequence right and Fort Guinnion follows the seventh battle in the Forest of Celidon both in geography as well as time, that would place it in southern Scotland.

Two more bits of toponymy will pin it on the map. The parish church in the village of Stow, which sits prettily on the Gala Water as it winds with the A7 towards Edinburgh, is called St Mary in Wedale. Buried in thick pinewoods a few hundred yards south is a rickle of stones identified on the Ordnance Survey as Our Lady's Chapel and near it Our Lady's Well.[23] In the *Old Statistical Account of Scotland* (a majestic work dealing with the fabric of the country in encyclopaedic detail), compiled at the end of the eighteenth century, the minister of Stow records 'a very fine perennial spring, known by the name of the Lady's Well, and a huge stone, recently removed in forming the new road, but now broken to pieces, used to be pointed out as impressed with the print of the Virgin Mary's foot.'[24]

The cartularies of the medieval Border abbeys confirm the existence of a church of St Mary in Wedale before their documents began in the early twelfth century, and there is some evidence that there was a pilgrimage shrine to the Virgin as early as the ninth century. The site is clearly very old indeed but it cannot with certainty have been a going concern when Arthur lived. However, there is some dubious help available. In the late twelfth or early thirteenth century, a monk in the priory at Sawley in North Yorkshire added some glosses to Nennius's text. This meant he clearly understood Old Welsh for he translated some of it into uncomfortable Latin. He has Arthur go on crusade (he was writing at the time of Richard I's doomed Third Crusade) to Jerusalem

[23] RCAHMS, *Selkirkshire* (1957).
[24] *Old Statistical Account of Scotland* (1791–2).

where he makes and has consecrated a replica of the Blessed Cross. This was to ensure Arthur's victory over the pagans. Then a last sentence which sounds like a repetition of an early tradition and which brings the little narrative back to earth with a local bump. 'And he himself [Arthur] carried the likeness of Holy Mary, the pieces of which were thus saved in great veneration in Wedale.' While that is much too specific a detail to have been invented, it proves nothing except the existence of an early tradition of Arthur fighting pagans near the village of Stow.

More comfort can be had from place-names, if looked at with care, and sense of how time rubs them smooth. Wedale is ancient and it is related to Guinnion. Because Stow is an Anglian name which means 'holy place', in itself a memory of the Dark Ages shrine to the Virgin Mary, Wedale is also thought to have been conferred by the incomers. Some Arthurian historians even incorporate its supposed Anglian meaning of 'dale of woe' into arguments supporting the placing of the Battle of Fort Guinnion in the valley of the Gala Water.[25] The Angles called it Dale of Woe because they lost to Arthur in that place. Too neat, I fear, and the Angles were rarely anxious to record a defeat. Wedale is a Celtic name, and a more thorough parsing will show even stronger support for a battle in the valley.

Around Stow there are a number of P-Celtic names which have been altered to fit into the mouths of the Q-Celtic speakers who settled by the Gala Water half a millennium after Arthur. *Tref* names, meaning 'settlement', became *tor* names, a Gaelic word for a hill or sometimes a rocky hill. Torsonce Hill is where the remains of the shrine to St Mary stands, hidden by trees, but in 500 it was a *Tref* name perhaps meaning the 'settlement of a prince or chief'. Torquhan a mile or so north was also a *Tref* name, as were several others close by.[26]

[25] W.F. Skene, *Arthur and the Britons* (reissued 1988).

[26] W.F.H. Nicolaison, *Scottish Place-Names* (1976).

Guinnion in P-Celtic came to be changed into Guidh-dail in Q-Celtic, which was in turn rendered as Gwedale, the valley of prayer. The latter element will bear a second look. *Dail* can also mean a field and anciently it could equally, just like the English word, stand for 'battlefield'. Everyone knows that Flodden Field has nothing to do with barley or pasture. With the right name or word alongside, 'field' means 'battlefield'. In the same way I think it likely that Gwedale, and its shortened Anglicized version of Wedale, means 'the prayer battle' or 'the holy battle' if the first element is pared back to the original P-Celtic gloss of 'holy'. This would fit well with Nennius's relative prolixity on the role of the Virgin and Jesus in gaining the victory over the heathens. And also add to the sense of mission that the armies of the Cymry unquestionably had. Not only was Arthur fighting to protect and secure his homelands, he also represented Christian enlightenment in its struggle against the forces of darkness and barbarity.

Wedale was also the valley of access to the north and to Edinburgh and while it may have suited Arthur to put on the clothes of Christianity to fit the place, his greater strategic purpose was surely to shut down a line of advance for the Angles. In winter the A7 by Gala Water can be a kinder passage to Edinburgh than Dere Street and the A68 up over the windy wastes of Soutra Hill. Arthur fought the invaders on the flat ground of Wedale because he had to, not especially because it saved a holy site from pagan hands.

There is an old hilltop fort to the north of Stow which Arthur could have used as his *castellum* as well as a Roman site slightly further away. And Nennius offers a clue to Arthur's battle tactics in the phrase '*pagani versi*', the pagans turned or were turned. Without bending the Latin too much to fit the hypothesis it sounds to me like the result of a successful cavalry charge.

A keen sense of the Roman past stands behind Nennius's next statement: 'The ninth battle happened in the city of the Legion.' Bald but clear. Identify the 'Urbs Legionis' and the location of the battle will be there. Several candidates are available: Chester, Caerleon and Colchester were all legionary headquarters.[27] But each had well-established names that appear repeatedly in the Roman record: Deva, Isca and Camelodunum respectively. All these are derived from local P-Celtic roots, and are different and particular. Looking again at Nennius's Latin, he wrote 'Urbs Legionis' or 'the city of *the* Legion'. Not 'the Legions' but '*the* Legion'. Deva, Isca and Camelodunum were headquarters to several named legions of the colonial garrison, but there was one place, which qualified as a city, that did become closely identified with a particular legion.

From 122 until the end of the Roman occupation of Britannia, York was the Northern Army Command and the headquarters of the Legio Sextam Victrix. There is no record anywhere, not even in the exhaustive lists of the *Notitia Dignitatum*, of the Sixth Legion ever being transferred from York. In time the Roman name Eboracum was sometimes replaced with 'Ad Legionem Sextam' or simply 'Ad Legionem'. It meant 'the place of the Legion' or more likely 'the city of the Legion'.[28]

This close association is not surprising. York was known throughout the west as a great imperial military base. Septimus Severus died there, his sons were proclaimed in the legionary fortress, as was Constantine in 306. Around that time the massive fortifications were augmented with huge polygonal bastions which still survive today. It is therefore clear that when reference was made in Britannia or Britain to the city of the Legion, they meant York.

Precisely because the city was Army Command North and because the empire valued Britannia so highly that in the fourth century at least six expeditions were launched to deal with the Picts, it is not surprising that Germanic mercenaries were stationed there in the fourth century. In fact one of the notable casualties of

[27] Peter Beresford Ellis, *op. cit.*
[28] Sheppard S. Frere, *Britannia* (1967).

the Barbarian Conspiracy of 367 was the Dux Britanniarum, a man with a German name, Fullofaudes. And his colleague, the Count of the Saxon Shore, also bore a German name, Nectaridus. He was killed by the Pictish war-bands.[29]

It is my contention that by the 490s Anglian settlers had combined with the descendants of German mercenary veterans to establish the embryonic kingdom of Deira based near York. There is evidence that the legionary *principia* was repaired several times in the fifth century, obviously by men who wanted to preserve it as a stronghold.

As a focal point, York was served by a network of roads north and south, and, less important, east and west. But geography set the strategic hub a few miles north at what is now the town of Catterick. That is where the Roman road system branched northwest over Stainmore to Carlisle, Galloway and Strathclyde, and almost due north to the Gododdin, the Tweed basin and Edinburgh. If the Anglians at York controlled Catterick then they could move easily against any and all of the northern kingdoms. That is why Mynyddawg of Edinburgh sent his cavalry south in 600 to confront the Angles. Behind the heroics and the florid language lay a cold-eyed military purpose. What was strategically important for the north in 600 was also vital for Arthur in the 490s. But unlike the warriors of Mynyddawg, Arthur defeated the embryonic kingdom of Deira and inhibited its growth for several generations. It was a key victory and possibly the reason why Arthur is so vividly remembered in 'The Gododdin', Aneirin's tale of defeat 100 years later: 'Gwawrddur would feed black ravens on the wall of a fortress, though he were not Arthur.' And perhaps the reference to feeding ravens – on the corpses of the defeated – is to the *principia* at York, Ad Legionem Sextam.

'The tenth battle happened on the bank of a river which is called Tribruit.' Another river battle at a place suitable for cavalry.

---

[29] John Morris, *op. cit.*

Tradition places this in southern Scotland but no clear toponymic case can be made.[30] Tribruit is not related to Teviot or any other river name in the region. Only tradition supports this, a faint echo of folk memory. All that is certain is that Arthur fought once again on the banks of a river. Ten battles won in the same way. Here is a reasonable conjecture of how these were planned.

Cavalry forces are good gatherers of intelligence. Long-range scouting parties could quickly and quietly locate an infantry army on the march. Following the Roman road system, still in good repair but probably lacking its wooden bridges, it was possible to occupy a covert position near a river which the foot soldiers would have to ford. At that point Arthur's herald blew the signal to charge and his cavalry emerged from the cover of the woods at the gallop. And then, about fifty yards from the startled infantrymen clambering out of the water, the troopers would kick for an extra burst of speed to make their impetus irresistible.

Arthur would choose his moment to the instant. Horses will always try to wheel away from an obstacle of any density, like a force of foot soldiers who have had time to form themselves into a spear-bristling shield wall. Disciplined infantry deployed in geography that will protect their flanks can always resist cavalry. On flat ground, by the banks of a river, it would have been very difficult for an infantry commander to avoid being outflanked even if he had had the time, the training and the presence of mind to get his men into a defensive formation. All the archaeological evidence is that Angles and Saxons were poorly equipped, depending themselves on surprise and ferocity for victory.

The Nennius list is taken from an oral source, most likely a praise-poem sung in the presence of Arthur or soon after his death. The alliterative 'Cat Coit Celidon' is a remnant of the original P-Celtic and three of the battle locations preserve a simple rhyme-scheme: Celidon, Guinnion, Badon. An early gloss on the location

---

[30] Peter Beresford Ellis, *op. cit.*

of the eleventh battle which 'was done on the hill which is called Agned' shows that there was a fourth element. In another version of the Nennius text Agned is replaced by the rhyming Bregion. Which in turn gives away the location. Bregion is a P-Celtic rendition of a Roman name.[31] Bremenium was an important outpost fort north of Hadrian's Wall and astride the arterial Dere Street.[32] It survives in an astonishing state of good repair close to the village of High Rochester. The plan is nearly square covering almost five acres and in places the stone walls rise fifteen feet from the surrounding ditch. The village green of High Rochester was once located inside the fortress and today there is still a scatter of relatively modern houses, one of which has the *principia* in its back garden, and a sheltered paddock for ponies in the north-east corner where the walls rise to six feet from the inside.

The walls would have been in much better repair in the 490s and Arthur could have hidden at least 300 horses in the stables and paddocks of the fort, while his scouts brought him reports of the advance of an Angle raiding party up Dere Street from York. Below the fort runs the River Rede and less than a mile away is Elishaw where the Roman Road used to cross the river by a wooden stilt bridge. Then, as now, there is a shallow ford where men could wade up to mid-thigh in the summer, higher in a spate or after winter rain.

It is logical to think of the battle at Bremenium as part of the same summer campaign that took Arthur's cavalry down to Catterick and York. But the order is wrong and Tribruit intrudes. Perhaps for poetic reasons these battles were sung out of sequence, and perhaps Tribruit is a place between Rochester and York where the Cymry scored a minor success, further weakening Deira before destroying the remainder of their army near its base.

Bremenium was and is an important strategic point. While walking round the ancient walls, I heard the sound of square-

[31] K. H. Jackson, *Language and History in Early Britain* (1963).
[32] Peter Beresford Ellis, *op. cit.*

Arthur's cavalry wait in ambush

bashing echoing in the upland air from the modern army camp by the main road, less than half a mile away. And at Otterburn, four miles south, there is another, larger camp. Battles were fought at or near Bremenium for millennia. Urien began his campaign against the Angles of Lindisfarne in the 580s by defeating them in this place, and in 1388 in a field by the modern roadside the Scots and the English fought the bloody Battle of Otterburn.

Tribruit and Agned/Bregion are Celtic names, as is the last of Nennius's sequence of twelve battles: the great and final victory at Mount Badon. 'The twelfth battle was at Badon Hill in which Arthur destroyed 960 men in a single charge on one day, and no one rode down as many as he did by himself. And in all these battles he emerged as the victor.' Add to this the note in the *Easter Tables* which had Arthur once again carrying 'the Cross of Our Lord Jesus Christ for three days and three nights on his shield and the Britons were the victors'. Gildas writes of '*obsessio Montis Badonicis*', a siege that was 'almost the last slaughter of the rascals'.

Three sources, much in agreement, for one event is remarkable for the period. It underscores Badon's importance as the crushing victory of Arthur, although none of the three historians says who the enemy were. But if the appearance of Christian iconography is any guide then they would have been pagans and probably Angles or, most likely, Saxons.

Badon also sounds like a siege by infantry or cavalry defending a mount or hill. Arthur's final charge is almost certainly on horseback and much better downhill than up. And such a charge would only succeed when an infantry shield wall was broken and turned and cavalry got behind warriors or forced them to run. That is when a real slaughter occurs, not in the grinding, pushing and shoving of hand-to-hand fighting with spear, sword and axe. Cavalry troopers have a telling height advantage over foot soldiers and can cut at their heads and upper body with tremendous downward force. While 960 is a symbolic/poetic number of three times 300 and three score, it does not smack of arithmetic hyperbole but rather of a large combined army utterly defeated, disabling military activity for a generation.

Badon was decisive, no doubt, but where was it? As Guledig Arthur led the British kingdoms in what sounds like a coalition. Cunedda's expedition to Wales shows the reach of the Gwyr Y Gogledd. Therefore when historians insist that Badon Hill was in England's West Country, possibly near Bath, they may well be right.[33]

Solsbury Hill near Batheaston is an attractive candidate. Standing by itself it is steep-sided and small enough to be defended for three days and three nights by a body of dismounted cavalry troopers. And there is enough room to corral their horses behind them. Despite a total lack of toponymic corroboration, it is a likely location.

A besieging infantry army would have needed to be very large to surround Solsbury Hill with no gaps in the cordon, and that was precisely the Saxons' problem. In British territory, near Bath, they would have great problems in feeding that number of men for more than three days. On Badon Hill a cavalry force could graze its horses and live off well-filled saddle bags for some time. Arthur may have waited until the besieging cordon was weakened by the dispatch of large foraging parties before he gave the order to mount and charge. Once broken the Saxon formation was lost and 'no one rode down as many as he did by himself'.

The great slaughter at Badon signalled the successful end of Arthur's long campaign all over Britain. For fifty years afterwards neither Angles, Saxons, nor Picts moved against the P-Celts. There was peace, but also consolidation. Half of what became England had been lost, from a diagonal between Hull in the north and Southampton on the south coast. But Arthur had achieved something unique in western Europe. Only in Britannia had the barbarians been stopped. Over the rest of the Western Roman Empire the Goths, Visigoths, Franks, Vandals, Alemanni and the others had

---

[33] John Morris, *op. cit.*

poured their hordes of warriors without check or hindrance. In 500 southern Scotland, Wales and west and north of England were all that remained of the empire.

Arthur failed, but he also defined the nations of Britain and in doing so set the dynamic of our polity, the tensions and character of who we are, formed by where we are. To the north, Arthur's victories allowed Scotland to remain a nation for another thousand years, long enough for its memory to be strong and to allow its rise again in the next millennium. To the west, Wales formed itself behind Offa of Mercia's Dyke and resisted the English for 700 years, long enough to remember its beautiful language to help us understand Britain as it was before the Romans came. The Irish fared worst, furthest from English power but most cruelly subjugated, starved, cleared off the land and still bleeding through ancient wounds.

After Arthur's death in AD 517, his immediate achievements were quickly forgotten as history was busily written by the winners. The *Anglo-Saxon Chronicle* reaches far enough back to note Arthur or his battles but, concerned overwhelmingly with events south of the Humber, it is silent and in any case not anxious to note defeats. Until Geoffrey of Monmouth wrote his *Historia* in 1138 Arthur was remembered only in Welsh and much of that the sort of florid stuff that yields little but the music of the words.

Only his name lived. Only the landscape remembered him. For he was a hero to the little people who walked their unnoticed lives in the valleys and over the hills of all of Britain. Despite their military mastery and inexorable success, the Anglo-Saxons did not supplant the P-Celtic-speaking peoples of England, Scotland or Wales. They could not. And these ordinary farmers and labourers remembered their last hero, liked to imagine that he had ridden his cavalry nearby. Hills, rock formations, lochs, cliffs, mounds even buildings got the name of Arthur. There are more than two thousand places all over Britain that have some, mostly imaginary, association with him. It is an extraordinary survival for a figure whose existence is only whispered at in historical record.

And yet that record is very telling; it holds a secret inside it which will be patent presently. First the evidence should be drawn quickly together. Nennius listed twelve battles. Eight of them were fought in or on the borders of present-day Scotland; four in Manau against the Picts, two in the greater Tweed basin and a further two in the hills around it. The mysterious Tribruit may be on the way to York, the city of the Legion, while Bassus may have similarly preceded the victory at Badon.

What this shows is an overwhelming bias to actions in the north, and when that is added to all the other evidence, there is little question that it locates Arthur's base in the south of Scotland, probably in the Tweed basin.

But where?

12

THE HORSE FORT

In the wintertime when the leaves are off the trees and the sun slants low, there is a view of ancient landscape that ties together all the strands of this story. It is a beautiful view and when the weather is warm enough to linger, old men sit on the benches provided by a thoughtful town council, puff their pipes and look out over the past. They sit on Calchvyndd, the chalky height of Catrawt and the Gododdin, translated into Scots as Chalkheugh Terrace in the little town of Kelso, also rendered from the original Old Welsh name. The greyish white of the chalk bank is gone now, planted with rhododendrons and buttressed by high retaining walls. The old men look across the broad River Tweed to a place they call the Fairgreen, and sometimes Friar's Haugh. Dotted here and there with hardwood trees, it is a wide sweeping meadow where cows and sheep pasture without the need for fences. This is because the Fairgreen is bounded by two rivers: the Tweed arcs south from the west until it meets the Teviot which itself turns south and then west to the Junction Pool. Perhaps 400 acres, the ground is never ploughed and hay very rarely taken. It is what horsemen call old turf, best for racing and when twice a year the point-to-point meetings are held, it is a rare day when the going is heavy.

The ground rises to a height in the centre of the haughland, a good place for the racegoers to watch the horses complete the circuit of jumps. The only place where the crowd is unsighted is to the west, where the ground dips down near the Selkirk to Kelso road. It is the narrow neck of the haugh where the two rivers almost meet and are separated by only 200 yards. And also by a long oblong mound rising to more than a hundred feet. The old men sitting on Chalkheugh Terrace can make out some massive remnants of masonry on its summit, particularly on the Teviot side where a wall runs almost continuous. Covered in trees now it can be difficult to visualize what stood there many centuries ago. Local people call it simply the Old Castle and because the road cuts between it and the haughland, few realize that these two places were one. And more, that they were important places central to Scotland's early history.

The Old Castle was Roxburgh Castle, built and expanded by the MacMalcolm kings of the twelfth century and on the mound where the racegoers stand there was a medieval city with four churches, a school, five mintmasters and the busiest export market in Scotland.[1] This was Roxburgh, and now no trace whatever remains, nor any ability to find some because no archaeology is permitted by the landowner, no aerial surveys have been taken. It exists only in the ancient documents collected and copied by the monks of Kelso Abbey whose whose ruins stand across the river.[2] It has been forgotten or ignored by generations of historians, perhaps because there is nothing to see and no opportunity to dig. Roxburgh lives on in an old county name, an aristocratic title and several traditions. St James' Fair was held there at least since 1113 and probably long before, but when the city disappeared, local people still held the fair until it was discontinued before the Second World War. This is why the old men with longer memories still call it the Fairgreen.

Even though the place lives on in names and words, the substance of Roxburgh has been entirely forgotten. It is truly a lost

[1] RCAHMS, *Roxburghshire* (1956).
[2] Alistair Moffat, *Kelsae* (1985).

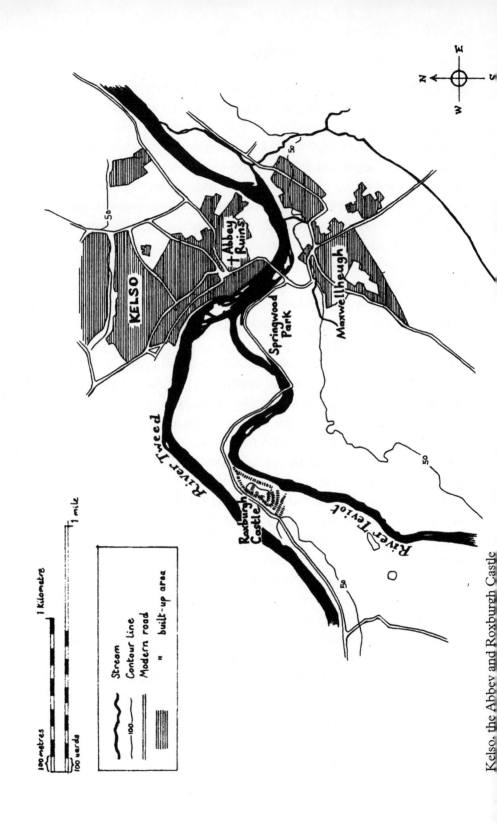

Kelso, the Abbey and Roxburgh Castle

city. All its voices are silent now, its stories lost in the grass where sheep graze and where twice a year horses thunder between the hurdles.

And yet it was a place of determinant importance to the whole history of Britain. It was the place where Arthur came back to, where he held his own power, where he kept safe his precious cavalry horses, where he drew the lines of communication together, where he sat in his castle hall feasting with his loyal warriors. It was, to use a mythic term, his Camelot.

Now this is a claim of some scale and a tale that will need to be told carefully. This is best done backwards. Beginning at the end I want to look briefly at traditions that are still, if barely, remembered now and then piece together the past from the decay of the old city, back to its medieval zenith and then using toponymy, Gododdin sources, military logic and the dictates of animal husbandry, I will show that in the 490s Arthur was Lord of Calchvyndd, the great Guledig of the P-Celtic kingdoms of the south of Scotland, the scourge of the Picts and the man who stopped the Angles and Saxons at Glein, Bremenium and Badon. From Roxburgh he and his Gosgordd rode out to fight to keep Scotland Scottish, Wales Welsh and parts of England Celtic.

Like ripples that persist long after the splash, the name and fame of Roxburgh has endured far beyond the substance. King David I MacMalcolm created the office of Sheriff of Roxburgh early in the twelfth century. It may have existed before but the first documents bearing the witness of Gospatrick, Sheriff, date from 1113, 1128 and 1147 and had the royal seal attached in the castle 'apud Rokesburgum'.[3] The same office persists today. The name also survived the local authority reorganization of 1974 and within Borders Region there is still Roxburgh District following the same boundaries set in the early modern period after medieval custom and practice. Even though the city has entirely disappeared the name of Roxburgh remains in frequent currency.

[3] *Kelso Liber* (*Liber S. Marie de Calchou*) (The Bannatyne Club) (1846).

There is another general observation possible here. In 1113 when David MacMalcolm was not yet king, he chose to found a community of French monks from Tiron in his Forest of Selkirk. In the first charter it is clear that he saw Roxburgh as his capital place; he held what later observers called the most powerful stronghold between Forth and Tyne; the town was sufficiently wealthy and busy to give forty shillings a year, a seventh part of the fishings, a seventh part of the produce of its mills, all the churches, all the schools and a substantial holding of town lands to the new abbey.[4]

David's titles included the English earldoms of Huntingdon and Northampton, but much more significantly he was also Earl of Annandale and Galloway, Prince of Cumbria and Earl of Teviotdale and Upper Tweeddale. Using the political geography of an earlier age he ruled the lands of Rheged, Selgovae and southern Gododdin.

David was raised at the court of the Norman King of England Henry I and thoroughly schooled in that culture. When he came to southern Scotland to rule over the vast sweep of territory, he immediately sought out its military and economic hub, the place he would make his power base. Roxburgh was already pre-eminent when the young earl decided to make it more so by extending the castle and striking Scotland's first coinage there.

The point is a simple one. Roxburgh was the most important place between the Lammermuirs and the Tyne, between western Galloway and the Berwickshire coast. Over the rest of Britain the old Roman centres tended to retain their pre-eminence: London, York, Chester and so on. But in southern Scotland and northern England, Trimontium decayed and Carlisle stagnated, while Roxburgh began to develop towards its early medieval zenith.

More detailed are local memories of the place. St James' Fair was the Christianized version of Lughnasa, held at the beginning of

---

4 *Ibid.*

Holy
Sepulchre

Market Street

St James' Church

Friary of
St Peter

RIVER TEVIOT

RIVER TWEED

W

S ——► N

E

Medieval Roxburgh and its castle

August. It was the culmination of the stock-rearing year with sheep and cattle sales and much else. And even though the city and the church of St James had both perished by the seventeenth century the ewes still lambed and farmers met in August on the Fairgreen to do business, just as they had done in the ditched enclosures at Eildon Hill North a millennium before.[5] When Trimontium fell into disrepair and became too difficult to maintain, the economic activity that surrounded it migrated downriver to Roxburgh, and when the sky gods of the P-Celts were replaced by the gospels, the great cattle fairs came to the haughland between Teviot and Tweed.

There are still people alive today who remember St James' Fair in the 1930s. By then it had become little more than an excuse for a picnic by the river with puppet shows, hoopla and other entertainments, although ancient memories were stirred when the provost of the royal burgh of Jedburgh came to cry the fair by ringing a handbell. He had to do it in the absence of an official from the old city and because nearby Kelso is not a royal burgh, and the handbell stood for the now silent church bells of Roxburgh. The only living remnant of the old fair was a continuing trade in horses and ponies carried on by the Muggers, or the Gypsies. The serious agricultural business had moved across the Teviot to the new Border Union Showground where purpose-built stands, pens, and ladies and gentlemen's toilets had been provided. Many hands are shaken, deals done, machinery bought and prizes won at the Border Union Show. It may seem a world away from the time when herdsmen drove their cattle through the fire at Eildon Hill, but it is still held at Lughnasa.

And the horse tradition seems indelible. Not only are they bought, sold and competed at the show but on the old Fairgreen, around the site of Roxburgh, they race twice a year. This is not a coincidence confined to this place. At Glein and Bremenium where

---

[5] A. Jeffrey, *The History and Antiquities of Roxburghshire* (1838).

Arthur chose killing grounds that were good for horses, there are still equestrian events held. Horse trials twice a year at Yeavering and annually between Rochester and Otterburn near an old ford over the River Rede. Doubtless these things have more to do with geography than history, or indeed folk memory, but to see horses gallop in places where Arthur charged his Gosgordd is an evocative sight.

More personal and therefore more pointed for me is a ceremony in which I took part when I was a young man. Each of the Border towns holds a Common Riding or a festival each year. Some are very ancient while others were created or revived only fifty or so years ago. Kelso holds its prosaically named Civic Week in mid July, elects a principal called the Kelso Laddie and then celebrates itself in a clutch of largely invented events over the space of a week. No one cares that the traditions are young, the purpose of the thing is to have fun and to understand something of the identity of the place, something of its history.

Hidden inside the calendar of mass rideouts, fancy-dress parades and torchlight processions is something very ancient, an unconscious link with Kelso's Celtic past. In 1986 I was asked if I would take part as one of the principals in the annual Whipmen's Ride. It was the twenty-fifth anniversary of the revival of the event and I was to be the Orator, the maker of a witty speech to the assembled company. I was honoured to be asked to do this; it was one of the most emotional days of my life. I had right- and left-hand men each with ten-foot horsewhips. As I paused for breath in my witty speech, both would crack their whips in the air and roar 'God Speed the Plough!' My audience paid attention. But that is to get somewhat ahead of things. In order to show how the Whipmen's Ride works in this story I shall recite brief details of the simple ceremonial and show its links to the lives of people who walked the same ground 1,500 years before.

In the early evening of the Friday of Civic Week the old curfew bell is rung to remind householders that they should put out their fires. Then horsemen and their followers on foot gather in Kelso Square where they elect 'My Lord Whipman' and give the Whipman's Flag into the keeping of the Kelso Laddie. Then a poem is recited. It has a title that no one understands, 'The Taddie Aus'. Here is the first verse.

> Alack! Ah alack for the auld Taddie Aus.
> We think o' them oft' as the May blossoms blaws.
> But they come nae again wi' the spring o' the year.
> To busk up oor toon in a gala day steer.[6]

This ritual and the poem tell an interesting story. At the Celtic festival of Beltane on 1 May domestic fires were put out before herdsmen drove their beasts up to the high pasture and to the summer shielings. But before they left they celebrated. Beltane was a sun and fire festival signifying the return of summer. And just as at Tarbolton (Tor-Beltane) where the young herds built an altar, the Kelso Whipmen elected a master of ceremonies who would officiate at the ceremony and adjudicate at the games and amusements that were to follow.

The poem's meaning is clear in one aspect. The Whipmen's Ride took place not in July but at the beginning of May. The town's records remember the Whipmen's Society in existence as early as 1650 but since most burgh records began about that time and traditions were things not much recorded, it is very likely that its history stretched much further back.

The 'auld Taddie Aus' is clearly a reference to the Whipmen, but what does it mean? Part of the ancient ritual of Beltane involved extinguishing the old fires of winter and lighting a new one, a 'need-fire'.[7] This was used also as a purification and on Eildon Hill North the P-Celtic herdsmen drove their frightened beasts between two fires. At the end of the night the herds scooped

[6] *Kelso Civic Week Programme* (1998).

[7] Sheila Livingstone, *Scottish Festivals* (1997).

up embers from the ashes or lit torches to take with them to light the new summer fires in the shielings. That is what 'Taddie Aus' means. Literally it is 'the Ash Daddies' or the men with the ashes from the Beltane fires.[8] Sometimes they would streak their faces, using the grey and black like warpaint.

After the ceremony in Kelso Square the cavalcade rides across to the site of the city of Roxburgh where they gather at the foot of an ancient wych elm. Nothing to do with witches (*wych* means 'pliant') it was a tree that the Celts incorporated into Word Ogham, an offshoot of Tree Ogham, and which had a powerful by-meaning associated with the strength and health of cattle and sheep. Over time these complex links decayed and the tree simply came to symbolize good luck for cows, sheep and horses. The original wych elm at Roxburgh was reputedly massive, measuring thirty feet in girth, and furniture and tools were made from its wood while it lived. In the era of the Gododdin, the Men of the Trees, such an elm would have been famous. At its site the Kelso Laddie cuts a sod from the old turf. This is another remnant of Beltane. The young men at Tarbolton did exactly the same thing when they built their altar to Bel, the Celtic sun god.

After the Orator has made his witty speech, horse races follow: ponies, trotting horses and great snorting thoroughbreds all compete in a series of classes. In the time of the old Whipmen's Society, there were also displays of horsemanship, much betting and, interestingly, both then and now, no so-called aids were allowed in the races, no whips, crops or spurs. And the prizes were worth having: riding and cart saddles.

All of the latter part of the ceremony is very reminiscent of the early horsemen's societies, their all-male membership, the secrecy and the lore of it all. The Whipmen existed as a sort of proto-trade union attempting to better their working conditions as the drivers of plough horses, carters and general farm servants, and that must have entailed confidentiality and exclusion.

[8] *Scots Dialect Dictionary* (Chambers, 1911).

But that was later. What is remarkable is the power of unconscious folk memory; the rituals of Celtic Beltane combined with powerful traditions of horse-knowledge and horsemanship. All of them taking place exactly where Arthur based his cavalry and four times a year remembered with his warriors the quarter days at Imbolc, Beltane, Lughnasa and Samhuinn. When we ride to the Fairgreen on the Friday evening led by My Lord Whipman, we ride with ghosts beside us.

On the far side of the Fairgreen stood the fair church of St James. Its bells rang for the last time in the middle of the seventeenth century; by 1649 there were only six communicants.[9] And in the nineteenth century the Duke of Roxburghe successfully resisted the temptation to fall in with fashion and retain the ruined aisle of St James which offered a romantic vista from the windows of Floors Castle. He decided that horse racing would look better and demolished the old church so that jockeys could enjoy an uninterrupted view of the next fence. Accordingly nothing at all of St James now survives except a tombstone, rescued from the cemetery and placed in Kelso Abbey. It and another offer a window into the workings of the old city.

'Here lies Johanna Bulloc who died in the year of Our Lord 1371. Pray for her soul' is inscribed on the recto side of one, while on the verso is carved a pair of sheep shears. The other stone is from the Franciscan Friary of St Peter which stood nearby the wych elm used in the Whipmen's Ride, and which was also flattened. All that can be made out on the face is the word 'mercer' but the stone is interesting. It was quarried near Tournai in France out of the distinctive *pierre bleue* limestone.[10]

The medieval wool trade underpinned Roxburgh's prosperity. Like much that thrives in commerce, it was a simple business. Sheep farming was organized on a semi-industrial basis by the great monastic houses of the Borders. Melrose, Jedburgh,

---

[9] RCAHMS, *Roxburghshire* (1956).
[10] *Ibid.*

Dryburgh and Kelso all controlled vast sheep ranches in the Cheviot and Selgovan Hills, in places that kept their P-Celtic names and where, like in Cumberland, the shepherds probably still spoke a form of Welsh. Each ranch produced a carefully calculated crop of wool. There exists a record of this compiled by a Florentine merchant called Pegolotti in 1340.[11] At Roxburgh market, under the keen eye of royal burgh tax officers, the wool packs were sold to Italian and particularly to Flemish merchants. The importance of the latter is remembered in the high incidence of the surname Fleming around Kelso. They carted the fleeces along the Via Regis, the King's Highway, which led to Berwick-upon-Tweed and ships bound for the cloth-making towns of the Rhine estuary. So that the wool could find its way easily to Roxburgh as well as from it, there was another Via Regis which led from Annandale up over Teviotdale and down to the old city.[12] Both of these were based on Roman roads. The regulations for Roxburgh's busy market were set as a paradigm for other emergent towns; the Leges Burgorum were applied to Dumbarton and elsewhere in the Middle Ages.

Because no archaeology is allowed and no plan survives it is extremely difficult to visualize the place or get a sense of how big it was. However, a careful and patient reading of the land grants made inside the town walls offers some clues. Three streets are mentioned. The Headgate led out of the east gate of the castle and at some point changed its name to King's Street, while Market Street ran crosswise from south to north. The arrangement was probably similar to Edinburgh where Castlehill runs out of the east gate of the castle before becoming the Lawnmarket and is then crossed by George IV Bridge. Not so steep-sided and smaller in scale than that, but similar.[13]

Roxburgh had a long circuit of walls, possibly only a wooden stockade since Tweed and Teviot already offered protection,

[11] Alistair Moffat, *Kelsae* (1985).

[12] A.R.B. Haldane, *The Drove Roads of Scotland* (1997).

[13] Alistair Moffat, *op. cit.*

which was extended at least once to include a new town which had grown up in the early twelfth century. Two churches stood within. In addition to St James there was Holy Sepulchre which, documents suggest, may have been a rotunda church. To the south of the walls stood the Friary of St Peter, founded in 1231 and deriving its income from control of the ford of the River Teviot. Friars Cottage, standing now at the north side of Teviot Bridge, still has the name. A fourth church, possibly the oldest, stood inside the castle walls. This was St John the Evangelist and an important place that saw audiences with papal legates, treaties signed and royal baptism.

King David I MacMalcolm knew that a growing economy needed more than high levels of production and wide distribution. He needed to create his own standard of exchange and in 1135 he caused Scotland's first coins of the Middle Ages to be struck at Roxburgh. Silver pennies were minted in sufficient number to allow numismatologists to discern the hands of five coin-makers working in the city.

An ability to count was also needed, and Scotland's earliest schools come on record in 1251 when a man called Thomas is noted as rector of more than one. If there were two then it is likely that they were attached to Roxburgh's municipal churches of Holy Sepulchre and St James.

If wool paid the bills then the castle protected the profits of the wool trade at Roxburgh. It was the initial *raison d'être* for the whole set-up. Placed at the narrow neck before the wide haughland opens up to be safely bounded by the two rivers, the castle's location impressed Henry VIII's general, the Earl of Hertford: 'It is one of the strongest seats of a fortress that I have ever seen.' Very large, on a steep-sided oblong mound closely bounded by Teviot and Tweed, Roxburgh Castle commanded a wide view on all sides. It had seven substantial towers, a donjon or keep in its centre, extensive barracks and stabling, a well and a church. State events were regularly staged within the walls and so impregnable was it thought to be that political prisoners and hostages were imprisoned in its dungeons.

One final part of the medieval picture remains to be drawn. David I originally founded his Tironian abbey at Selkirk on the River Ettrick near the hamlet of Lindean. He was persuaded to uproot the French colonists and bring them downriver to Kelso 'near Roxburgh' as the documents have it. The kingdom was prospering, the economy expanding and David needed a civil service to help run it efficiently. Abbeys produced literate, numerate and educated men who owed everything to the king, whose probity and loyalty were unquestioning. But why did he not plant the new church by the town of Roxburgh, at his elbow?

The reasons are nowhere written down and seem to be implied in religious tradition and precedent rather than administrative logic. It is clear that there was a pre-existing church at Kelso dedicated to St Mary. Like Cuthbert's Church at Old Melrose, it stood in a loop of the river, an allusion to the hermetic inclination of the early Celtic Church. Not an island like Iona or Lindisfarne cut off from the sinful temporal world, but almost. The comparison with Melrose is significant in another way. When David I brought Cistercian monks to build a new abbey in 1136, they moved it from the loop of the Tweed where the site may have been too restrictive. But they kept the dedication to St Mary. The Tironians did the same thing at Kelso. Remembering the ninth-century tradition of a pilgrimage shrine to the Virgin at Stow in Wedale and Arthur's bearing her likeness on his shield at Guinnion, and at Badon, is there a whisper of a cult of St Mary in the Borders in the Dark Ages?

At all events David I lavished gifts on Kelso, their value incalculable in modern terms, and quickly made St Mary's the wealthiest and most politically significant abbey in all Scotland.[14] Her abbots were statesmen, her priors preferred to great ecclesiastical office

[14] Alistair Moffat, *Kelsae* (1985).

and the double cruciform design of the church made Kelso the largest and most impressive ecclesiastical foundation north of Durham.

The medieval glory of Kelso and the power of Roxburgh lasted for only two centuries. In 1296 Edward I of England turned his armies north and began 300 years of intermittent but brutal Border warfare. Roxburgh and Kelso lay too near the frontier to prosper; the castle was occupied by the English for nearly 100 years and the abbey was burned and looted repeatedly. By 1460 Roxburgh Castle was destroyed by the Scots in an artillery fusillade which killed King James II in a fearful accident, when a cannon burst near where he was standing. He had wanted to destroy Roxburgh so totally that should it fall into English hands again, it would be useless to them. The town began to decay in the fourteenth century, and by the mid seventeenth century the growing town of Kelso had taken over many of its functions as a market. In the eighteenth century Roxburgh's buildings and churches were used as stables and cow byres and by 1800 there was nothing to see, no stone left standing on another save the ruined arches of St James and the Friary of St Peter.

But whatever the historical reason, and by any measure, the complete disappearance of Roxburgh is astonishing. Because there is nothing to see, no tour of the ruins available, no physical investigation allowed, this great city and all that happened within it has been ignored or underplayed by historians. No one goes there except local people looking for a good walk, or punters attending the point-to-point races twice a year. In every sense Roxburgh is a lost city.

Be that as it may, it is important to be clear about the connection to this present narrative. Context is the answer. When the city first comes on record as such a substantial and vibrant centre, it must have been a going concern for a considerable time before 1113. Its military significance is obscured by time but no one in the Middle Ages missed it and before that its virtues as a stronghold would have been recognized. Economically it is clear that the wool trade was operating in some volume before the monks arrived in the early 1100s with their tally sticks. Relative political stability followed Malcolm II MacMalcolm and King Owain of Strathclyde's victory at Carham over the Northumbrians in 1018, but even before that the castle and town were in existence. The evidence needs a little background.

In 617, after the Gododdin rout at Catterick in 600, Edwin united the Angles of Deira in Yorkshire and Bernicia in Northumberland into the army of Northumbria. Twenty years later they captured Edinburgh and overran the Tweed basin which they held until Carham. In that time the Angles conferred many new place-names; some of them recall actual events such as at Pallin's Burn where St Paulinus baptized the heathen aristocracy of Northumbria.[15] That happened in 627 and since Pallin's Burn is only twelve miles from Roxburgh, it shows how close the Angles had encroached only a century after Arthur's death.

As in modern political takeover, only the previous élite suffered immediately and most P-Celtic peasants were left on the land they cultivated. The incoming ruling class needed to eat just as the outgoing did and it would have been foolish to drive food producers away. Instead the Anglian chiefs seized places that offered control, and one of them made straight for the strongest fort in the Tweed basin and gave it and the settlement around it his name.[16] He was an aristocrat called Hroc. Like *hrosa* for 'stallion', *hroc* is an early animal name and it means 'rook'. The old P-Celtic name died and soon the place became known first as Hroc's Burh then Rokesburg and later Roxburgh. It is impossible to date this event but given the importance of the site and the dateable taking of Edinburgh in 638, Hroc must have made himself master of Roxburgh early on in the Anglian occupation of the Tweed basin.

As ever, names of places whisper secrets. When the Anglians

[15] James Campbell (ed.), *The Anglo-Saxons* (1982).
[16] Mike Darton, *The Dictionary of Place-names in Scotland* (1994).

conferred new names they were very often after people. This was in contrast to P-Celtic names which mostly described geography and sometimes function. Just as Dodin's Tun replaced Tref yr Llin near Edinburgh in an earlier example, Hroc stamped himself on a place whose former name described what happened there. The ghost name of Roxburgh never completely faded and in several disparate places it is also called Marchidun, Merchidun or the Marchmound.[17] In lazy ignorance I had believed that this was a reference to its proximity to the marches between England and Scotland, rather as in the aristocratic title the Earl of March acquired from his ancestors' role as marcher lords.

Taking the earlier form Marchidun, the last element is familiar as a P-Celtic word for a fort. There are many 'duns' in Celtic Britain and I had missed a simple reference. It led me to open dictionaries to find the first element. *March* or *Marc* has nothing to do with frontiers. In both P- and Q-Celtic it has a very specific meaning: *marc* is a 'cavalry horse, a charger, a steed'. *Marchog* is a 'cavalry warrior', *marcslaugh* is a 'war-band of cavalry warriors'.[18] There are many historical references. But one crystal thing was clear: Marchidun means 'cavalry fort'. And it meant that before Hroc made Roxburgh his place in the early seventh century.

At first I found the name puzzling. Forgetting the old town and the haughland, I wondered about the practicality of keeping horses enclosed in a place so steep-sided and confining where feed and water would have had to be handled in large quantities up the castle hill. But as soon as I looked at an aerial photograph everything fell into place. Roxburgh, or Marchidun, is a perfect place to base a large cavalry force. The logistics tell the story by themselves.

When armed and mounted, Arthur's cavalry was a fearsome, almost irresistible force if massed in numbers on the right ground, choosing its moment to strike. When dismounted they were very vulnerable indeed, much more than their infantry opponents. If a

---

[17] A. Jeffrey, *The History and Antiquities of Roxburghshire* (1838).

[18] Edward Dwelly, *The Illustrated Gaelic-English Dictionary* (reprinted 1994).

foot soldier is surprised all he has to do is reach for his spear and shield and he is ready to defend himself. If a cavalry warrior is threatened with sudden attack he has first to arm himself, then catch his horse which may be some distance away, then he has to get a saddle and bridle on it, and then at last he can mount and be ready to fight. That in turn dictated much about the organization of horseback warfare.[19] First and most vital a secure, defensible, difficult-to-access base was needed to house dismounted warriors overnight and also, near at hand, another safe, probably fenced area was needed which had pasture and water for horses. Both of these places, finally, needed good all-round vision to allow early warning of attack. Few sites like that exist.

Large ramparted hill forts often enclose a wide area where both men and horses can be safe but very often water has to be brought up or existing wells are too piddling to provide the 400 or so gallons that 300 horses need every day. Good for overnight but useless for much longer, hill forts that were large enough to accommodate the animals often had long perimeters which were impossible to defend against concerted attack, particularly under cover of darkness. Something Venutius and his Brigantine and Selgovan warriors discovered to their fatal cost at Stanwick 300 years before.

Roxburgh is a perfect place for a cavalry fort. The castle mount is very steep, and shows signs of having been made steeper on the northern side where what looks like a dry moat may have been a Dark Ages ditch; the modern road makes it very difficult to visualize. And its perimeter could be easily defended by 200 to 300 well-organized soldiers. In any case, sentries could see for up to two miles on every side. On the south the River Teviot comes very close to the foot of the mound, while on the north the Tweed is only 150 yards away. By itself the castle mount is a superb place for a stronghold.

But sitting at the narrow neck of a huge area of haughland bounded by two large rivers, it has no parallel with any other site in

---

[19] John Morris, *The Age of Arthur* (1973).

Britain. There are upwards of 400 acres of pasture with drinking water all around. Not only do the Tweed and Teviot keep horses in, they are too deep, except in one place, for men to cross without boat or bridge. At the narrow neck at the east end of the castle mound, where the Headgate would have started, there is an interesting archaeological detail. Laid bare by the roots of an old chestnut tree are the first few courses of a massive stone wall. The Tweed is only 150 yards to the north and that point would have been the prime place to throw a defensive wall across the neck of the haugh. Any attacker would have had to risk a sort of crossfire from running the gauntlet of 200 yards of the castle ramparts before they reached a wall built at that point.

The haughland is so large that with careful management several cuts of hay could have been taken to provide winter feed when the campaigning season was over. And there is also enough room for a herd of brood mares to live all the year round, supplying replacement mounts as they were needed. And by the rivers there are tracts of flat ground for breaking and schooling and for getting both horse and rider fit for the summer.

My contention is that Arthur used this uniquely suitable place for his base, but also he did so using Roman training techniques mixed with Celtic horse lore augmented by what seeped into Borders horse culture from the training schools of Trimontium. But there is a much more secure and recent Roman military connection to be traced to Roxburgh.

After the Barbarian Conspiracy of 367, Count Theodosius set prefects over the P-Celtic kingdoms. He cannot have expected these men to impose their authority without some sort of military backing and since by the end of the fourth century most Roman frontier troops were mounted, it is probable that they commanded troops of cavalry. Paternus Pesrut, the man with the red cloak, was given authority over the southern Gododdin in the Tweed basin. My belief is that he did not consider reoccupying Trimontium because he needed a legion to do it and all he had was an *ala* or

Marchidun circa AD 500

wing of 300 cavalry (the same number of Gododdin warriors who rode to their deaths at Catterick). For reasons of logistics I think he built a fort on the castle mount at Roxburgh and ran his horses on the haughland. If only military common sense and toponymy was behind this claim then it might be less than substantial. But the choice of Roxburgh as base for Paternus Pesrut is underpinned by a remarkable and recent find of Roman coins.

Directly opposite Roxburgh Castle on the south bank of the Teviot lies the old Springwood Estate. It used to belong to the Douglas family who had built a beautiful country house, now sadly demolished. The grounds are now occupied by a caravan site and a retirement village, while the field bordering the Teviot is often ploughed and sown for barley or hay. Field walkers and a very learned and persistent local historian have found more than 300 Roman coins in Springwood and fifty-four of these date from the time of the Emperor Valentinian of 364 to 378, the man for whom Theodosius renamed the province Valentia. The coins are not gold or silver or objects of any sort of intrinsic value. Most are bronze and measure half an inch across like five pence pieces or cents. Neither treasure, nor booty, they are the small change of a money economy and they arrived at Roxburgh in the pouches of Roman soldiers. And, more, they were found not in the castle mount or on the haughland where archaeology is forbidden but on a site separated by a wide river from the centre of Roxburgh.

In 1996, protruding from a rabbit scrape, field walkers found a fascinating object in Springwood Estate. A copper alloy terret, a piece of horse harness which may date from as late as the fifth century. Its condition implies that it wore through and was discarded. It is a tantalizing glimpse of cavalry activity at Roxburgh and as a piece of high-quality horse gear, its discovery confirms the wealth of the area.

Archaeologists also found traces of what may be a Roman fort near the remains of old Springwood House and a series of small square enclosures which look like dwellings. They are arranged in two lines and they border a stretch of hitherto uncharted Roman road which leads arrow-straight to the riverbank opposite the east gate of Roxburgh Castle. There must have been a bridge – otherwise the road had no purpose whatever. Working backwards, there are also clear signs of a Roman road, punctuated by signal beacon points, travelling along the south bank of the Tweed as far east as the village of Cornhill in present-day England. And on the north side of the Teviot there is another road picking up the line of the one that stops at the riverbank and then goes west along the south bank of the Tweed, joining Dere Street near the village of Maxton. Third- and fourth-century coins have been found at Maxton and on the south side of the Teviot near Springwood.

In fact Roman copper coins of the third and fourth centuries have been found in other places in the Borders: at Borthwickbrae, Lauder, Peebles, Newstead, Dryburgh, Lilliesleaf and Tweedmouth, all on or near the Roman road system through the area. This currency circulated in Scotland after 212.

If this is what can be uncovered by knowledgeable and careful local people from an area not central, but adjacent to the main site, what lies under the feet of the grazing sheep and cows at Roxburgh?

More important, these extraordinary finds place Paternus Pesrut and his cavalry at Marchidun, at the Cavalry Fort at the end of the fourth century. The northern genealogies recite that Paternus's father was a man with the famous Roman name of Tacitus, and then tell that he had a son called Aeternus. Who, in turn, fathered a man who took a famous P-Celtic name. He was Cunedda, the great leader who led his cavalry to rescue Wales. I believe he led them out of the gates of Marchidun down what became the Via Regis for the wool trade into the Eden valley and Carlisle, and then south.

There is no doubt that the Gododdin knew this place. They gave its neighbour across the Tweed to the east a name that has come down to us. Calchvyndd, or the chalk cliff, used to be clearly visible from Marchidun as Arthur's warriors looked out over their grazing horses.

After his triumphant final expedition from Roxburgh to win the crushing victory at Badon in 499/500 Arthur had one more battle to fight. Here is the entry from the *Easter Tables*, giving the correct date: '517 The Battle of Camlann, in which Arthur and Medraut fell: and there was plague in Britain and Ireland.'

Medraut became the Mordred of legend, Arthur's bastard son by his sister Morgan, and tradition holds that they were enemies at Camlann, what Tennyson called 'the last dim, weird battle of the West'. I believe that Arthur led the Gosgordd out of Marchidun down the Via Regis into the Eden valley just as Cunedda had done before him. And near Arthuret where the slaughter drove Merlin into the Wood of Celidon, he found Mordred's army. Camlann means 'crooked glen' in P-Celtic and the Roman name for Castlesteads on Hadrian's Wall was Camboglanna, which means exactly the same.[20] Like Arthuret in 573 this was a battle between rival factions of the Men of the North, and in it Arthur was mortally wounded. The romances of Geoffrey of Monmouth and Malory tell that the dying man was brought back to Avalon, the Isle of Apples, where his wounds were bound up, and where he died. And then Excalibur was hurled into a pool to be caught by a hand and arm clothed in white samite.

Now there is a documented place at Marchidun, on the haughland, near the Junction Pool where Tweed and Teviot join, a place the Celts believed sacred, which was called Orchairt. The place where apples grew on a fertile peninsula that fails to be an island by 200 yards of geology.

Perhaps not. But the burden of the story is clear. Arthur led the cavalry of the Men of the North, the only native British kingdoms capable of concerted resistance to the three enemies of Britannia. In a brilliant campaign centred on the Scottish Border country, he rode out from his horse fort to defeat them all, to allow the nations of Britain to form, and to sow the seeds of glory.

[20] Michael Wood, *In Search of the Dark Ages* (1981).

I3

THE LANDS OF
AIR AND DARKNESS

In compiling this narrative I excluded any argument that relied heavily on tradition or on a folk memory not given substance in another way, in a place-name for example. To finish, however, I want to deal with matters unprovable, and with intuition, with coincidence, with rootless tradition and with extended conjecture. Often it is something on the edge of reasoned argument that sparks a connection, or that encourages a second and harder look at a text or a map. Having shone as bright a light as I could bring on the lost kingdoms of southern Scotland, and on Roxburgh, their lost city, I want now to look at the hinterland, the places behind such facts as are assembled, and make a brief journey into the lands of air and darkness.

But first an aphorism to set this on a sound footing; something, in fact, from the sober world of behavioural science, where everything begins from first principles, everything observed and noted, and no conclusion drawn without every sensible test of logic fully applied.

The story concerns the African weaver bird. Behavioural scientists captured a number of these birds in the wild. They were noted for their construction of elaborately woven nests suspended from a branch like a woollen sock. The scientists kept the birds in captivity and as successive generations were born, they did not introduce any nesting materials into their cages, providing instead a foam rubber saucer for them to brood on. Then they took the great-great-grandchildren of the original wild weaver birds and put them into different cages with nest-building material strewn on the floor. When the mating period began, the birds took the straw, twigs and moss and built perfect sock-shaped nests.

It was a remarkable thing. No one had taught them to do this, they had no parents to observe, they had never even seen a weaver bird nest. DNA memory at work. The brain of an adult weaver bird is no bigger than my thumbnail. What memories lie in our huge brains? What is certain is that we remember more than the weaver bird, even if we do not realize it or simply mistrust what folk memory prompts in us.

I use that plain but striking story to underscore one claim I cannot back with any sort of detailed evidence, toponymic or otherwise. In the Scottish Border country we have a long history of understanding horses. Like all other agricultural areas it is only two generations since horses powered machinery, pulled carts or carried men as they worked the land. Scotland was quiet and green then, before the roar of the internal combustion was heard everywhere.

But in the Borders there is something unique, something significant for this story. Every summer each small town holds a festival; most are called Common Ridings. Four towns can trace them back 500 years. They all involve the same principle: a group of mounted townspeople ride out to patrol the common land, the territory that they hold in common. Even when that no longer exists, as in most burghs, the tradition of the rideout still holds. In all the ceremonies a young man is elected to carry the town flag and to be in some ways the symbol of its independence, and at several points he leads a great tearing charge of all his mounted followers, generally where the ground is good.

Nowhere else in Britain do the Cives, the Citizens, the Cymry still do this. I believe that the mounted Common Ridings of the Scottish Borders are the folk memory of Arthur's cavalry, the Gosgordd.

How you interpret that is largely a matter of taste but one curious survival offers a scrap of documentary reassurance. In the town of Hawick, home of one of the oldest Common Ridings, there is a statue at one end of the High Street of a mounted survivor from the skirmish of Hornshole after the Battle of Flodden in 1513. Carved on the plinth is the town motto: *Teribus Ye Teriodin*. Although natives of Hawick are called Teris, no one knows what it means. In fact it is a P-Celtic phrase, more correctly rendered *Tyr y Bas y Tyr y Odin*. Literally it means 'Land of Death and the Land of Odin', and I believe it is an ancient connection with the legends of the Ride of the Dead, sometimes known in a variant as the Wild Hunt. Odin led the Ride of the Dead, collecting souls as they rode through the night sky. Perhaps something that originated with the high flight of wild geese, the Gabriel Hounds, who scream their calls as they stream across the sky at twilight. In later versions, Arthur replaced Odin as their leader.

The Wild Hunt is sometimes called Odin's Host and it is said that he rode to find the souls of men slain in battle or sometimes he led the spectral huntsmen as they careered through forest glades on headless horses chasing a ghostly hart.

On a statue dedicated to the sons of Hawick who fought at Hornshole and also fell at Flodden, a memory of the Ride of the Dead is a remarkable thing to see. A small droplet from the deep well of folk memory. And, more, a motto in P-Celtic a millennium and a half after it was the common tongue of the countryside, after Arthur rode to victory at Glein, Bremenium, Caledon and Badon.

Like all ceremony, the Common Ridings had a serious and even dangerous purpose behind them. Selkirk is the best example. Through a series of royal grants the common land around the town which belonged to all its citizens had become a large area of almost

22,000 acres. Not only could the townspeople graze and water their cows, sheep and horses on it, from the more upland parts they had the right to cut peats for winter fuel. Peat Law to the north-west remembers this practice. However the people of Selkirk and their burgesses had to fight hard to retain the common, which was pressed on all sides by greedy aristocrats who believed that bits of it belonged to them, and also that ordinary people had no real right to the ownership of land. John Muthag, a provost of Selkirk, was killed when he tried to gain legal backing to evict encroaching aristocrats in 1541, and in 1668 the townspeople rioted when the Riddels of Haining tried to appropriate parts of the Southern Common. This was class warfare, sharply fought.[1] The lairds were wealthy and powerful, their ancestors inserted into positions of ownership by Anglian and Norman incomers. The townspeople were ordinary people whose strength lay in unity and persistence. Among them the traditions of the P-Celts survived, because they were all they had. The Lord of Whipmen cuts the Beltane sod because his ancestors did the same thing in the same place more than a millennium before. When the Teris line the streets of Hawick to cheer on the riders and their Cornet, they did so in the past to encourage them to fight for their rights. 'Aye in common' they shout. And they mean it.

Folk memory is very strong in the Borders; each year on the second Friday after the first Monday in June, Selkirk sings the same songs, at the same time, in the same place and weeps the same tears for all that experience in one place. Five hundred years the records reach back but for much longer before that ordinary people remembered where they came from and recited their traditions without any need to write them down. I once tried to buy a tape of the Selkirk Common Riding songs. 'What do you need a tape for?' said the shop assistant, shaking her head. 'We all know them.'

Among the Q-Celts of modern Scotland, this sort of folk memory has a name. They call it the *beul-aithris* which literally

[1] John M. Gilbert (ed.), *Flowers of the Forest* (1985).

means 'mouth-history' and has come to be a synonym for tradition. But originally it signified all that passed from one mouth into another: stories, songs, poems, place names and proverbs. The *beul-aithris* for the Gaels, and similar mechanisms for P-Celts, represented a huge store of inherited information which they needed for practical as well as cultural reasons. Consequently it was very accurate with none of the overtones of invention now carried by the phrase 'oral tradition'. Given what we now understand about the written word and its unreliability and partiality – no one would be comfortable with the *Sun* newspaper as a record of British political history since 1970 – the transmission of information through the *beuli-aithris*, even across millennia, should worry no one. Even when these become intertwined as in Geoffrey of Monmouth or in Thomas Dempster's astonishing assertion that British kings in southern Scotland 'had worn the purple', it is often better to listen for the voices of ordinary people who have long vanished into the darkness of the past, rather than set store by a fact simply because someone decided to write it down.

There is a tradition in Selkirk that offers a conclusion. At the end of the Common Riding morning, the flags are paraded and then flourished in a ritualistic style on a dais so that everyone can see. Watching the standard-bearer cast his flag in the Market Square and then listening to the pride and dignity in 'The Liltin'', a lament for the dead at Flodden played in absolute silence, a local man turned to me with tears in his eyes. 'Aye,' he said, 'we come from nothing small.' And he was right. For this is not a history brittle with relics, it is about people and a pulse of memory that beats unbroken down a hundred generations.

BIBLIOGRAPHY

This is not intended as an exhaustive bibliography but rather as a guide for those who might want to read further. It would have been near-impossible to list everything I had read in pursuit of Arthur, so what follows is not arranged into primary and secondary sources but in what seemed to me to be a sensible order of importance and value. The first section lists works which I referred to repeatedly and the second includes material which was very helpful. For the sake of simplicity and ease of access, I have for the most part excluded reference to periodicals and books no longer in print and included the most recent work on this historical period where possible. This is a bibliography for browsers in bookshops and borrowers from the public libraries.

Anderson, A.O., *Early Sources of Scottish History* (1990)
Anderson, A.O., *Scottish Annals from English Chroniclers* (1991)
Bede, *Ecclesiastical History of the English People* (Penguin, 1955)
Bede, *The Life of Cuthbert* (Penguin, 1965)
Beith, Mary, *Healing Threads* (1995)
Darwin, Tess, *The Scots Herbal* (1996)
Dixon, Karen, *Roman Cavalry* (1994)

Dryburgh Liber (Liber S. Marie de Dryburgh), The Bannatyne Club (1847)

Dwelly, Edward, *The Illustrated Gaelic-English Dictionary* (reprinted 1994)

Frere, Sheppard S., *Britannia* (1967)

Geoffrey of Monmouth, *The History of the Kings of Britain* (Penguin, 1966)

Gildas, *De Excidio et Conquestu Britanniae* (Phillimore, 1978)

Guest, Lady Charlotte (ed.), *The Mabinogion* (1906)

Hale, Alan, *The Border Country, A Walker's Guide* (1993)

Kelso Liber (Liber S. Marie de Calchou), The Bannatyne Club (1846)

Livingstone, Sheila, *Scottish Festivals* (1997)

Malory, Sir Thomas, *Le Morte d'Arthur* (Penguin, 1969)

Melrose Chronicle (trans. Joseph Stevenson) (1850)

Melrose Liber (Liber S. Marie de Melros), The Bannatyne Club (1837)

Moffat, Alistair, *Kelsae* (1985)

Morris, John, *The Age of Arthur* (1973)

Murray, J.A.H. (ed.), *Thomas of Ercildoune* (1875)

Nennius, *Historia Brittonum* in J. Morris, *The Age of Arthur* (1973)

Nicolaison, W.F.H., *Scottish Place-Names* (1976)

RCAHMS (Royal Commission on the Ancient and Historical Monuments of Scotland), *Roxburghshire* (1956)

RCAHMS (Royal Commission on the Ancient and Historical Monuments of Scotland), *Selkirkshire* (1957)

RCAHMS (Royal Commission on the Ancient and Historical Monuments of Scotland), *Peebleshire* (1967)

Scots Dialect Dictionary (Chambers 1911)

Skene, W.F., *Four Ancient Books of Wales* (1868)

Stephens, Thomas, *The Literature of the Kymry* (1849)

Stewart, R.J. and Matthews, John (eds.), *Merlin Through the Ages* (1995)

Vegetius, *Epitoma Rei Militaris*

Watson, W.J., *The Celtic Placenames of Scotland* (1926)

Williams, Gwyn A., *Excalibur* (1994)

Aburron, Yvonne, *The Enchanted Forest* (1993)

Alcock, L., *Arthur's Britain* (1971)

Ambleton, R., *The Outpost Forts of Hadrian's Wall* (1983)

Anderson, A.O. and M.O., *Adomnan's Life of St Columba* (1961)

Anglo-Saxon Chronicle (ed. and trans. Michael Swanton) (1996)

Armit, Ian, *Celtic Scotland* (1997)

Ashe, G. (ed.), *The Quest for Arthur's Britain* (1971)

Augustine of Hippo, *The Anti-Pelagian Treatises* (ed. F.W. Bright) (1880)

Bain, J., *Calendar of Border Papers* (1894)

Bannerman, John, *Studies in the History of Dalriada* (1974)

Barrow, G.W.S., *Robert the Bruce and the Community of the Realm of Scotland* (1965)

Barrow, G.W.S., *The Kingdom of the Scots* (1973)

Barrow, G.W.S., *Kingship and Unity Scotland 1000–1306* (1981)

Black, Ronnie, various articles in the *West Highland Free Press* (1997/8)

Blair, Peter Hunter, *An Introduction to Anglo-Saxon England* (1970)

Barber, Chris and Pylatt, David, *Journey to Avalon* (1997)

Burday, Gordon, *Farmers, Temples and Tombs* (1998)

Caesar, *De Bello Gallico* (ed. Locks) (1842)

Campbell, James (ed.), *The Anglo-Saxons* (1982)

Chadwick, N.K., *The Celts* (1970)

Chadwick, N.K., *The British Heroic Age: The Welsh and the Men of the North* (1976)

Coe, Jon B. and Young, Simon, *The Celtic Sources for the Arthurian Legend* (1995)

Coghlan, Ronan, *The Illustrated Encyclopaedia of Arthurian Legends* (1991)

Craig Brown, T., *History of Selkirkshire* (1885)

Curle, A.O., *The Treasure of Traprain* (1923)

Currie, Andrew M., *Dictionary of British Placenames* (1994)

Darton, Mike, *The Dictionary of Place-names in Scotland* (1994)

Davies, Norman, *Europe* (1996)

Delaney, Frank, *The Celts* (1986)

Dent, J. and McDonald, Rory, *Early Settlers in the Borders* (1997)

Dio Cassius, *Roman History* (ed. Boissevain) (1895)

Dorward, David, *Scotland's Place-Names* (1995)

Douglas, Sir George, *A History of the Border Counties* (1899)

Duncan, A.A.M., *Scotland – The Making of the Kingdom* (1975)

Dunning, Robert A., *Arthur – The King in the West* (1988)

Elliot, Walter, *The Trimontium Story* (1995)

Ellis, Peter Beresford, *Celt and Saxon* (1993)

Foss, Michael, *Celtic Myths and Legends* (1995)

Foster, Sally M. (ed.), *The St Andrews Sarcophagus* (1998)

Fraser, G.M., *The Steel Bonnets* (1971)

Gilbert, John M. (ed.), *Flower of the Forest* (1985)

Gillies, William (ed.), *Gaelic and Scotland* (1989)

Glennie, J.S., *Arthurian Localities* (1869)

Goodrich, N.L., *King Arthur* (1986)

Graham, Frank, *Dictionary of Roman Military Terms* (1989)

Haldane, A.R.B., *The Drove Roads of Scotland* (1997)

Heslop, R.O., *Northumberland Words* (1892)

Holmes, Michael, *King Arthur, A Military History* (1996)

Hutton, Ronald, *The Pagan Religions of the Ancient British Isles* (1991)

Jackson, K.H., *A Celtic Miscellany* (1951)

Jackson, K.H., *Language and History in Early Britain* (1963)

Jackson, K.H., *The Gododdin: The Oldest Scottish Poem* (1969)

Jeffrey, A., *The History and Antiquities of Roxburghshire* (1838)

Jenkins, Elizabeth, *The Mystery of King Arthur* (1975)

Jocelyn, *Life of Kentigern* (ed. J. Pinkerton) (1789)

Kelso Civic Week Programme (1998)

Lamont-Brown, Raymond, *Scottish Folklore* (1996)

Livingstone, Sheila, *Scottish Customs* (1996)

Lynch, Michael, *Scotland – A New History* (1991)

Morris Jones, J., *Taleisin* (1918)

Neat, Timothy, *The Summer Walkers* (1996)

Neville, Gwen Kennedy, *The Mother Town* (1994)

O'Brien, Conor Cruise and Maire, *Ireland – A Concise History* (1972)

Old Statistical Account of Scotland (1791–2)

Oliver, J.R., *Upper Teviotdale and the Scotts of Buccleuch* (1887)

Omand, Donald (ed.), *The Borders Book* (1995)

Pennant, Thomas, *A Tour in Scotland* (1776)

Phillips, G. and Keatman, M., *King Arthur, The True Story* (1992)

Prebble, J., *The Lion in the North* (1971)

Ridpath, G., *The Border History of England and Scotland* (1776)

Ross, Stewart, *Ancient Scotland* (1991)

Skene, W.F., *Celtic Scotland* (1870)

Skene, W.F., *Arthur and the Britons in Wales and Scotland* (republished 1988)

Smout, T.C., *A History of the Scottish People* (1969)

Smout, T.C. (ed.), *Scottish Woodland History* (1997)

Smyth, A.P., *Warlords and Holy Men, Scotland AD80–1000* (1984)

Soutra Cartulary (Trinity House of Soutra), Advocates Library

Stenton, F.M., *Anglo-Saxon England* (1943)

Strang, C.A., *Borders and Berwick* (1991)

Tacitus, *Agricola* (ed. J.G.C. Anderson) (1922)

Tennyson, Alfred, *The Idylls of the King* (1859)

Tolstoy, Nikolai, *The Quest for Merlin* (1985)

Tough, D.L.W., *The Last Years of a Frontier* (1928)

Wacher, John, *Roman Britain* (1980)

Wade-Evans, A.W., *Nennius' History of the Britons* (1938)

Wainwright, F.T. (ed.), *The Problem of the Picts* (1955)

Watson, Godfrey, *The Border Reivers* (1974)

William of Malmesbury, *The Acts of the English Kings* (1947 edn)

Wood, Michael, *In Search of the Dark Ages* (1981)

INDEX

Figures in italics indicate line drawings.

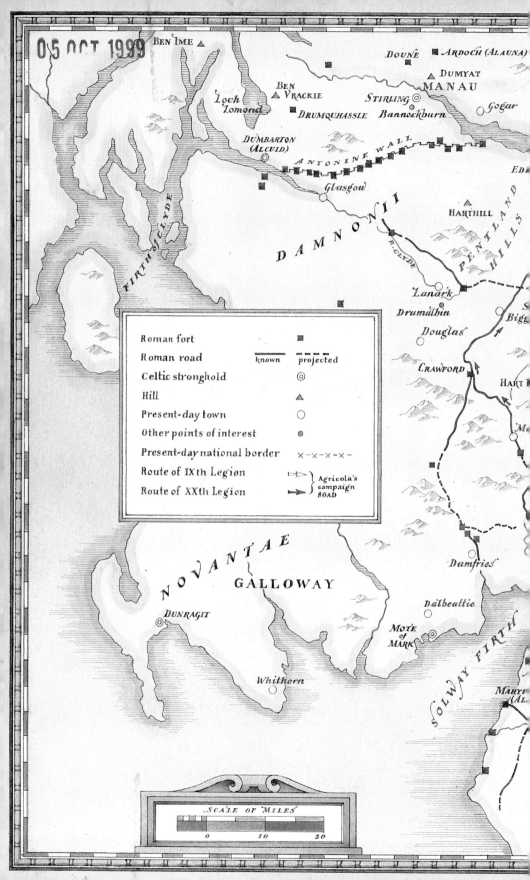